ON THE LEVEL

ON THE LEVEL

Discovering the Levels of Biblical Relationships Among Believers

Richard I. Gregory
& Richard W. Gregory

IFCA PRESS
2005

ON THE LEVEL

Discovering the Levels of Relationships Among Believers

Published by IFCA Press, a division of IFCA International, P.O. Box 810, Grandville, MI 49468. To learn more about IFCA International, visit our website at www.ifca.org

To order more copies of this book, visit www.ifcapress.com or call 800.347.1840

Cover design by Jim Connelly Studio

ISBN 0-9766838-090000

Printed in the United States of America

DEDICATION

To Carol and Patricia,

Our wives, partners in ministry, and faithful servants of the Lord, whose encouragement and prayer greatly motivated us in the writing of this book.

ACKNOWLEDGEMENTS

Harold Kregel – for his repeated appeal for the book. His friendship and encouragement, exhortation and reminders served us well in the motivation to get this book written. We miss him as He is already with the Lord.

Les Lofquist – for his faithful encouragement and exhortations concerning the importance of this book. His assistance in reading, editing, and publishing the text has made him a principal reason this book exists.

Dan Fredericks – for his analysis of the material of the book and the encouraging recommendation that the book be used in church study groups.

Bobbie Raught – for her expertise in editing the material. She spent scores of hours reviewing and correcting.

Jim Connelly – for the layout, artwork, and cover.

Roy Sprague – for his help in reading the text and providing helpful suggestions in the editing process.

Nate Osborne – for his help in reading the text and providing feedback concerning the content.

Saints at Byron Center Bible Church – for their gracious release of their pastor so that he could use his time in the writing of the book. Their "holding on to him loosely" is a tribute to their awareness of how they can serve the Lord in their stewardship of their pastor.

CONTENTS

FOREWORD

This book is a call to purity and balance. It represents that truth of God's Word which has fallen upon the rocks of neglect in today's American Church. For this reason it was a book that had to be written.

The call to purity

This is clear. God calls the follower of Jesus Christ to purity. We are called to holiness (1 Thessalonians 4:7; 2 Timothy 1:9). We are to be holy as He is holy (Leviticus 19:2; 1 Peter 1:16). We are to present our bodies to Him in the pursuit of holiness (Romans 12:1). Our old man was crucified that we should no longer be slaves to sin (Romans 6:4-7). The new man is created in holiness (Ephesians 4:24). "*Let us cleanse ourselves from all defilement of flesh and spirit, perfecting holiness in the fear of God*" (2 Corinthians 7:1).

The call to purity is the acknowledgment that God has called believers out of the world in order to maintain a personal and corporate purity in the midst of this world. Separation from sin is implied in the very word church: the Greek word *ekklesia* ("church") means "a called-out assembly."

In Christ's letter to the church of Pergamos, He warned against tolerating those who taught false doctrine (Revelation 2:14-15). Concerning a brother who persistently sins and refuses to repent, the Lord Jesus commanded that we lovingly discipline him (Matthew 18:15, 17). This concept was repeated by the Apostle Paul (1 Corinthians 5:1; 1 Timothy 5:19-20; 2 Thessalonians 3:1-6). Concerning doctrinal truth, we are to guard the Gospel as a sacred trust (1 Timothy 1:1-11, 6:20; Galatians 1:1-9). We are to refuse to allow any unbeliever to have ministry in the local church (2 John 9-11; 1 John 4:1-6). We are to refuse false teachers to teach and spread their error in the local church (Romans 16:17, 18; Titus 3:9-11; 2 John 9, 10). We are to warn and speak out against false doctrine and false teachers (Philippians 3:1-3; Acts 20:27-31; 1 Timothy 4:1-16; 2 Timothy 3:1-17). We are to preach and teach sound doctrine continually (2 Timothy 4:1-5). We are to refuse to cooperate in ministry with those churches and organizations that teach and promote doctrine contrary to the doctrine of the Word of God (Romans 16:17, 18; 2 John 9-11). As Charles Spurgeon summarized during his own struggle with doctrinal error and compromise in the Nineteenth Century English church: "Complicity with error will take from the best of men the power to enter any successful protest against it ... It is our solemn conviction that where there can be no real spiritual communion, there should be no pretense of fellowship. Fellowship with known and vital error is participation in sin." (*The Sword and the Trowel*, November 1887.)

In our own days of doctrinal carelessness and toleration here in the Twenty First Century American church, the doctrine of biblical separation is mocked by many, ignored by most. But it is clearly taught throughout Scripture. Believers of all ages have received the same call to purity.

The call to balance

This is clear. The call to balance is given along side of the call to purity. The doctrine of biblical separation does *not* require Christians to avoid all contact with unbelievers. Like the Lord Jesus, we should befriend the sinner without partaking of the sin (Luke 7:34). Paul expressed a balanced view: "*I wrote you in my last letter not to associate with immoral people; I did not at all mean with the immoral people of the world . . . for then you would have to go out of the world*" (1 Corinthians 5:9-10). In other words, we are in the world, but not of it (John 17:11, 14-15).

The call to balance also means that we should exercise biblical separation with a humble, gracious spirit in such a way as to strengthen the body of Christ. After instructing Timothy to protect the church from false teaching (1 Timothy 1:3), in the same context Paul wrote: "*the goal of our instruction is love from a pure heart and a good conscience and a sincere faith*" (1 Timothy 1:5). We see the same kind of balance in Paul's second letter to Timothy. After very strong words regarding the false teaching of Hymenaeus and Philetus (2 Timothy 2:16-21), Paul instructed Timothy to pursue love and peace (2:22), to refuse to be quarrelsome (2:23-24), and to teach and correct with patient gentleness (2:24-25). That is balance!

But it seems balance is so often absent from the church today. Extremes are all too common. Mean spiritedness is found on one extreme. Undiscerning tolerance is found on the other extreme. I am so grateful for this book with its call to purity and balance. It carefully presents truth which has been largely forgotten in today's American Church.

I found the authors' concept of the Pyramid of Responsibility to be extremely helpful in understanding the various levels of relationships within the Body of Christ. It has clarified in my own thinking the biblical responsibilities demanded of believers on each level. Understanding the levels of the Pyramid of Responsibility and the responsibilities of each level will help maintain proper Christian attitudes in applying the principles of biblical separation. Believers cannot escape the biblical mandate that we must distinguish between the holy and the unholy. Yet, at the same time we are to be discerning and separated from sin, we are also to be loving toward one another. The Pyramid of Responsibility in biblical relationships will help us keep the call to purity in proper biblical balance.

I am most eager to commend this book to all of God's people. We need it.

Les Lofquist
IFCA International Executive Director

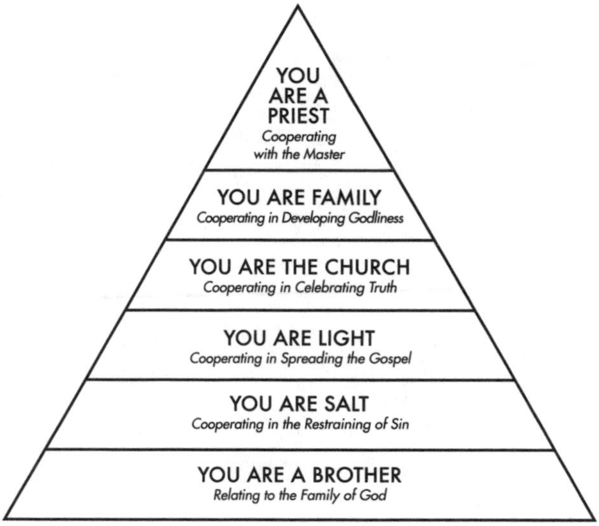

PYRAMID OF RESPONSIBILITY

The mandates of biblical relationships

INTRODUCTION

MAKING A DIFFERENCE

Tiptoeing through the minefields encircling the relationships within the Body of Christ is enormously daunting. It seems that at any moment the dreaded event of stepping in the wrong place will trigger a mine that Satan has laid to disrupt fellowship between believers. As successive issues detonate, the Body of Christ is often divided, and the loss of its vitality prevents brethren from being effective in representing Christ Jesus. Some of these mines are important areas of truth and doctrine that must never be viewed as negotiable. Others are incidental matters that ought not to inflict the damage they do. Some believers conclude that the risk of crossing the field is too high. Consequently, they want little to do with attempting to relate to the entire Body of Christ. They stay where it is safe and allow the rest of the Body of Christ to do the same. As a result of this protectionism and exclusivity, their impact is greatly diminished.

Other believers are so desirous of enjoying relationships with the entire Body of Christ they become indiscriminate. These believers seem to care little about the issues and the damage that compromising their doctrinal beliefs brings. By the time they reach the other side of the minefield, there is little genuine Christianity left. As a result of their inclusiveness, they have little to offer in terms of meaningful fellowship in Christ.

Many who are in the midst of this minefield are grasping for answers that will enable them to determine how they can avoid compromise while enjoying the relationships for which God holds them responsible. These individuals are full of questions such as: With whom may I fellowship as brothers in the Lord? With whom may I cooperate as the salt of the earth? With whom may I reach out with the light of the Gospel? With whom may

I worship within the context of the local church? With whom may I enjoy a true family relationship? With whom may I enjoy the intimacy of marriage? Are there any relationships that include no one except me and the Lord? Each of these questions sharpens the focus in relationships and brings a believer to a more limited level of responsibility. Whereas a person might be able to enjoy *personal fellowship* with a brother in the Lord, he might not feel able to join his local church. Whereas a believer might be able to join with another believer as "salt" by opposing abortion, he might not be able to serve together with him as "light" in evangelizing the lost with him.

Holiness and the biblical doctrine of separation

Although all of His attributes are essential, the holiness of God is revealed as His basic attribute (Isaiah 6:3). This is uniquely important since holiness is used as a name for God (Proverbs 30:3). In addition, God swears by His holiness (Psalm 89:35). Honoring God's holiness, by recognizing that we are to be separated unto God, is the most basic, practical doctrine for the believer to embrace. Throughout this book, the term *separation* is therefore used in its biblical sense. Ezekiel 44:23, in speaking of the priest's role, says: "*Moreover, they shall teach My people the difference between the holy and the profane, and cause them to discern between the unclean and the clean*". (See also Leviticus 10:10; Ezekiel 22:26). The biblical doctrine of separation requires that believers "*make a distinction*" between the sacred and profane, the pure and impure, the obedient and disobedient and ultimately between good and evil.

Certainly, holiness must be viewed as indispensable in the life of every believer (Hebrews 12:14). God commands that His followers be holy: "*And like the Holy One who called you, be holy yourselves also in all your behavior; because it is written, 'You shall be holy, for I am holy*'" (1 Peter 1:15-16). Thus, the doctrine of biblical separation must be seen as the practical application of the truth that God is absolutely holy. However, the appropriate focus of believers is to strive to be like the One who is holy – not merely different from those believed to be unholy. Simply separating from the ungodly or disobedient does not *in itself* make one a biblical separatist. If the character of God and heart of God are not being reflected in one's attitudes, the biblical doctrine and purpose of separation is being defiled, not fulfilled.

If God separates Himself from evil, can the believer be holy "*like the Holy One who called you*" without separating himself from evil? In this regard, since God himself is a "separatist," those whom God places "upon this earth to represent Him would be required to be holy (separated) as well. They would be expected to mirror His character."[1] However, too often in attempting to emulate the character of God by separating from evil, believers have dishonored the name of God by misrepresenting Him in spirit. With harshness and bitterness they have castigated, vilified, and denigrated people with whom they have disagreed – all in the name of the holy God. What is missing is the heart of the holy God, whom they strive to emulate, for He gave His own Son to reconcile those who are at enmity with Him. His heart is to redeem, restore, reconcile, and recover a relationship with those who are estranged from Him.

While emulating God's holiness by striving to separate from evil, we cannot dismiss our duty to emulate His desire to see those who are disobedient "*come to their senses and escape from the snare of the devil, having been held captive by him to do his will*" (2 Timothy 2:26). To affirm oneself by catching another in error does not represent God's heart since "*rejoicing in unrighteousness*" discredits one's claim of genuine love (1 Corinthians 13:6a). At the same time, those who would repudiate the doctrine of separation in favor of integration (as is true of the New-Evangelicals)[2] must also be identified as incongruent with the heart of God.

Purpose of this book

This book is designed to provide believers with the understanding that there are varying levels of relationships within the Body of Christ, each with differing responsibilities. Although somewhat inclusive on the broadest level (our brotherhood in Christ), relationships become increasingly limited as one moves toward the individual's standing before the Lord (priesthood of the believer). Thus, the most limited level of relationship is the priesthood of the believer, a level so exclusive that no one except the individual believer and the Lord are able to enjoy it. Confusing the limitations of one level with those of another is where the majority of detonations occur in the minefield of biblically mandated relationships between believers. Seeking to apply the freedoms intended for a "lower" level to a level designed to be more limited produces inclusivism and compromise. Likewise, seeking to impose the restrictions intended for an "upper" level to a level designed to be broader brings exclusivism and unwarranted schism. Therefore the Pyramid of Responsibility of biblically mandated relationships must be understood and applied as believers seek to emulate our holy and loving God.

What happened?

Through the years our family has been privileged to be a part of a community of believers who enjoyed being together. Our family history includes a sprawling Victorian home in a small town in northeastern Pennsylvania. The family included grandmother, aunt, parents and nine children. Although there were thirteen living together, the memories of a wonderful family life with caring parents and very interactive children taught all of us a great deal about unity-in-diversity. This extended beyond personal interaction within our home and included church involvement.

The patriarch of the family was an old fashioned Methodist and the matriarch was raised a Baptist. Early in their marriage they began attending a Pentecostal assembly where a dear friend of theirs was the pastor. Later, when a Bible Church began in our town, our whole family became a part of that fledgling ministry, even though we would occasionally attend the Presbyterian church out of an appreciation for the preacher's messages. Those were days when denominational labels were less of an obstacle to fellowship. Prior to the encroachment of liberalism, there was an awareness of the breadth of the Body of Christ and a safety in celebrating it.

Those years were a transitional time in the life of the church. As the years progressed and the Fundamentalist/Modernist controversy crystallized, theological consistency became a vital issue. In this tumultuous period, relationships among genuine believers became strained as some biblical responsibilities were overlooked in the attempt to keep the church pure from the encroachments of liberal theology. Brothers in the Lord, both pastors and laymen, were forced to make choices to leave denominations that had come under the control of liberalism or to remain in them trying to recapture fidelity to the Word of God and the true testimony for Jesus Christ.

Thus, the controversy became sharp not only between those who denied the faith and those who defended the faith, but also between genuine Christians who differed on what approaches were appropriate in contending for the faith. This was complicated by the fact that the liberals resented the efforts to maintain theological purity by many who refused to leave their churches. These believers were often viewed as divisive and the most persistent were forced out. Furthermore, those who left, either by choice or pressure, questioned the spiritual vitality of those who insisted on remaining. This critical atmosphere produced the exchange of unkind words and unbiblical judgments, where motives of the heart were questioned. This practice ignored the admonition of the Apostle Paul to the

Ephesian believers: "*I implore you to walk in a manner worthy of the calling with which you have been called, with all humility and gentleness, with patience, showing tolerance for one another in love, being diligent to preserve the unity of the Spirit in the bond of peace*" (Ephesians 4:1-3).

Maintaining a Christ-like spirit is imperative regardless of the occasion – even when confronting those who are attempting to destroy the truth. It is incumbent on the believer to carefully follow the example of Jesus in making a difference – on the one hand denouncing apostates with great passion and forthrightness, on the other reaching out with compassion to the publicans and sinners.

True believers rejoice when they experience genuine Christian fellowship. It is good for brothers to be able to share in the glories of Christ together. The Psalmist observes in Psalm 133:1, 3: "*Behold how good and how pleasant it is for brothers to dwell together in unity ... for there the Lord commanded the blessing – life forever.*"

Yet the pages of church history are littered with fractures caused by cultural, doctrinal and personal differences. Somewhere the Church lost a basic understanding of the meaning of genuine Christian fellowship. In her quest to preserve organizational unity she forgot that genuine Christian fellowship is founded upon, and centered in, a common belief about and devotion to Jesus Christ.

Just as the doctrine of Christology is primary in one's salvation, so Christ must be at the center of all true biblical relationships. This necessitates mutual surrender to the Scriptural revelation concerning His person and work. The "can't we all just get along" mentality (which declares that as long as we embrace "Jesus" we are all pulling in the same direction) will not do. *The basis for unity is not an abstract "Jesus" that is subjectively established in one's private experiences, but is rather the truth about the Son of God specifically revealed in Scripture.* The Apostle John states in the beginning of his first epistle that our fellowship with one another is dependent upon our fellowship with the Lord. This can also be said of biblical unity. This essential unity makes authentic Christian fellowship different from all other relationships.

An elusive concept

The unity that the Scripture expects believers to pursue can be a very elusive concept. There are varying approaches in attempting to understand the nature of unity. Often it is viewed subjectively implying oneness in spirit, interests, and feelings among individuals. At other times it is viewed objectively as the commonness of purpose regardless of other diversities. Some believe that unity is intrinsically an organizational word with the result that differences are sublimated to a united commitment to organizational ecumenism (as illustrated by the National and World Councils of Churches). Others do not see organizational union as necessary since they view the unity Christ referred to in John 17 as being spiritual. They believe all who are truly in Christ Jesus enjoy a common salvation and are members of a spiritual family called The Church. Differences in identifying the foundation and visible expression of unity have led to a variety of interpretations of Jesus' prayer in John 17:21, "*that they may all be one*." When John penned these words of Jesus, believers were being forcibly expelled from the synagogues and antagonism against them was harsh. John did not record this prayer in order to promote a sociological or organizational unity. His desire was that his readers might understand the heart of Jesus, who wanted unity based on the gift of God's Word which alone is truth (John 17:14-17). It should be noted that being a part of the spiritual body of Christ, to which all true believers belong, provides the foundation for true biblical unity. Achieving this true biblical unity demands that one not merely know the truth, but that one be possessed by it. This characteristic of truth captivates believers by virtue of Christ's claim on those who trust Him.

John R. Edwards makes a very impressive observation in his discussion of the use of the term *homothumadon* ("of one accord") in the writings of Luke and Paul. He notes the contrast between the unity-in-diversity experienced in the early church and the unity-in-diversity concept being promoted today. He writes,

> The unity-in-diversity rhetoric of mainline churches today leaves the impression that the ground of unity is unity itself. The church, however, cannot attain unity by looking to itself, nor by adapting to changing social norms, nor by diluting or dismantling its theology in hopes of achieving a broader or more generic consensus. The true unity of the church is an alien gift of God from outside, reflecting both God's nature and governance. The church is indeed diverse, but the goal of the church is not diversity. It is rather unity with God, which is a gift of the Spirit when the church seeks to live in conformity with God's will as revealed in Scripture.[3]

The question then, is: "How can believers responsibly relate to one another when there is such diversity?" Finding the common ground for God's gift of true biblical unity demands a careful examination of the relationships maintained by the Lord Jesus. Jesus chose twelve men to be his ministry team. There was great diversity among them. He chose two sets of brothers who were fishermen (Peter & Andrew, James & John), a political zealot (Simon the Zealot), a publican (Matthew), a skeptic (Thomas), a man with a businessman's acumen (Phillip), a reflective thinker (Bartholomew or Nathaniel), Matthew's brother (James, the son of Alphaeus), a thief and traitor, (Judas Iscariot) and a little known disciple named Thaddaeus. Although none were men of great reputation, they were obviously diverse in their expectations.

Some of these men were quietly reflective and inquisitive. Others, like Peter, were forward and aggressive. It seems as if they all had ambition to be the "greatest." Two of them, James and John, employed their mother to intercede with Jesus on their behalf for favorable position in His kingdom, much to the aggravation of the others (Matthew 20:20-24). Judas openly second-guessed Jesus about the use of funds when the precious ointment was used to anoint Jesus (John 12:4-5). Peter openly confronted Jesus about what he perceived to be the error of his prediction that He was to suffer and die at the hands of the Jews (Matthew 16:22). The strife among them continued to simmer despite the Lord's rebuke in Mark 10, and Luke refers to it in his discussion of the Last Supper. It would be interesting to know how many conversations Simon the Zealot and Matthew, the employee of the Romans, had concerning their former pursuits.

Indeed, there is a call to unity and even to a certain degree of uniformity. However, as R.C. Sproul in his book *Getting the Gospel Right* explains:

> This is not a drab, colorless uniformity that forces people into molds that rob them of their individuality. That sort of uniformity is not redemptive but dehumanizing. The goal of Christian sanctification is not the loss of personality or individuality such as promised in religions that seek the absorption of the self into some world-soul, by which the self is engulfed by the whole and swallowed up in oblivion. For the Christian this union with and conformity to Christ enhances his personal self, not annihilates it. The church is the ultimate embodiment of the motto *e pluribus Unum*.[4]

Only the operation of God's grace could produce the unity necessary for the twelve Apostles to focus on the task the Lord would give them: to provide leadership in spreading the Gospel to all people groups. Only the indwelling presence of the Holy Spirit could effect the operation of that grace. They would face theological and cultural differences in the early church that had the potential of thwarting the fulfillment of the Great Commission given by Jesus before His ascension.

History has demonstrated some instances when believers became so estranged from one another that the only thing unbelievers could see were the sinful attitudes displayed and the uncharitable, scathing words that were exchanged. Many times differences were superficial. But some differences were over very basic questions of essential doctrine.

The relationship between two reformers

During the Sixteenth Century, Protestants and Roman Catholics debated crucial issues such as the ground of salvation, the nature of justification, the means of grace, imputed righteousness, and the famous concepts of *sola fide* and *sola Scriptura*. Even in the midst of these great debates, genuine believers were dividing over issues that legitimately affected which level of relationship they could enjoy but should not have resulted in schism.

One such argument focused on the nature of the elements used in Communion. The Lutheran and the Reformed leaders met at Marburg, Germany in 1529 to conduct the first conference designed to unite Protestants around a common doctrinal statement. Luther and Zwingli represented the two groups respectively and were able to come to agreement on fourteen of the fifteen doctrinal points that the conference addressed. However, Luther's disposition and dogmatism promoted a sharp division over the nature of the elements in Communion. The inability to agree to disagree in love would continue to make unity impossible. Luther continued to attack those who believed that the elements of Communion were only symbols of the body and blood of Christ. Because of the intensity of this disagreement, Luther sought no level of relationship with Zwingli whatsoever. Historian Philip Schaff notes that shortly before Luther's death he continued to overwhelm Zwingli and his followers "with terms of opprobrium, and coined new ones, which cannot be translated into English. He called them heretics, hypocrites, liars, blasphemers, soul-murders, sinners unto death, bedeviled all over. He ceased to pray for them and left them to their fate."[5]

Zwingli, on the other hand, had a much more conciliatory attitude toward Luther and begged him to come to some expression of unity. However, Luther resisted saying, "if they would have unity, let them agree with me." It is as though Luther decided that the restrictions which necessarily characterize the highest level of the priesthood of the believer had to be applied to every level of relationship within the Body – even the lowest level of fellowship between brothers. Zwingli seemed to have a better spirit. He was characterized by Rupert Meldenius' famous Seventeenth Century motto: "in essentials unity, in non-essentials liberty, in all things charity."[6]

This is a prime example of the lack of understanding of the importance of biblically responsible relationships. Luther and Zwingli were both committed to the same essential doctrines of Protestantism as was demonstrated by the Marburg Colloquy's fourteen points of agreement. Yet Luther refused to call Zwingli a brother and even doubted his salvation. Because of a disagreement on a doctrine not essential to redemption, Luther maligned Zwingli as a heretic. Luther displayed no awareness of the various levels of relationships that exist within the Body of Christ.

Although this point of difference may have limited Luther's ability to conscientiously join with Zwingli for the celebration of the Lord's Supper, it ought not to have caused him to negate the validity of Zwingli's salvation. How tragic! Yet this has been repeated over and over through the years because, like Luther, many believers have failed to recognize that relationships within the Body of Christ do not demand total agreement on all matters of doctrine and practice. There exist, within the scope of Christian relationships, various levels of intimacy and intensity that produce corresponding responsibilities. Just as Christ had levels of relationships within the twelve, setting apart Peter, James and John as his inner circle, so believers must recognize that God does not intend that every relationship within the Body be equally intimate and intense. It is necessary for each believer to identify the levels of relationships and the responsibilities each demand.

Although each believer is responsible to every other believer to recognize their value as brothers in Christ, many mistakes have been made because the various levels of relationship within the Body are ignored. When this is the case, there is inevitable confusion concerning the responsibilities believers have toward one another. It is important to recognize that as relationships within the body of Christ become more focused in intensity, biblical responsibilities correspondingly increase. Careful study of the Word of God will reveal the progression of responsibilities God expects believers to fulfill. These responsibilities begin with one's relationship to all believers, and culminate with the enjoyment of the Lord alone through the priesthood of the believer.

Ours is an attempt to identify the various levels of relationships within the Body of Christ based upon the biblical responsibilities that each level demands of believers. Understanding these levels and the responsibilities each invokes will help maintain proper Christian attitudes in applying the principles of biblical separation. Believers cannot escape the biblical mandate to distinguish between the holy and the unholy and the sacred and the profane. The holiness of God demands this. Having the spiritual disposition to make that distinction is vital to the fulfillment of God's expectation that we be a people separated unto His name, while at the same time loving one another. The following is a breakdown of those levels with their corresponding responsibilities in a Pyramid of Responsibility in biblical relationships.

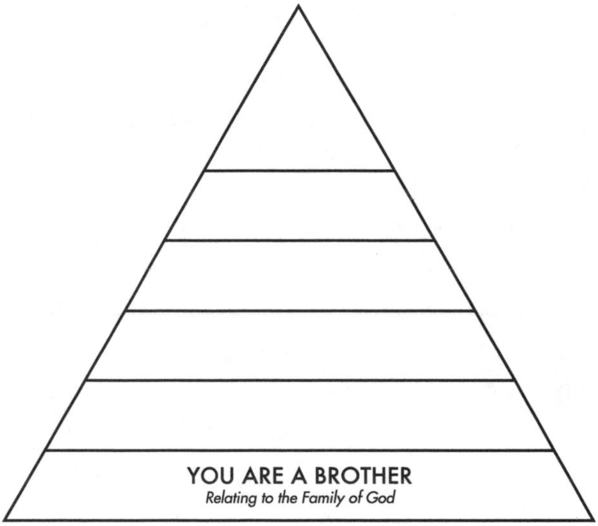

PYRAMID OF RESPONSIBILITY

The mandates of biblical relationships

CHAPTER ONE

YOU ARE A BROTHER

Relating to the Family of God

Growing up in a home with plenty of children was a healthy experience. As in any household, we had our share of squabbling. But our differences were overcome by the fact that we belonged to each other. We were family. We were brothers and sisters. Our family grew and more children were born. Each new child became a source of change and caused the older children to make adjustments. They lost their individual bedrooms and had to share closet space. Beds were replaced by bunk beds. We had to learn to share socks and tee shirts. It was a kind of joke in the family that the first one up in the morning was the best dressed. We learned that a family is an ever-changing organism. The change in years, numbers, personalities and experiences resulted in a dynamic that demanded response from all involved.

Family: unity in diversity

The flexibility necessary to make adjustments in relationships is essential if unity in the midst of diversity is to be maintained. The question one faces in such cases is, "How flexible do I have to be?" Being flexible is hard for some. Tragically, there are those who demand adjustments from others but respond negatively to those adjustments asked of them. Some are not equipped with the disposition to adjust to any changes and are limited by their own preferences. Others cannot get beyond certain incidents or personalities and are held captive by their own reactions. They refuse to recognize the need for maintaining close bonds and family identity. Consequently, they drift farther and farther apart and the concept of being brothers and sisters no longer carries with it a deep sense of belonging and responsibility. Parents are neglected and siblings live their lives untouched by those with whom they shared their formative years. Although this has not been our personal experience, our years in the pastorate have provided numerous examples of family estrangement. In such cases individualism reigns, bitterness thrives, and each family member devotes himself to his own pursuits while caring little about the responsibilities of being a part of an extended family.

This same dynamic has developed within God's family. As each generation passes, it is possible to lose family identity while the Church fragments into a variety of denominations, interest groups, para-church organizations and independent fellowships. The adherents to various expressions of the Church forget their common heritage in Christ Jesus. Understanding all genuine Christians are brothers demands the exercise of great discernment and biblical love. Every believer is responsible to recognize the value of each redeemed sinner. To neglect the relationships and corresponding responsibilities that exist in Christ ignores the work of grace He has performed. The relationship each believer has to his brothers in Christ carries specific responsibilities, regardless with which expression of the visible church they are identified.

The problem believers face in fulfilling these responsibilities is in distinguishing between true brothers in Christ and those who have joined the visible church but have never been truly redeemed. As the visible Church de-emphasizes the Gospel and the historic doctrines of the Word of God, there will be more and more professing Christians who fail to possess a genuine saving relationship with Christ. This threatens the ability of some believers to fulfill their biblically-mandated and Spirit-driven responsibilities to cultivate relationships with brothers with whom they differ. Since the division of the wheat and tares is impossible until the Day of Judgment (Matthew 13:24-43), some may cynically dismiss their responsibility to relate to other genuine believers as too dangerous because those believers do not conform to their "brand" of Christian expression. In such cases, these believers may not concern themselves with the responsibility to honor the entire Body of Christ. Although it is necessary to be discerning, it is essential that every believer genuinely seek to resolve the question: "Are you truly my brother?"

Discerning differences

Admittedly, exercising spiritual discernment is not easy. It takes a measure of commitment to the "one anothers" of Scripture. Paul reminds the

Roman believers that "*we, who are many, are one body in Christ, and individual members one of another*" (Romans 12:5). Therefore, we are responsible to "*be devoted to one another in brotherly love; give preference to one another in honor*" (Romans 12:10). "*Be of the same mind toward one another; do not be haughty in mind but associate with the lowly. Do not be wise in your own estimation*" (Romans 12:16). He instructs them to "*accept one another, just as Christ also accepted us to the glory of God*" (Romans 15:7) and because "*you are full of goodness*" you are "*able to admonish one another.*" (Romans 15: 14). Recognizing the responsibility spiritual discernment places upon believers, brothers in Christ should take special care not to overlook, quickly judge or reject other true believers. Catching someone doing something right should be regarded as a virtue. Unfortunately, this virtue has been replaced, in the minds of many, with the disposition to expose someone doing something wrong. Believers must seek balance in these pursuits.

Characteristics of apostates

It is not necessary to conclude that there must be universal acceptance of anyone who merely claims to be part of the Body of Christ. Clearly the Scriptures teach that there are those who "*have crept in unnoticed, those who were long beforehand marked out for this condemnation, ungodly persons who turn the grace of our God into licentiousness and deny our only master and Lord, Jesus Christ*" (Jude 4). Jude provides clear statements throughout His epistle that apostates can be recognized through various beliefs, attitudes and practices that identify one "*devoid of the Spirit*" (Jude 19).

However, it should not be the disposition of believers when exercising spiritual discernment to eagerly classify other believers as apostates. In many cases, true believers are either untaught, immature in the faith or naively entangled in associations that are spiritually unhealthy. There is a vast difference between an immature or errant brother and an apostate. Genuine Christian love demands that true believers warn those who are not properly identified as apostate but are beginning to manifest characteristics inconsistent with genuine devotion to the Word of God and the testimony of Jesus Christ. When the following characteristics begin to be observed in people's lives, those who are discerning must care enough to understand that if unchecked, they commonly lead to apostasy.[7]

- **Impenetrable Hearts** - they have hearts that become insensitive to the truth (Hebrews 3:7-19).

- **Indulgent Habits** - they demonstrate repeated susceptibility to temptation (Ephesians 2:2-3; Matthew 13:22).

- **Intimidation** – they are concerned about personal safety more than faithfulness to Christ Jesus (Matthew 13:21; 24:9-12).

- **Interference** – they are easily distracted from the truth by listening to false teachers (Matthew 24:11-12).

- **Infatuation** – they are lured away from Christ by means of worldliness (2 Timothy 4:10).

- **Indifference** – they neglect the necessary diligence in pursuing Christ in the Word (Hebrews 2:3).

- **Inoculation** – they become so accustomed to being in the environment of the Church that they no longer are aroused in spirit (Hebrews 6:4-5).

- **Isolation** – they begin to dismiss their need to gather with believers and dishonor the Lord's Day (Hebrews 10:25).

As the above characteristics become dominant in people's lives, there are additional indications they have become apostate. These traits become more pronounced and the true believer can more easily recognize one who is not truly part of the Body of Christ. These are the ungodly people who were once thought to be believers, but have fallen away from the faith. John describes them as those that "*went out from us, but they were not really of us, for if they had been of us, they would have remained with us; but they went out, so that it would be shown that they were not of us*" (1 John 2:19). The traits of these people include:

- **Impiety** – a practical as well as verbal denial of the grace of God (Jude 4).

- **Insubordination** – a refusal to submit to the Lordship of Jesus Christ and the authority He has invested within the spiritual leadership of the Church (Jude 4; 2 Peter 2:1).

- **Imitation** – a "form of godliness" that fails to focus on and bring glory to the Lord Jesus Christ (2 Timothy 3:4-5).

- **Innovation** – a dissatisfaction with the truth of God's Word and a desire to add their own perspectives as though they were from God (1 Timothy 4:1).

- **Intolerance** – a refusal to hear sound doctrine and a demand for teachers who will merely affirm their errant priorities (2 Timothy 4:3-4).

- **Indulgence** – an inability to restrain oneself from the love of self which leads to the insatiable desire to satisfy one's lusts (2 Timothy 3:1-2).

- **Imposition** – an insistence that others follow their innovations (1 Timothy 4:3).

- **Impudence** – a defiant attitude toward the Word of God and a blatant dismissal of biblical authority (2 Timothy 3:8).

When one or more of these characteristics become dominant, there is clearly an inability for the believer to enjoy oneness in Christ Jesus with the apostate. In such cases, sincere believers are unable to enjoy a kindred spirit that ought to exist between individuals within the family of God. But there are times when these traits are not yet dominant, making discernment difficult; the tares look so much like the wheat that clear distinctions are impossible. The Lord Jesus addresses this in Matthew 13:24-43. MacArthur suggests that the tares in this passage are

> probably darnel, a type of weed that can hardly be distinguished from wheat until the head matures. In an agricultural setting, sowing darnel in someone else's wheat field was a way for enemies to destroy someone's livelihood catastrophically. It pictures Satan's efforts to devastate the church by mingling his children with God's, in some cases making it impossible for believers to discern the true from the false.[8]

There is such a thing as bramble that is easily distinguished from wheat and needs to be sorted out from the wheat. However attempting to remove tares from the wheat is impossible because of the great similarity in appearance. Since this is the case, the Lord instructs us to patiently await His work of sorting them out. He says: "*Allow both to grow together until the harvest; and in the time of the harvest I will say to the reapers, 'First gather up the tares and bind them in bundles to burn them up; but gather the wheat into my barn*'" (v. 30). Whereas we have to be patient with reference to tares, we must be uncompromising with reference to the bramble that is easily distinguished from the wheat.

The Church as God's family

When Jesus declared to his disciples, "*I will build My church; and the gates of Hades will not overpower it*" (Matthew 16:18), He shared His intention of calling out from humanity a people who would be a family of believers. The declaration is loaded with theological truth and tremendously practical in its application. The Lord identifies Himself as the architect and artisan in the creation, composition and completion of this great family, His Church. She is to be a communion of people cleansed by His own blood. She is kept by the power of God through faith alone in His finished work on the cross and is empowered to bring glory to the Father by submissive obedience to the truth of God's Word through the indwelling Holy Spirit. Each individual who becomes a part of God's family is the Father's special gift to the Son. When the Church is completed, the Son will present her, without spot or wrinkle, back to the Father as a final tribute of His commitment that God may be all in all (1 Corinthians 15:27-28).

This marvel of God's grace and mercy is universal in her character, local in her expression, militant in her calling and triumphant in her destiny. The Church is pure and spotless, yet in her temporal manifestation, she encompasses imperfect human beings who are in need of abundant grace and mercy. Her future standing is viewed as perfect but her present state is fraught with frailty. The Church is visibly manifested in specific local assemblies of believers. She is commissioned to bring glory to God through worship, prayer, fellowship, discipline, evangelism, mutual care, equipping for service and the conducting of baptism and the Lord's Table. She is God's chosen instrument to fulfill His Great Commission and superintend His work in the world until Jesus comes.

Becoming a part of the family

Through the centuries various views have developed regarding the nature of the Church and how one becomes a part of God's family. The Reformation addressed these theological issues of ecclesiology (the doctrine of the church) and soteriology (the doctrine of salvation). Roman Catholic theology teaches that one becomes a part of Christ's Church, and thus obtains salvation, through baptism, confirmation and regular participation in the necessary, designated sacraments. They teach justification is by faith ... but it is a process that must be maintained through the sacraments and can at any time be interrupted by the presence of mortal sin. In such cases, confession and absolution must take place before the process begins again. Final entrance into Heaven comes only after a complete cleansing from venial sins has taken place through suffering in Purgatory. One can never be certain he is going to heaven, for according to "St Peter's Catechism" produced by the Roman Catholic Church in 1971, "It is a sin of presumption to say you are saved and sure of heaven."[9]

The Protestant Reformation challenged the Roman doctrine of progressive justification with its cry, "The just shall live by faith." Salvation was obtained "by faith alone in Christ alone." Justification, the Reformers argued, was the forensic decree of God whereby one's sin is imputed to Christ and Christ's righteousness is imputed to the believer through the exercise of faith alone in Christ alone. Conversion (or "being saved," as it is often designated), is instantaneous and permanent. The object of saving faith is the finished work of Christ. Justification is grounded in His death, burial, resurrection and intercession in behalf of all who repentantly acknowledge their sinfulness and trust the merits of Christ alone for personal salvation. Thus, one becomes part of the Church through the regenerating decree of God, which is congruent with the trust one puts in Jesus Christ through believing the Gospel message concerning Him.

An exclusive Gospel

The Reformers' message is very discriminatory. It excludes all who come to God any other way than by faith alone in Christ alone. It excludes those who would trust in their righteous deeds. It excludes all who would trust in their baptism, church membership or righteous life as reasons why they should be a part of God's family. The historic doctrine of salvation preaches a Gospel that points to what the Lord Jesus Christ accomplished once and for all on the Cross and in the Resurrection. It does not point to what man has done or is doing to gain God's favor. The biblical message of salvation is God-centered, not man-centered.

For many years there was basic agreement on the Gospel among Protestants, teaching that it is "by faith alone in Christ alone." But with the arrival of Higher Criticism and the application of developmental evolutionary thought to the Scriptures, the biblical foundation of the Gospel was eroded. Even today, with the development of a "New Perspective on Paul" among some Evangelicals, the historic doctrine of justification is being reconsidered.

The historic Gospel provided a problem for liberal theology. Liberalism's Social Gospel was centered on the assertion that man's nature was essentially good and preached a message designed to revolutionize society through education and social reformation. The socially-based Gospel of the liberal and the biblically-based Gospel of the grace of God are mutually exclusive. Yet the liberals of the early Twentieth Century insisted on an ecumenical union with all professing Christians. If that ecumenical union was to be achieved, some adjustments in the conflicting Gospel messages had to be agreed upon and some accommodations had to be made by those who initially resisted those adjustments. This was essentially what took place in Protestant denominations. If denominational unity was to be maintained, then doctrinal tolerance had to be promoted, and accommodation had to be made to include a variety of views. In addressing this spirit of tolerance and accommodation, Dr. D. Martyn Lloyd-Jones wrote:

> Is it right to tolerate in the same church people whose views on the essentials of the faith are diametrically opposed? Is it right in the light of the New Testament teaching that we regard such people as "brethren," that we refer to people who never darken the doors of a place of worship as "lapsed Christians" simply because they have been baptized when infants? Is that compatible with the New Testament teaching with regard to the church, and her unity, and her discipline and her life?[10]

Could those whose lives have no evidence of regeneration be called brothers? Ecumenical thirst for union would answer an enthusiastic, "yes!" The Evangelical/Fundamentalist conclusion was a resounding, "no!"

To achieve their ecumenical goals, the liberal community promoted a view that baptism is the visible sign of being a Christian, and, therefore, New Testament ecclesiology requires the practice of unity with all who are baptized. The liberals affirmed that the Anabaptist view was incorrect (church membership was for true believers only) and they taught the multitudinous view of the Church (Christianity encompasses the company of the baptized).[11]

The troublesome question arose. Should accommodation and toleration on the part of Evangelical/Fundamentalists be practiced in their denominations in order to avoid denominational division? The answer to that was mixed. Some desired to win back their denominations for the truth. Others viewed the principle of "*come out from among them and be separate*" (2 Corinthians 6:17) as the controlling principle dictating action. Consequently, there were true brothers who remained in compromising alliances within their denominations while there were other brothers who left in order to start new denominations and fellowships committed to the Word of God and an unadulterated Gospel. Thus, brothers in Christ found themselves divided, and the consequence of the division led to open conflict. Again, the question had to be asked, "Are you truly my brother?"

The family divided

It is hard to limit relationships with brothers in Christ. It seems to go directly against the desire of the Lord for His Church. Had He not instructed believers to love one another as he loved them? Did He not say that love would be the mark of the Christian? This is the dilemma many true believers faced, for there are other places in the Scripture where believers are clearly commanded to limit relationships with brothers. The Scripture mentions several:

- **Disorderly Brethren** - "*Now we command you brethren, in the name of our Lord Jesus Christ, that you keep away from every brother who leads an unruly life and not according to the tradition which you received from us.*" (2 Thessalonians 3:6)

- **Divisive brethren** - "*Now I urge you, brethren, keep your eye on those who cause dissensions and hindrances contrary to the teaching which you learned, and turn away from them.*" (Romans 16:17)

- **Decadent brethren** - "*... I wrote to you not to associate with any so-called brother if he is an immoral person, or covetous, or an idolater, or a reviler, or a drunkard, or a swindler – not even to eat with such a one.*" (1 Corinthians 5:11)

- **Disobedient brethren** - "*If anyone does not obey our instruction in this letter, take special note of that person and do not associate with him, so that he will be put to shame.*" (2 Thessalonians 3:14)

- **Disputing brethren** -"*If anyone advocates a different doctrine and does not agree with sound words, those of our Lord Jesus Christ, and with the doctrine conforming to godliness, he is conceited and understands nothing; but he has a morbid interest in controversial questions and disputes about words, out of* *which arise envy, strife, abusive language, evil suspicions, and constant friction between men of depraved mind and deprived of the truth, who suppose that godliness is a means of gain.*" (1 Timothy 6:3-5)

- **Determined brethren** -"*Reject a factious man after a first and second warning, knowing that such a man is perverted and is sinning, being self condemned.*" (Titus 3:10)

- **Disciplined brethren** - "*If your brother sins, go and show him his fault in private; if he listens to you, you have won your brother. But if he does not listen to you, take one or two more with you, so that by the mouth of two or three witnesses every fact may be confirmed. And if he refuses to listen to them, tell it to the church; and if he refuses to listen even to the church, let him be to you as a Gentile and a tax-collector.*" (Matthew 18:15-17)

- **Defiant brethren** - "*Among these are Hymenaeus and Alexander; whom I have handed over to Satan, so that they will be taught not to blaspheme.*" (2 Timothy 4:14-15) "*Alexander the coppersmith did me much harm; the Lord will repay him according to his deeds. Be on guard against him yourself, for he vigorously opposed our teaching.*" (1 Timothy 1:20)

The concept of limiting relationships and association in all of these cases actually illustrates what biblical love is all about. Kenneth Wuest shares his insights on the meaning of the Greek word *agapao*. He notes that the word:

> speaks of a love which is awakened by a sense of value in an object which causes one to prize it. It springs from an apprehension of the preciousness of an object. It is a love of esteem and approbation. The quality of this love is determined by the character of the one who loves, and that of the object loved. [12]

Understanding *agape* love as the recognition of intrinsic value that makes an object precious helps us perceive the meaning of the Apostle John's observation, "*If someone says, I love God and hates his brother, he is a liar; for the one that does not love his brother whom he has seen, cannot love God whom he has not seen*" (1 John 4:20). A fellow believer is precious in God's sight. That is why He gave His only begotten Son, for that sinner's salvation. If God so valued a sinner as to bring him into His family, how can one say a brother has no value?

Genuine love is not a matter of feeling; it is placing the same value the Lord places on his redeemed ones. Jesus declared: "*This is My commandment, that you love one another, just as I have loved you*" (John 15:12). If one highly values his brother, he will carefully follow the instruction to "*admonish one another*" (2 Thessalonians 3:15) so that a brother will have all the resources necessary to understand his sin and to see the consequences sinful behavior has on godly relationships. Sin breaks fellowship with other believers. If one is not willing to deny himself the personal benefit of another's fellowship because of that brother's sin, he does not demonstrate the true character of biblical love for that brother.

The Apostle Paul clearly incorporates the demonstration of love found in limiting a relationship with a brother. He instructs the Thessalonians: "*If anyone does not obey our instruction in this letter, take special note of that person and do not associate with him, so that he will be put to shame. Yet do not regard him as an enemy, but admonish him as a brother*" (2 Thessalonians 3:15). The emphasis of this section is that we are to identify the particular way in which a brother is errant in failing to obey the Scriptures. We are to make sure there is no participation with him in that error. The phrase "*do not associate with him*" literally means "to mix it up." Louw suggests:

> In translating terms referring to association, one may employ a number of different kinds of expressions, for example, "to have something to do with," "to keep company with," "to go around with," "to join in doing things together," or "to become a companion of." Sometimes association is spoken of in terms of the impression made upon others, for example, "to be seen often together," "to be regarded as close friends," and even idiomatically as "to be another person's shadow."[13]

The error needs to be spotlighted and avoided and no encouragement is to be given to a brother who is in error. In order to incite him to lose respect for his error ("*be put to shame*"), we must identify the error and then refuse to affirm him in it. However, he is not to be regarded or classified as an enemy (literally "a hostile"). In other words, we are not to conclude that a brother who fails to obey "what is written" is an antagonist, nor are we to show hostility toward him. This is the great danger in the appropriate relationship with an errant brother: allowing one's contempt for error to splash onto one's perspective of the person caught in that error. Scripture, however, instructs us to demonstrate our familial concern for our brother by "admonishing him" (literally "*to put in mind, to admonish, warn, advise*").

The spirit in which this is done is crucial. 1 Corinthians 13:6 teaches that love "*does not rejoice in unrighteousness, but rejoices in the truth.*" Christians cannot delight when they have "caught" a brother who is errant – announcing to everyone his particular problem under the guise of "*taking special note of that person.*" Instead, they should approach brothers who are overtaken in some fault with tremendous humility and the desire to see them restored (Galatians 6:1). The specific priorities of this humble approach are found in 2 Timothy 2:24-26. Repentance from error and rescue from the snare of the devil should be the underlying motivations within those reaching out to them. In appealing to members of the family of God who have gone astray, there are certain temperaments that must be maintained according to 2 Timothy 2:24-26. They include:

- **Civility** - "*The Lord's bond-servant must not be quarrelsome*" - the truth of God's Word is not demonstrated with an abusive, harsh, argumentative approach to those who differ with the Word of God. Literally, this reads, "It is not necessary to be quarrelsome." For a person to adopt the spirit of the world in contending for the faith belies their confidence in the power of the Word. It also places the responsibility to convert an errant brother upon their own persuasive or punitive skills. This is not the spirit of godliness that we must have as we appeal to our brothers.

- **Compassion** - "... *but be kind to all*" - referring to gentleness or outward mildness in handling someone. This is used only one other time in the New Testament in 1 Thessalonians 2:7 describing the tenderness of a mother with a child. The argument from the Scriptures is not enhanced whatsoever by a spirit of austerity.

- **Competence** - "... *able to teach*" - the emphasis made here to concentrate on God's Word in preaching and teaching clarifies it as a primary duty of spiritual leadership. In addition, there are some who understand "apt to teach" in 2 Timothy 2:24 to mean "teachable" since it occurs in the midst of a list of dispositional character qualities (1 Timothy 4:6, 11, 13; 5:17; 2 Timothy 2:15, 24,25; 4:2; Titus 2:1).

- **Composure** - "... *patient when wronged*" - describes the servant of the Lord as one who is able to maintain an attitude of patient forbearance without resentment toward those who are in opposition. The term comes from *anechomai* (to hold up) and *kakon* (evil) and describes a person who is able to take upon himself the ability to carry a relationship even when the opposing person responds inappropriately.

- **Caution** - "… *with gentleness*" - we are to possess "power under control" and approach people with whom disagree with meekness, knowing they are often the very ones for whom our ministry is most urgent. Paul essentially warns us not to undermine our confidence in the sufficiency of Scripture by resorting to any harsh treatment. The ability to control oneself in the face of harsh treatment is one of the greatest evidences of confidence in the sufficiency of Scripture

- **Correction** - "… *correcting those who are in opposition*" - we are to use the Word of God in a kind, gentle, meek, and loving way to refute those who are in opposition to God's Word. This emphasizes the responsibility to show how a person in error can be reconciled both to the truth and to his brothers in Christ. The term here describes those in opposition and conveys that they have deliberately chosen to oppose – or they have set themselves up in opposition to the truth. Even when disagreement is deliberate and obnoxious, brothers are to reach out to those with gentleness and meekness in order to see them restored.

If we cannot show these characteristics of compassion toward brothers who differ, how are we ever going to show genuine compassion to the enemies of God? In order for these qualities to be demonstrated, a continuing concern needs to exist for these brothers. It is incumbent upon the community of believers to reach out to sinning brothers with the truth and with an appeal to turn from those errors with which faithful servants of God cannot "mix it up."

Example of biblical love for brothers

On March 29, 1994 a group of Christian leaders released a document they had signed calling for cooperation between Evangelicals and Roman Catholics in a number of different areas. It was called *Evangelical and Catholics Together: The Christian Mission in the Third Millennium* (hereafter referred to as ECT or ECT Accord). Many quickly protested such cooperation as an indication of apostasy. At the time, we were involved in the leadership of a fellowship of independent churches known today as IFCA International. At the 1994 Annual Convention of the IFCA, we considered our responsibility to the men who signed the ECT Accord. A resolution was unanimously adopted and we decided that a letter should be written to each of the signers providing them with a copy of the resolution and sharing our concern. As brothers, the IFCA International resolution called upon them to reconsider their action and recognize that the ECT Accord represented a compromise of biblically authentic Christianity. The following is a copy of the letter sent along with the resolution to each of the signers. (Also see Appendix Four: *IFCA International Resolution on Evangelicals & Catholics Together: The Christian Mission in the 3rd Millennium.*)

August 8, 1994
Dear,

The Independent Fundamental Churches of America is a fellowship of 752 member churches and over 1200 pastors and Christian workers across America representing some 320,000 people in our churches. Our 65th annual convention was held recently in Santa Rosa, California. The enclosed resolution on "Evangelicals and Catholics Together: The Christian Mission in the Third Millennium" was adopted unanimously and represents our great concern that the unity and cooperation called for are being pursued for sociological reasons rather than as an expression of oneness in truth. It is apparent that the great biblical doctrines of soteriology are necessarily trivialized in this pursuit. Unity that does not find its source in common understanding of the clear teaching of the Word of God must minimize truth and eventually make adjustments to any truth that inhibits the accomplishments of its purpose. Cooperation within an unholy alliance, no matter how noble its cause, is clearly contrary to the teaching of the Word of God.

We prayerfully call upon you to rethink your commitment to the propositions in this document that are very damaging to the propagation of the truth and the overall work of God.

Sincerely,
Richard. I Gregory
Executive Director, IFCA

Needless to say, the signing of the ECT Accord by forty noted Evangelical and Roman Catholic leaders caused no small stir among the Fundamental/Evangelical community of believers. Many other individuals and organizations called upon the signers of the ECT Accord to reconsider their action. One of the most effective was the effort of apologist John Ankerberg. In conjunction with his television program, he announced in early January 1995 that he would conduct a seminar to be held on February 8, 1995 with three Christian leaders at the Coral Ridge Presbyterian Church in Fort Lauderdale, Florida to analyze the ECT Accord. Participating were D. James Kennedy, the pastor of the host church; R.C. Sproul, founder and chairman of Ligonier Ministries and professor at Knox Theological Seminary; and John MacArthur, the pastor of Grace Community Church in Panorama City, California. Transcripts, video tapes and audio tapes of the symposium were widely distributed. At issue was the ECT's apparent disregard of Evangelical doctrinal distinctives and historic Roman Catholic official statements about *sola fide* and *sola Scriptura*. Ankerburg produced a six-part video series of this seminar (titled "Protestants and Catholics: Do They Now Agree?"), and aired it on six consecutive Sunday evenings starting March 5, 1995.

Appeal through private meetings

Private meetings were scheduled between the ECT signers and these notable ECT critics. The expressed purpose of the meetings was to appeal biblically to the signers to clarify the statements in the ECT Accord that seemed to disregard the theological differences between Protestants and Roman Catholics and limit evangelism. As a result of these passionate appeals to the ECT's signers, Charles Colson of Prison Fellowship Ministries requested a meeting specifically for the purpose of trying to avoid a serious rift in the Evangelical/Fundamentalist community of believers.

The meeting was held January 19, 1995 also at Coral Ridge Presbyterian Church in Fort Lauderdale, Florida. The gathering included, Colson, Campus Crusade for Christ's founder Bill Bright, and theologian J.I. Packer (all ECT signers). Also at the meeting were ECT critics John MacArthur, R.C. Sproul, John Ankerberg, D. James Kennedy and author Michael Horton. The meeting was moderated by Moody Bible Institute's president Joseph Stowell, with assistance from church historian John Woodbridge.[14] The result of the meeting was a two hundred fifty word Clarifying Statement signed by William R. Bright, Charles W. Colson, Kent

R. Hill, and James I. Packer. Although the ECT's critics who attended the meeting did not sign the statement, they helped to write it. It was reported in an article in *Christianity Today* that MacArthur later observed:

> "I'm very glad for the second document. I'm glad [Colson, Packer and Bright] had the opportunity to clarify what is clarified there. It still doesn't go as far as I would have hoped." He [MacArthur] remains steadfast in his belief that evangelical ECT signers ultimately should "recant." "The bottom line," he says, "is that Roman Catholicism is another religion." [15]

A different approach

Not all agreed that appealing to the ECT signers was the best way to relate to brothers with whom you disagree. Caustic articles and sermons by some separatists decried MacArthur and the other ECT critics for even talking to the "compromisers" who signed the ECT Accord. In their view, the effort to reach out to "compromising brothers" exposed the ECT critics to be themselves compromisers. Further, they concluded that anyone who had any relationship with ECT critics were also guilty of compromise.[16] In this approach the characteristics of second and third degree separation became very evident. In addition, the intimidating and watchful eye of "the defenders of the faith" roamed to and fro seeking to catch anyone who violated their relational standards.

These brothers have a very restricted and focused view of the responsibilities true brothers have to one another. It appears that their practice is to label as compromisers or apostates all who are violating biblical principles (as they understand them). Therefore, they denounce and expose them. In this approach, the character of true biblical love, which calls for admonishment with continuing responsibility (2 Thessalonians 3:14-15), seems to be absent which calls.

Conclusion

True believers have a responsibility to regard all other believers as objects of the love of God in Christ Jesus. Each must say: "If God loves them, so must I." This love recognizes their value as brothers. It requires that believers fulfill the responsibility to encourage brothers toward godliness and to admonish them when they are in error. When a true brother fails to respond to admonishment, it may be necessary to demonstrate true biblical love by limiting relationships in order to bring them to repentance.

It is never biblical to destructively attack a brother, with the motive of exposing him, in order to promote the correctness of one's own view.

When the church finds it necessary to exercise discipline because of sinful conduct or attitude, it is incumbent upon brothers not to take upon themselves the responsibility to get in between the church's discipline and the sinning brother in the name of showing love. God's declared method of restoring a brother must not be compromised. The process of appeal given to us by the Lord in Matthew 18 teaches patient, relational reaching out (in order to "gain your brother") rather than impatient exposure (in order to rid the body of undesirable "compromisers"). There may come a time when the "leaven" will have to be removed, after appeals have been unsuccessful in bringing repentance. However, fulfilling the responsibility brothers have to brothers includes the exercise of true biblical love, endeavoring to keep the unity of the Spirit in the bond of peace based upon fidelity to the Lordship of Jesus Christ and the authority of His Word. This is the very basic relationship in the Body of Christ.

Thus, at this lowest and most common sphere of relationship within the Body of Christ, believers are to relate to one another as part of the same family. They are to love one another, appeal to one another, and admonish one another. They are to fellowship with one another on an individual basis, granting acceptance to those who may differ but who confess Christ Jesus as Lord and Savior. Although there may be no room for the more intense fellowship levels such as cooperative evangelism or ecclesiastical participation, there is room for personal fellowship in Christ Jesus. It is inappropriate to participate in corporate worship and evangelism with those whom we have significant doctrinal differences. But the willingness to discuss respectfully in personal conversation these differences in theological convictions should not be considered compromise.

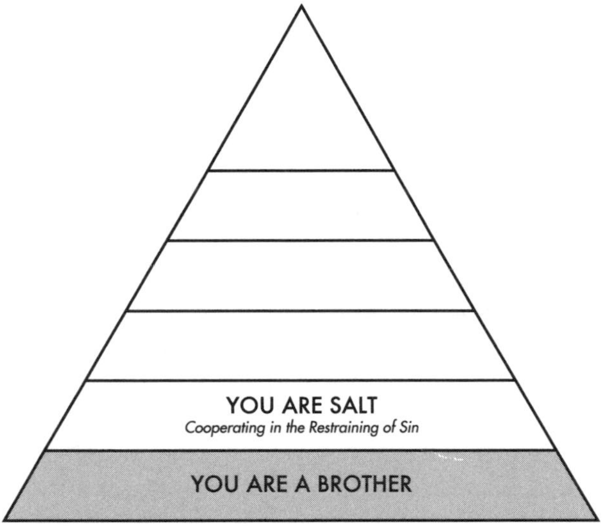

PYRAMID OF RESPONSIBILITY

The mandates of biblical relationships

CHAPTER TWO

YOU ARE SALT

Cooperating in the restraint of sin

Believers have always had difficulty determining just how involved they should be in the affairs of community and government. This has been especially true since the landmark Scopes Trial in 1925 when the debate between creationism and evolution entered the courtroom in Tennessee. During this time of cultural upheaval, historic Christianity was being assaulted by scientific theory, social change and theological liberalism. Many Christians built protective walls around their families and decided to drop out or limit participation in community, social and political activities. Many no longer participated in the political process and confined their social involvement to their churches. Their opportunities to be salt and light in society (Matthew 5:13) were consequently severely limited and their reclusive attitudes toward society opened them up to criticism.

Liberal theology seized the day and promoted a Social Gospel that defined the command to "*go into all the world*" to mean promoting health, human rights, and helping the poor. Applauding the government's willingness to provide for the needs of its citizens, liberal theologians declared that their agenda for the Church and the new found social agenda of the government were one and the same. Partnering with the social welfare programs, food programs, and work relief, liberal denominations found great delight in seeing "Christianity" advanced. Instead of seeing the Gospel as good news of reconciliation to a holy God through the redemption available in the blood of Christ, theological liberals saw it as good news of relief from poverty and respect for individual rights.

This severe capitulation by the liberals and the twisted focus of their denominational priorities became the object of tremendous concern for Fundamentalists. The idea of a Social Gospel was repudiated, and those possessing a commitment to the true Gospel withdrew from relationships that entangled them in such superficial social pursuits. Unfortunately, many Fundamentalists went too far and identified all social involvement as a distraction. They left the involvement in social issues to the Liberals and withdrew from addressing society's dilemmas under the guise of faithfulness to the true Gospel. While the Liberals emphasized, "*Let us do good to all people...*" (Galatians 6:10a), the Fundamentalists would emphasize, "... *and especially to those who are of the household of the faith*" (Galatians 6:10b). Hence, the Fundamentalists' emphases led them to internalize their focus and programming – and removed them from interacting with the world to alleviate the problems faced by a sinful world. The Fundamentalists' perspective was often essentially: "What do you expect? Seek first the Kingdom of God and all these things will be added to you" (Matthew 6:33). "We are not going to alleviate the consequences brought about by sin through some social bandage. Only the Gospel will heal the problem!" Although such a perspective does find some biblical basis, it is not tempered with the spirit of grace and love that God Himself portrays.

Where is the balance to be found in all of this? How involved ought the believer to be in social concerns and governmental issues? Many within Fundamentalism, while suffering humiliating attacks from both Liberals and the New Evangelicals, concluded they had to withdraw from the mainstream of society and culture in order to preserve the integrity of the Gospel. Some developed a fortress mentality to protect themselves from potential compromises. Although focusing on purity is an essential priority of true religion, so are social concerns: "*Pure and undefiled religion in sight of our God and Father is this: to visit orphans and widows in their distress, and to keep oneself unstained by the world*" (James 1:27). Jesus called upon the Father to preserve His followers not by disengaging them from the world where they were to represent Him, but by keeping them from being overwhelmed by evil. "*I do not ask You to take them out of the world, but to keep them from the evil one*" (John 17:15).

Jesus desires that God glorify Himself not through isolating His people, but by protecting them as they are engaged in representing Him in the world. Jude concludes his book with a glorious tribute to the work of God while His children engage unbelievers. Warning believers to hate "*even the garment polluted by the flesh*" (Jude 23b), he repeatedly emphasizes the need to display mercy to those who are struggling in sin. He encourages us not to abandon them by assuring us that God "*is able to keep you from stumbling and to make you stand in the presence of His glory blameless with great joy*" (Jude 24).

Consistent with this priority is the instruction given to believers by the Lord that they serve Him by being the "*salt of the earth*" (Matthew 5:13a). His intention is that believers' testimonies be evident as they live among those lost in sin. When a person is born again, by being reconciled to God, he possesses influence in the world and behaves like salt. The effects of salt include:

- **Salt Enhances Flavor** - the testimonies of believers are designed by the Lord to influence the world by bringing the joys of life into greater focus. As believers live consistently godly lives, those who are lost are able to taste the blessings of the Lord through the lives of believers lives. One of the issues that intensifies the apostate's accountability before the Lord is through contact with the godly, they have "*tasted of the heavenly gift and have been made partakers of the Holy Spirit, and have tasted the good word of God and the powers of the age to come, and then have fallen away …*" (Hebrews 6:4b-6a). Walking uprightly and faithfully under the Lordship of Jesus Christ produces not only the believer's joy of fellowship with God, but also the ability of the lost to observe the believer's life restored to God's intended "flavor." The bitterness and blandness of alienation from God becomes a means of dissatisfaction, and the enjoyment of God's blessing becomes something to be desired.

- **Salt draws out infection** - as the testimonies of believers are observed by the lost, the shame of sinful behavior grows in the lives of the lost. "Most methods of curing depend on dehydration whether by evaporation as in drying in the sun and wind or over smoky fires, or by extraction of fluid from the tissues by osmosis in the case of the treatment with salts. Common salt, which is chiefly used, and the chemicals absorbed from smoke also have specific bactericidal affects."[17] Like a wound is caused to sting by contact with salt, so too, the consciences of the wicked begin to feel the sting of shame as they come into contact with the "*salt of the earth.*" A certain "burning" is felt by those who would otherwise feel comfortable in their sin. If left to itself, the world would continue to fester in the infection of its own sin. However, through the agency of godly people, infection can be drawn out so that ultimately, the power of the Gospel might produce healing.

- **Salt creates thirst** - as the testimonies of believers are observed by the lost, a thirst is created in those who begin to recognize they are dry and need a drink. Differing from enhancing taste, creating a thirst serves as a motivation to satisfy the craving for proper water.

- **Salt preserves from decay** - as the testimonies of believers are observed by the lost, the advance of decay is greatly reduced. "Although micro-organisms are usually thought of as causing spoilage, they are capable under certain conditions of producing desirable affects, including oxidative and alcoholic fermentation. The micro-organisms that grow in a food product and the changes they produce are determined by acidity, available carbohydrates, oxygen, and temperature. Untreated meat, for example, molds and putrefies; the addition of salt causes different organisms to grow."[18] In order for bacteria to grow, there must be moisture. As the moisture is removed through the process of osmosis, the environment for bacterial activity is reduced. Essentially, the "moisture" of sin is reduced through the application of salt. The believer restrains the culture from its decay toward lawlessness.

In line with these observations, believers, as the possessors of the Holy Spirit, serve as influences that restrain sin. In reality, the Holy Spirit is the Restrainer. However, He indwells believers and executes restraining influence through them: "*And you know what restrains him [the Man of Lawlessness] now, so that in his time he will be revealed. For the mystery of lawlessness is already at work; only he who now restrains will do so until he is taken out of the way. Then that lawless one will be revealed …*" (2 Thessalonians 2:6-8a). This is the work of the Holy Spirit as He keeps evil in check through the Church that He indwells. When the church is removed from the world through the Rapture, the Holy Spirit (the obstacle to the Antichrist) will also be removed. In the meantime, the Holy Spirit is restraining sin.

There has been much debate about the difference between restraining sin through blocking the agenda of lawlessness and providing the solution to lawlessness through the redemption that is in Christ Jesus. Certainly, the only answer to the lawlessness waiting to overwhelm the world is the preaching of the Cross and personal faith in Christ Jesus. He is the *only* solution to the problem. However, it is by means of the presence of the Holy Spirit in the world – primarily through indwelling and empowering the Church – that lawlessness can be restrained. Whereas overcoming lawlessness is the outcome of the people of God serving as light, restraining it is the outcome of the people of God serving as salt.

Confusing these two issues causes people either to withdraw from the involvement in engaging the world with the purpose of restraining of sin, or to indulge themselves in society believing that it will "turn things around" and bring in righteousness. Reconstructionism, for instance, teaches that the way in which the world will eventually become Christianized is by means of the "transformation" of every area of life according to the principles of Theonomy (bringing society under the laws and penalties of God revealed in the Old Testament). This is an example of salt with no light.

On the other extreme are those who believe the Church needs to accept the world in whatever form it takes and minimize whatever differences might exist with the world by embracing the culture. Instead of confronting the cultural aberrances, they befriend the culture in order to proclaim a mono-dimensional Gospel of "love." This is an example of light with no salt. Either way is unacceptable and keeps the church from fulfilling its objectives.

Jesus warns His followers they should be careful not to lose their effectiveness. He says: "… *if the salt has become tasteless, how can it be made salty again? It is no longer good for anything, except to be thrown out and trampled under foot by men*" (Matthew 5:13b). In the context of this passage, He is stating there are ways salt can become contaminated. Such contamination renders the salt without value except as a means by which pathways can be kept free from vegetation. How can the "*salt of the earth*" lose its effectiveness?

- Corruption (loss of credibility)
- Compromise (loss of contrast)
- Cloistering (loss of contact)

Thus, believers must be involved in preserving a culture free from the decadence that neglect enhances while carefully preserving their commitment to the holiness of God. It is at this point the believer comes to realize not everyone who claims to be a Christian is able to be included in the attempt to serve as the salt of the earth. Certainly the vast majority of people who are truly born again, regardless of their specific affiliation or denomination, will be able to serve the Lord as salt. However, there are those who would be called brothers in the Lord who are corrupt, compromising, or who have cloistered themselves so discriminately from the world that they are no longer relevant. To partner with them would discredit and undermine the effort to see morality and ethics preserved. Such brothers should not be sought or included in the band of obedient believers. It is for this reason that this second level of separation is more restrictive than the first level of brotherhood.

TYPES OF ACTIVITIES AS SALT

Humanitarian / Social contributions

When it comes to answering the call of the Lord to do good unto all men, there is room for brothers to respond commonly from a diversity of positions. He is the Lord of all and each believer has the duty to respond in His name. It is in this realm that the passage in Luke 9 is best applied. The disciples observed a man who was using the name of Jesus to restrain sin by casting out a demon. They tried to stop him because he was not following along with them. Jesus confronted their exclusivity by declaring: "*Do not hinder him; for he who is not against you is for you*" (Luke 9:50). Clearly this principle cannot be broadened into the upper levels of relationships and responsibilities dealt with later in this book. It pertains to the restraining of evil. Compromise occurs when people attempt to apply this principle to areas of separation where God expects believers to be more restrictive. It is on the level of serving Him as "*the salt of the earth*" that this principle is most appropriately applied. The following are some illustrations of ways in which believers are able to band together and honor one another's efforts to serve the Lord as "*the salt of the earth.*"

- **Blood drives** - If the local denominational church were to sponsor a blood drive because the community blood bank is dangerously low on their supply, it would be appropriate for all Christians, regardless of affiliation to participate. It would not be a compromise of Fundamentalism for me to walk into a denominational church and give blood. Some people might feel that they ought not to give blood at a denominational church because they would be compromising even by being seen at the location. Therefore, they refuse to give at that location and will either not give at all, or seek another location. Although a believer should not feel comfortable going to such a place to worship together with a church that is compromising, to serve as salt through the good deed of blood donation is not profane.

- **Food pantries/Clothing distribution centers** - If a community possesses a local food pantry, it would be very appropriate to provide food for stocking the shelves. When economically challenged people visit the pantry to receive relief of their deprivation, it is appropriate that they see individuals and churches that are willing to "do good unto all men." Even gathering food and clothing at church and announcing the church's ability to cooperate in such humanitarian relief initiatives would be helpful and godly. There are some, however, who feel as though they would be compromising to participate in a local food pantry because there are churches with whom we could not cooperate on the light level that also participate in making contributions on the salt level. Since they feel the need to separate from such churches or denominations, they withdraw from participating in the name of a pure Gospel. However, they fail to see the difference between the levels of salt and light.

- **Shelters for the poor or battered** - Most communities have shelters for people who are homeless or who are suffering from abusive relationships and are in need of protection. Individuals and churches that provide contributions to those shelters are able to do so in the name of Christ and recognize they are serving the Lord as the "salt of the earth." Again, they should not fear they will somehow violate the holiness of God by giving a cup of water to the least of these. Rather, Jesus praised those who extended themselves to those in need and affirmed that to do so demonstrated the reality of their faith. There were no qualifications or restrictions, but when they saw someone in need, they sought to meet it. He stated:

> *Come, you who are blessed of My Father, inherit the kingdom prepared for you from the foundation of the world. For I was hungry, and you gave Me something to eat; I was thirsty, and you gave Me something to drink; I was a stranger, and you invited Me in; naked, and you clothed Me; I was sick, and you visited Me; I was in prison, and you came to Me." Then the righteous will answer Him, "Lord, when did we see You hungry, and feed You, or thirsty, and give You something to drink? And when did we see You a stranger, and invite You in, or naked, and clothe You? When did we see You sick, or in prison, and came to You?" The King will answer and say to them, "Truly I say to you, to the extent that you did it to one of these brothers of Mine, even the least of them, you did it to Me* (Matthew 25:34-40).

It would not do for a believer to ask a person in need of a piece of bread (just to be safe) whether someone from another denomination had already given them a drink of water.

SOCIAL ISSUES

Homosexuality/HIV

One of today's relevant social concerns is the problem of homosexuality and its related impact upon society and culture. The agenda of the radical homosexual community is to create the impression that homosexual relationships are normal and to claim the constitutional protections attendant to such a status. As the sin of homosexual behavior becomes accepted through lobbying, blatant advertisements, and intimidations, it will desensitize the culture through repeated exposure. The impact on society will inevitably cause ours to follow every other culture that has embraced this sin. In *The History of the Decline and Fall of the Roman Empire*, British historian Edward Gibbon (1737-1794) identified homosexuality as one of the key characteristics of the moral decline that contributed to the disintegration of Rome. From a historical and moral point of view, resisting the encroachment of the homosexual agenda is essential if believers are to serve as salt.

It must be reiterated that the solution to the homosexual problem is the Gospel. However, since Scripture declares that God does give *some* "over to a depraved mind" (Romans 1:28), they will not respond to the Gospel. Therefore, the enmity against God represented by their agenda must be resisted and its sin restrained. However, in serving the Lord as the "*salt of the earth*" believers must demonstrate genuine concern rather than hostility for the souls of those captivated by homosexual lust. Believers should cooperate together in an attempt to thwart the deterioration of morals and marriage that results in the implementation of the homosexual agenda.

In our attempts to reach out to homosexuals, we found a tremendous willingness among believers from a diversity of churches to cooperate for the purpose of resisting the demoralizing effects of homosexuality in our community.[19] Many denominational leaders shy away from involvement, claiming it would "merely bring division" or "the Scriptures are not clear" or "current 'scientific research' opens too many questions for them". Genuine believers within their churches will see the shallowness of their commitment to serve as salt and step outside the guidance of their leaders to do what is right.

This is what we encountered in one of our ministries when we stood firmly against the agenda of radical homosexuals who asserted God's "genius" in creating them with sexual confusion. When an attempt was made to force the issue in our local High School, united appeal was made to the local school board. That appeal called upon the school board members to yield to the God who had placed them in their positions of authority. We asserted God is profaned when He is blamed for the condition described by Him in Scripture as an abomination (Leviticus 18:22). Such an appeal, although made with gentleness and love, was branded as bigoted and hostile by some within the community. Salt certainly burns a wound as the process of osmosis draws out the infection.

Since the impact of the "*salt of the earth*" will often burn as it is applied, demonstrating the love of Christ to homosexuals is crucial. On one occasion during a convention in Wichita, Kansas, we were approached by a man in great distress. When we began talking with him, he shared how terrified he was at the news he had just received that his "partner," with whom he had lived for two years, had been HIV positive for the past year and a half. He was broken and distressed – scared to death by the prospect that he also was HIV positive. Over a meal at a nearby restaurant, the man listened to the Gospel and committed his life to Jesus Christ. He then agreed that the best thing to do was to go home and reconcile with his estranged parents. We provided him a bus ticket to Cedar Rapids, Iowa. One of the realities we faced was the fact that there were few churches that would welcome him as a brother and provide for him a haven.

Many within the Church at large are more fearful of the dangers of AIDS than they are burdened for the souls of the infected. On various occasions, people who were once enslaved by homosexuality have expressed their deep appreciation for the message of love that we preach because they have personally experienced the power of the blood of Jesus Christ to deliver them from their bondage.

Abortion/Family planning

Another area of upheaval in our society where the "*salt of the earth*" needs to be applied is that of the sanctity of human life. As the people of our culture dismiss God's creative handiwork (claiming unborn babies are merely "masses" or "tissue" they are free to "excise" and discard), true believers must clarify this profaning of God's prerogatives as Life-giver. We must restrain such profanity. Banding together with other believers to restrain the abortionist agenda from corroding the moral commitments of our culture is an important Christian responsibility.

There must be no question in the mind of a believer that God will never bless taking the life of a child while it is safe in the haven of its mother's womb. The opposite is true – slaying children is a cause for His specific indignation and wrath because the lives taken are made in His image. Thus, it is His very Person that is profaned by the abortionist. Whereas they claim that they are exercising the "freedom of choice," they fail to understand they are actually eliminating God's choices and obligating Him to dispense justice and vengeance upon those who would defy Him. Allowing one's culture to so putrefy in the eyes of God without attempting to preserve it through the "*salt of the earth*" is to fail in our God-given responsibility.

Thus believers from various theological perspectives are able to band together to resist such cultural abomination. Participating in crisis pregnancy centers, local adoption agencies, sanctity of human life organizations such as Right to Life or Baptists for Life, local "Life Chain" demonstrations, and similar initiatives to promote awareness of the sanctity of life is necessary for the believer to serve as the "*salt of the earth.*" Advocating "abstinence only" reproductive health in local school systems is appropriate. In one of our ministries, we were able to serve on a committee of community representatives responsible for approving the reproductive health curriculum used in the school district. Through our appeal, our district approved an abstinence only program with reference to sexual responsibility. However, there were various representatives from denominational groups participating as well. It is not justifiable to charge with compromise those who participated in this kind of activity. Cooperation occurred on this level as the "*salt of the earth.*"

A word needs to be given here regarding the extent of activity that is deemed appropriate. There should never be an occasion where the laws of God-given authority are violated in the attempt to restrain sin. Indeed, we are told in Scripture that it is better to obey God rather than men (cf. Acts 5:29). However, to defy God-given authority is to defy God Himself: "*Every person is to be in subjection to the governing authorities. For there is no authority except from God, and those which exist are established by God. Therefore whoever resists authority has opposed the ordinance of God; and they who have opposed will receive condemnation upon themselves*" (Romans 13:1-2). It is not that there can be no appeal to governing authorities; we are encouraged to do so. However, we cannot justify ourselves in "civil disobedience" through the claim that we are serving as the "*salt of the earth.*" There is no command in Scripture to defy governing authorities who give freedom to their people to personally disobey God's commands. However, should the government personally direct a believer to abort a child (such has been the case in some countries like China), the situation would be different. Such a command is inappropriate and should be defied. But, defying government because someone else is violating a Scriptural command is also inappropriate. Therefore, such activities as an "Operation Rescue" attempt which trespasses on private property, or violating restraining orders, participating in or giving approval to abortion clinic bombings or the murder of abortionists would be things that result in receiving condemnation by God.

Cloning/Genetic engineering

The people of God have the responsibility to call upon our culture to honor the distinct privilege of God as the Lord of life. The endeavor to marginalize God and usurp His prerogatives brings insult to Him. In the early chapters of Genesis, after men began to repopulate the earth following the flood, the defiant nature of man was made evident on the plains of Shinar. They did not find contentedness as servants of God, for there was a great desire to "*make for themselves a name*" (Genesis 11:4). They displayed a great desire to break free from dependency on God. Genesis states: "*the Lord came down to see the city and the tower which the sons of men had built. The Lord said, 'Behold, they are one people, and they all have the same language. And this is what they began to do, and now nothing which they purpose to do will be impossible for them*'"(Genesis 11:6). In saying this, the Lord is describing the attitude that prevailed in the minds of deviant men. He knew they felt as though they were capable of doing whatever they pleased.

It was not the building of a structure that was offensive to the Lord. It was their attitude of self-reliance and defiance against Him which led them to believe that "nothing which they purpose to do will be impossible for them." Their sense of pride in their ability to achieve resulted in an arrogant independence from the Lord. The mercy of God intervened and thwarted their efforts by confounding their ability to communicate with one another. He drew linguistic boundaries and established the basis upon which racial distinctions would be developed. As a result, men were scattered and the over-estimation of their abilities diminished.

One of the lessons the people of God learned through the displeasure of God at Babel is that just because men can do something does not mean that they should. Just because they could build an impressive tower and display their self-dependence and their ability to achieve great things by working together, does not mean that it was appropriate. When the capabilities of men, whether in technology, biology, or any other discipline, cause them to circumvent their duty to honor God that pursuit becomes an offense to God. This is similar to the circumstance we face today with cloning and genetic engineering. Simply because cloning has been proven to be possible does not mean it is an appropriate pursuit. As the ethics of such a pursuit are discussed, believers must engage in the debate. Christian medical professionals from every denominational background ought to be involved in the discussions on the research and bio-ethical levels.

All such questions as these need to have answers provided by Christian intelligence and biblical sensibilities: the sanctity of human life versus the freedom to experiment with cloned embryos; the contrast between the being created after the image of another's DNA and the one created in the image of God; the propriety of procreation outside the context of marriage; the broadening of the "benefits" of abortion; and the process of the "selective reduction" of embryos For Christians to withdraw themselves from the process of cultural debate is to fail to fulfill the responsibilities given by God to serve as the "*salt of the earth.*"

Redefining the family

The family is the most basic institution of human society. There is a direct correlation between the degeneration of the family and the consequent degeneration of culture. Most of the trends that are bemoaned in our society may be traced directly to the problem of a disintegrating family. If an explanation is needed for the exponential rise in the in the problems of crime, drug addiction, illiteracy, teen pregnancy, school shootings, homosexuality, and the like, one need only look to the collapse of the family. There is a direct cause and effect relationship. Because of divorce, incest, infidelity, feminism, single-parenting, work-a-holism, materialism, abortion, pornography and poor communication, the family, as God intended it to be, is an endangered species.

God's design for society is that it be built upon families which exist as one man and one woman, united in a monogamous relationship for life (Mark 10:6-9). God entrusts to them the stewardship of children as a means by which to bless them (Psalm 127:3). The family must remain a priority. The role of parents is to represent the Lord to their children and to "*bring them up in the discipline and instruction of the Lord*" (Ephesians 6:3b). Thus, a parent is not free to exercise independent priorities and opinions that fail to properly represent the Lord. All authority (including parental) is established by God as a means by which He is to be represented (Romans 13:1). As a family embraces a lie, their ability to function is debilitated, and as a result the culture disintegrates.

Deceptions that bring a family into instability are to be confronted by those who would serve as "*the salt of the earth.*" We are told in Titus 1:10-11 that "*there are many rebellious men, empty talkers, and deceivers, especially those of the circumcision, who must be silenced because they are upsetting whole families, teaching things they should not teach for the sake of sordid gain.*" Here Paul tells Timothy that the deceptions which are "*upsetting whole families*" (literally "cause to fall, overturn, or destroy")[20] cannot be tolerated. The solution Paul gives to Timothy regarding the danger of these destructive teachings is that those who advocate them must "*be silenced.*" Hence, believers who will be obedient to the Lord as "*the salt of the earth*" will necessarily seek to discredit the errors that advance the destruction of the family.

There are many such false teachings, denigrating the family, being used to destroy the basis of a stable society. One of the former presidents of the New York chapter of the National Organization for Women declared that "marriage is legalized servitude, and family relations are the basis for all human oppression."[21] The definition of marriage itself has come under the scalpel of social reformers who endeavor to normalize homosexual unions. These attacks are so rampant in American culture that activist courts in Hawaii, Vermont and Massachusetts have forced their citizens to recognize same-sex unions. The ultimate damage done to society through such measures is so evident that the United States Congress is considering a Federal Marriage Amendment to the Constitution which reads:

> Marriage in the United States shall consist only of the union of a man and a woman. Neither this constitution or the constitution of any state, shall be construed to require that marriages or the legal incidents thereof be conferred upon any union other than the union of a man and a woman.[22]

Although this legislative action does not address all of the issues surrounding God's intention for marriage, it does limit what can be construed as constituting marriage.

Not all the attacks on the family are as blatant. There is a need for the Christian community to band together as "*the salt of the earth*" and oppose the attempts to redefine marriage and the influences that are destroying the integrity of the family unit. Organizations such as Focus on the Family and American Family Association provide a rallying point whereby education, networking, and resources can be received and Christians empowered to stand against the degeneration of the family. But the solution to the problem of the disintegrating family ultimately is not social reform. The only solution is for individuals to be reconciled to God through personal faith in Jesus Christ. Redemption is the solution, not political reform. However, actively representing the revealed purposes of God for the family will assist in impeding the decay of our culture. Being "*the salt of the earth*" demands that believers be engaged in debunking the perceived validity of falsehood.

POLITICAL ISSUES

Voting

One of the first duties of any citizen in a democratic republic is to fulfill the responsibilities placed upon him by his government. The foundation of a successful representative government is for the citizens of that government to participate and express their voice through voting.

There are many Christians who, for a variety of reasons, have purposefully decided to neglect this duty. Some believe that, since no candidate completely represents their Christian beliefs, they should vote for no one. They withdraw from the process because they believe that to vote for someone who does not align with all of their views would be compromising their faithfulness to the Lord. Others believe that since God establishes those who are in authority, they do not want to risk voting against God's will by supporting the wrong man. Consequently, they prefer to vote for no one rather than vote mistakenly against God's man. Others believe, since the solution to the ills of society does not rest in politics, they ought to stay out altogether and invest solely in the dissemination of the Gospel message.

Is it compromise for a believer to vote? Because of the instructions given by the Lord in Romans 13, we know that it is the responsibility of believers to allow their voice to be heard through the balloting process. As they vote, it is their duty to represent the biblical priorities revealed in Scripture. It is tragic when some believers focus on secular priorities while ignoring the spiritual values that ought to determine their vote. This was true when Bill Clinton was reelected as President of the United States in 1996. Some expressed to us their opinion that his immoral conduct, as an individual, could be overlooked because of the way the economy was flourishing. Some even declared that, despite his deviances, God was blessing our nation's economy.

Such temporal and secular considerations ought never to govern the priorities of a believer. Believers have the responsiblity to "glorify the Lord" as they cast their ballot. God instructs us that "*whether, then, you eat or drink or whatever you do, do all to the glory of God*" (1 Corinthians 10:31). Thus, a believer ought to ask the question: "How can I represent the interests of God's glory in the way that I vote?" At times, a believer's vote might be just as concerned with restraining evil as it is about exalting righteousness. There may be times when neither candidate offers a desirable platform, but one platform is so far away from what is right that it must be defeated. However, if believers completely withdraw from the process of voting, then the environment created will be without restraint and the festering nature of evil will merely putrefy the culture.

Candidacy

Another place where believers are able to make significant contributions in the restraint of evil is in serving in public office. The Scriptures teach that a society governed by the ungodly is under great disadvantage: "*When the righteous increase, the people rejoice, but when a wicked man rules, people groan*" (Proverbs 29:2). The guidance provided by the ungodly allows a culture to tumble headlong toward judgment.

However, when righteous men lead, there is great advantage: "*Where there is no guidance the people fall, but in the abundance of counselors there is victory*" (Proverbs 11:14). Thus, believers who give themselves in service to the Lord as "*the salt of the earth*" by representing Him in governmental positions bring blessing to a nation. Believers are told that one of the marks of a godly man is that he is exalted to sit even in the gates of the city, which was a position of great influence in ancient societies (Proverbs 31:23; Deuteronomy 16:18). Believers are able to properly serve the Lord as "*the salt of the earth*" by running for public office at any and all levels of government.

The people of God need to offer themselves as candidates for school boards, township councils, mayoral offices, as well as seats on commissions, in Congress, in the Senate, and governorships. At any level in the political process, believers should exert the influences necessary to restrain evil by representing the righteousness of God. Certainly, having believers in public offices will not produce righteousness in the lives of the people being governed. This is only possible through the power of the Gospel and the transformation of lives through regeneration. However, sin and evil can be restrained through the influences of godly people in public office.

Legislation

The purpose of legislation is to restrict sin. In the passage providing us understanding on the relationship between the governing authorities and the responsibilities of believers, the Apostle Paul declares: "*rulers are not a cause of fear for good behavior, but for evil. Do you want to have no fear of authority? Do what is good and you will have praise from the same; for it is a minister of God to you for good. But if you do what is evil, be afraid; for it does not bear the sword for nothing; for it is a minister of God, an avenger who brings wrath on the one who practices evil*" (Romans 13:3-4). The purpose of legislation is to restrict the freedoms that men possess to exercise evil (which is checked only by accountability). A culture can never be made righteous through legislation. The advancement of morality cannot be accomplished through legislation. Legislation merely restrains immorality.

For this reason, believers who would obey the Lord by being "*the salt of the earth*" will support legislation that confronts evildoers and restrains their freedoms. The call for believers to disassociate from attempting to legislate morality is an irresponsible delusion. Certainly, we cannot look to legislation to conform people to the standards of God. However, to absent believers from the process of legislation is to create a vacuum wherein immorality can and will prosper.

Political leaders, on whose shoulders rest the responsibilities to approve legislation, need to hear from believers. Contacting state and federal legislators, participating in petition drives, compiling and distributing political voting records, and similar educational helps are properly performed by believers of all denominational backgrounds. Certainly political leaders who are believers ought to sponsor legislation that represents biblical values and priorities that honor God.

Conclusion

Throughout this section, we have observed various ways believers are able to band together for the purposes of enhancing flavor, creating thirst, and drawing out infection, and preserving from decay. Engaging in social issues on a variety of levels is necessary for the people of God to fulfill their role as "*the salt of the earth.*" It is also necessary to recognize that social reform is not the solution to the problems brought upon a culture by sin.

However, there is danger in striving to serve as "*the salt of the earth*": one can become so consumed with the effort that preservation of morality becomes an end in itself. Certainly, efforts that fall short of presenting the

Gospel as the solution fall short. This is where a great deal of confusion often occurs. It may lead to a Social Gospel (which is the error of the liberals) or it may lead to an isolationism that abandons the social process in favor of the next level of discussion – being the "light of the world." Both of these errors disable the purposes of God for the believer's impact in the world.

Another danger is the development of a familiarity between believers who feel free to cooperate with one another on the "salt level" but they ought not to cooperate on the "light level." Because of a blurring of lines, some may begin to cooperate with one another on both levels. This leads to compromise and cooperative evangelism. This is essentially what produced the compromises in the *Evangelical and Catholics Together* agreement. Christian leaders who were involved in attempting to be "salt," became so friendly they decided that they could also cooperate together as "light." This is certainly not acceptable, for it violates various biblical principles and doctrines that will be discussed in the next chapter. However, because there are some who blur the distinctions between these two levels, we should not dismiss God's expectation that His children work together as the "*salt of the earth*."

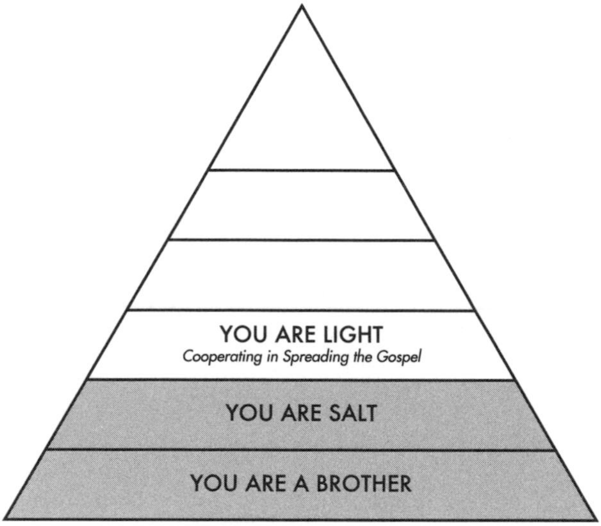

PYRAMID OF RESPONSIBILITY

The mandates of biblical relationships

CHAPTER THREE

YOU ARE LIGHT

Cooperating in spreading the gospel

The preaching and preservation of the Gospel is a sacred trust. In fact, the Apostle Paul shared with the Thessalonian Christians that the responsibility is so great that those entrusted with the Gospel must be "tested" and found faithful (1 Thessalonians 2:2-4). He had been set apart for his life's work, in the purpose of God, before he was born. Nevertheless it was necessary for Paul to be proven before he was permitted to engage in the ministry. After his conversion, he spent two years in the Arabian Desert, about ten years in his native Tarsus and then three years of practical experience with Barnabas in Antioch. All of this was before the church entrusted him to take the message of the Gospel of the grace of God to the Gentiles.[23]

It should surprise no one that faithful Christians should be extremely careful about entering into any relationship that would compromise the integrity of the Gospel. As seen in The Pyramid of Responsibility, each successive level of relationships within the body of believers is more limited. Whereas one might be able to cooperate with other believers on the "salt" level, relationships on the "light level" must only include those committed to maintaining the integrity and purity of the Gospel message.

The one thing that should unite all true believers is the light of the Gospel of the glory of Christ who is the image of God (2 Corinthians 4:3). However, uniting to herald an unclear message produces confusion. Since the declaration of the Gospel is a noble task, the message must not be adjusted for theological biases or cultural whims. Obedient believers respond to the commission of the Lord Jesus to "*go into all the world and preach the gospel to all creation*" (Mark 16:15). This Gospel, however, is continually under siege by the Evil One.

Since true faith comes by hearing and hearing by the message concerning Christ (Romans 10:17), Satan employs all of his wiles to keep men from hearing the message of the Gospel clearly. Because the Gospel is so primary to the Christian message, believers are charged with maintaining its purity. They face the challenge of preserving the integrity of the Gospel where it is being perverted by church traditions, theological additions and pragmatic omissions. This requires appealing to those who muddle its clear message and confronting those who substitute another gospel in its place.

THE HINDRANCE TO COOPERATIVE RELATIONSHIPS

Assaults on the Gospel

Assaults on the Gospel are nothing new. The Apostle Paul, in the First Century, was deeply concerned with preserving the integrity of the Gospel message. Can you imagine how discouraged he must have felt when he found it necessary to write to the Galatian believers: "*I am amazed that you are so quickly deserting Him who called you by the grace of God to a different gospel, which is really not another; only there are some that are disturbing you and want to distort the Gospel of Christ*" (Galatians 1:6-7). He knew these Galatian believers with Jewish backgrounds were struggling with the assault on their culture by a Gospel that included the Gentiles. They had a hard time accepting the fact that these new Gentile believers were not being required to meet the ceremonial demands of the Law of Moses. He knew from personal experience how the Gospel of the grace of God invoked strong feelings among the Jews.

The doctrinal concept that a person is justified by faith alone in Christ alone, but sanctified by one's own faithfulness, was much more in line with their Jewish way of thinking. He appealed to them with the direct question "*This is the only thing I want to find out from you: did you receive the Spirit by the works of the Law or by the hearing of faith? Are you so foolish? Having begun by the Spirit you are now being perfected by the flesh?*" (Galatians 3:2-3). There are some today who muddle the clarity of the Gospel in certain expressions of theology such as popular Arminianism. Establishing cooperative relationships in the declaration of the Gospel with those who hold such a view would be confusing to believers in our churches. But there also have been assaults on the Gospel that demanded outright confrontation and repudiation.

Two such heresies that brought a great deal of turmoil to the church in the Fourth and Fifth Centuries were:

- **Arianism** - Arius was a presbyter in Alexandria, Egypt early in the Fourth Century. He taught that God the Father alone is eternal, and Christ was created out of nothing as the first and greatest of all creatures through whom all other things were created. Yet because of the power and honor delegated to Him, He was to be regarded as God and was to be worshipped.[24] This heresy spread rapidly and almost totally captivated the church in the early Fourth Century. God raised up Athanasius, the Bishop of Alexandria, to oppose and expose this heresy that had overtaken the church.

- **Pelagianism** - Pelagius, a monk from Britain, was a popular preacher in Rome from A.D. 401-409. He sought to encourage lax Christians who felt they could not fulfill God's commands because of the frailty of their flesh. He told them God commanded nothing that is impossible and everyone may live free from sin if that was their desire. He believed the human will was created capable of choosing good or evil and that man's free will emancipated him from God. Redemption was not necessary. In fact, the followers of Pelagius eventually concluded that individuals no longer had to deal with God, but only had to deal with themselves alone. God only re-enters at the last judgment.[25]

The Gospel message continues to be manipulated and corrupted with doctrinal aberrations often promoted by men of influence, even as Arius and Pelagius used their considerable influence to spread heresy so long ago. All would do well to heed the warning of the Apostle Peter to the early Christians: "*False prophets also arose among the people, just as there will be false teachers among you who will secretly introduce destructive heresies, even denying the master who bought them bringing swift destruction upon themselves. Many will follow their sensuality and because of them the way of truth will be maligned*" (2 Peter 2:1-2). It should not surprise us that this pattern was present in the Fourth and Fifth Centuries and is present in the Church today.

Cooperative evangelism

The great evangelists of the Nineteenth Century, with the exception of Charles Finney, declared the Gospel with clarity. But when liberalism began to infest the major denominations in America, with its Social Gospel and desire to make Christianity compatible with the modern mind, the leavening of the Gospel in America began. The great Prayer Meeting

Revivals of the mid 1800s and the emerging Bible Conference ministries of the late Nineteenth and early Twentieth Centuries were cooperative efforts of Christians from many denominations. However, all were committed to the authority, inerrancy and sufficiency of Scripture and the integrity and purity of the Gospel.

When Billy Graham attempted, in the latter half of the Twentieth Century, to duplicate the mass evangelism efforts of D.L. Moody and Billy Sunday, he found himself caught in unholy alliances with liberals willing to use him to pad their pews. Ian Murray's book *Evangelicalism Divided* very carefully outlines the growing problems with Graham's methods. Murray quotes from William Martin's biography of Graham, *Prophets With Honor*, and addresses Graham's response to his critics:

> He doubtless intended to keep himself and his crusades free from Modernist contamination, but success weakened his resolve. As non-Evangelicals watched the streams of people who responded to his invitation, they wanted to channel at least a trickle of them into their own churches. As they saw that it was possible to cooperate with his crusades without having him attack their beliefs from the pulpit, they began to join in the invitations, and when he agreed to come to their cities, to volunteer for committees ... Increasingly, and particularly after extensive cooperation with liberal state churches in England, Scotland and on the Continent, Graham came to accept, then to welcome, then virtually to require, cooperation with all but the most flagrantly Modernist Protestant groups, such as Unitarian, or such bodies as Mormons and Jehovah's Witnesses, whose teaching excluded them from Evangelical and mainline denominations.[26]

Originally, it was not the desire of most Fundamentalists to separate from Billy Graham. His fiery preaching, burden for souls, and obvious success made them very reticent to "touch God's anointed." He became a popular hero to those who hungered to see souls saved. However, the New York Evangelistic Crusade in 1957 became a defining moment for them. Graham refused the invitation of conservatives led by Dr. Jack Wyrtzen and accepted the invitation offered by the liberal Protestant Council of New York City. This illustrated the Neo-Evangelical repudiation of the biblical doctrine known as "separation."

The Neo-Evangelicals were committed to finding areas of agreement and cooperation with professed theological liberals. This approach legitimized liberals as genuine Christians even though they openly denied the great fundamentals of the faith. This inclusivism contributed to the theological deterioration that would eventually bring Graham to profess that Roman Catholics are genuine believers and, in an interview with Dr. Robert Schuller, state that the heathen are not lost. [27]

The issue of ecumenical evangelism became an issue that began to divide rather than unite the Church. Some genuine believers chose to turn a deaf ear and willingly closed their eyes to obvious unholy alliances. They did this in the name of reaching men for Christ. Although none would deny that people were saved, the pragmatic approach taken by genuine believers to justify participation with unbelievers in the name of reaching souls for Christ, contributed to the demise of doctrinal standards in many churches and the lack of spiritual discipline in the pursuit of holiness in individual lives. "Doctrine divides" was the excuse that many used to justify their disobedience. Darkness reigns when the light is diminished and that light is eventually extinguished by a corrupted and compromised Gospel message.

Establishing cooperative relationships in the declaration of the Gospel, if couched in a pragmatic philosophy of "the end justifies the means," will lead to disobedience and an attitude that sound doctrine will stand in the way of reaching men for Christ. I once spoke to one of the signers of the *Evangelical and Catholics Together Accord* and a leader of a popular Christian student movement. He told me, "If we are to reach the world for Christ by the year 2000 we are going to need the help of the Roman Catholics to do so." I replied, "With what Gospel?"

Christian education

The early Twentieth Century found many believers desiring to learn more about the Word of God. The publication of the Scofield Reference Bible in 1909 coupled with the Bible Conference and Prophetic Conference Movements, provided a resource for laymen which proved to be a thorn in the side of liberal pastors being trained in denominational seminaries. Liberalism was seeking to make Christianity more compatible with the modern mind. In the process of doing so, major doctrines of the Word of God were either being ignored, denied or explained away. This upset the majority of laymen and a good number of older pastors. They no longer trusted their denominational schools and seminaries, so they began to support independent Bible Institutes, Christian Colleges and independent Seminaries. This was spurred on by the growth of the missions movement following the Second World War. Many from these liberal denominations attended these new schools to train for missionary and pastoral ministries. Disenchanted believers left their denominations to form new churches, many times for all the right reasons but with very wrong attitudes.

I remember some young believers coming to me and sharing that their denominational church had a new pastor whose preaching ridiculed some of the sacred doctrines of the Word of God. They wanted my help to start a new church. There were about twenty young couples involved. I told them I would be glad to do so if they would do certain things. I wanted to protect them from developing the "wrong attitudes and a critical spirit" that often accompany people who leave a church. I requested that they ask for an appointment with the elders of their church along with the pastor. At this appointment, they should graciously explain that they no longer felt in complete agreement with the church because of the doctrinal positions being promoted by the pastor. If the elders supported the pastor in his error, then they should ask permission to leave with the church's blessing to begin a new congregation. If the elders refused to grant their blessing, then they could graciously leave knowing that they had not reacted, but had responded. Unfortunately, they did not follow my advice, so I did not feel free to help them in their effort (which by the way, never successfully materialized).

These emerging churches were often driven together by their common devotion to the "Fundamentals" (as presented in the landmark series *The Fundamentals* which was produced from 1910-1915 and distributed free of charge to over three hundred thousand people). The Fundamentalists considered liberalism as the common enemy. When our Fellowship, now called IFCA International, began to organize in 1929 the doctrinal statement could be written on a 3 x 5 card. With their focus on their common enemy, they did not see doctrinal and philosophical differences as important as they would under different circumstances in the future. Presbyterian, Baptists and Independents shared in Prophecy, Missionary and Bible Conferences. Christian Colleges and Bible Schools appealed to the broad base of Fundamentalists and recruited board members, faculty and students from very diverse backgrounds.

But this early unity was hard to maintain as the institutions matured and relationships became more refined. Training institutions that were once formed to train Christian workers shifted their emphasis as a new generation of leaders emerged and the influences of Neo-Evangelical inclusivism began to be felt. Christian Colleges and Seminaries that once were vigorously committed to the authority and inerrancy of the Word of God, began to employ faculty and enroll student bodies that no longer reflected the commitment of the schools' founders. James Hunter in his book, *Evangelicalism: The Coming Generation*, notes from his study of nine popular Christian colleges and seven evangelical seminaries:

> At one level one can simply view the historical and institutional dynamics of Christian higher education as merely a reflection of broader changes in the Christian community. These changes, then, are a consequence of other sociological and historical factors. While this is undoubtedly true to some extent, it is probably more accurate to say that Christian higher education is involved in a dialectical process—not only an effect but a cause of these changes as well. At this level we can see the multiple ironies of Christian higher education. On the one hand Christian higher education evolved into precisely the opposite of what it was supposed to be, that is, into bastions of secularity if not anti-Christian sentiment. Contemporary Christian higher education, on the other hand, produces the unintended consequences of being counter productive to its own objectives, that is, it produces individual Christians who are either less certain of their attachments to the traditions of their faith or altogether disaffected from them. Education, to the degree that it is not indoctrination, weakens the tenacity with which Evangelicals hold on to their world view. In sum, Evangelical education creates its own contaminating effects. And the more Christian higher education professionalizes and bureaucratizes (that is the more it models itself institutionally after secular higher education), the more likely this process will intensify.[28]

Educational choices are one of the most difficult ones facing parents as they raise their children. To make educational choices without understanding that education is not a means to an end, but a preparation for life, risks making choices that will have lasting negative consequences. Many Christian educational institutions no longer reflect the reasons for which they were founded. It is important that parents consider carefully the product a school is producing before choosing to establish a cooperative relationship in the life preparation of their children.

Christian institutions of higher education may seek to establish cooperative relationships in order to enhance the quality of their institutions and provide accountability and accreditation. The parameters established in such cases may be adjusted to reflect commitment to the integrity of the Gospel, basic doctrinal agreement and to excellence in education.

Missions

The passion for world missions has always been a hallmark of the Fundamentalist/Evangelical movement. The missionary vision that came out of the Nineteenth and early Twentieth Centuries was an example of the cooperative effort of local churches and individual Christians who offered themselves and their resources in order to take the Gospel to the far reaches of the world. But within the framework of the missionary enterprise the modern ecumenical movement found its birth. Following the London Missionary Society (1795) which included various missionary boards in England, there were numerous missionary societies and conferences held in the Nineteenth Century such as:

- the Conference of all denominations (1810) called by William Carey in South Africa

- the American Board of Commission for Missions (1812)

- the Evangelical Alliance which met in London (1846) and included 800 delegates and 50 denominations

- the Great Missionary Conference in London (1888) which was attended by 1879 delegates and 139 missionary societies.

All of the above were thoroughly fundamental in theology, though rather diverse in doctrinal beliefs. However, as the Nineteenth Century came to a close, the effect of liberalism began to be seen in the missionary movement. The Foreign Mission Conference of North America was held in 1893 and included 23 mission boards. It was to grow to 80 before the 1910 conference. It continued to exist and in 1950 it became the Division of Foreign Missions of the National Council of Churches. In 1895, the World Student Christian Federation met and was led by John Mott, J.H.

Oldham, Nathan Soderbloom and William Temple. All were to become strong ecumenical leaders. In 1900, the Ecumenical Missionary Conference was held and was the largest mission conference held up to that time with 2500 delegates and 162 mission societies. However, the 1910 World Missionary Conference held in Edinburgh, Scotland was the most significant ecumenical conference. It had 1206 missionary delegates chosen by mission boards and societies, not by local churches or denominations. The conference sought to strengthen and encourage ecumenical leaders. It also appointed a continuing committee that later became the International Missionary Council. It met every four years and the evolution of its message gave evidence of the influence of liberal theology and the Social Gospel. It eventually merged with the World Council of Churches in New Delhi in 1961 and became the Department of World Mission and Evangelism. Ecumenism was born out of a desire to reach the world. The resulting de-emphasis on doctrinal purity and integrity of belief was the flower that eventually brought forth the fruit of compromise and apostasy within the ranks of such a noble endeavor.

The emergence of faith missions can be traced to the Niagara Conferences in the late Nineteenth Century where A.T. Pierson, editor of the *Missionary Review of the World* and J. Hudson Taylor of China Inland Mission constantly urged their listeners to pledge support to foreign missions. The result was a heightened interest in missions by laymen and local church leaders. When information of liberalism's growth among missionaries began to filter back from denominational mission fields, conservatives became alarmed. Consequently, conservative denominational churches and their pastors began to look to non-denominational faith mission boards as partners in their missionary endeavors. This response by conservatives caused some denominations to become alarmed at the trend.

The progress of ecumenism in world missions began to alarm many of the conservative mission societies. Consequently, in March of 1917 a meeting of several mission agency leaders took place. The Interdenominational Foreign Missions Association's (IFMA) historical records make the following observation: "The meeting occurred as the flowers of the Fundamentalist/Modernist Controversy were ready to bloom and the conservative mission agencies no longer felt comfortable with and able to work within the growing ecumenical movement....Having been born in the environment which produced the Fundamentalist /Modernist Controversy, it was no surprise that the issues of separation and cooperation were constant points of reference in IFMA discussions."[29] This original motivation carried over to the proposed merger of the IFMA with the more inclusive Evangelical Foreign Missions Association (EFMA).

The EFMA was organized in 1947. This generally coincides with the emergence of the National Association of Evangelicals. The EFMA differed from the IFMA in that it included mission agencies from denominations and its doctrinal requirements were not as restrictive. Consequently, when a merger was suggested, the IFMA felt that the value of organizational independence and its close relationship with organizations like the Independent Fundamental Churches of America would have been jeopardized. While the IFMA and the EFMA were "similar in most doctrinal areas and evangelical commitment, the IFMA's reservations were over the areas of maintaining its distinctiveness and the Pentecostalism which was included in the EFMA."[30]

The Evangelical/Fundamentalist mission effort found itself divided along doctrinal lines, with the understanding of biblical separation becoming a very important difference. However, as the decades of the Twentieth Century passed, these differences seemed to be less important to many of the mission agencies in the IFMA. Increasingly more cooperative working relationships between the IFMA and EFMA began to grow. Beginning in the 1960s, they merged several of their committees and began holding their annual meetings in the same location. "While the question of cooperation versus separation did not disappear from the IFMA thinking, its focus was directed toward achieving the work of evangelism rather than maintaining proper separation."[31]

Though many of the conservative mission agencies were not troubled by the IFMA/EFMA relationships, others felt that the drift toward de-emphasizing doctrine and emphasizing "getting the work of evangelism done" was a slippery slope. But where were they to turn? There was another association called The Associated Missions. It provided an association for conservative denominational mission agencies that did not feel comfortable with the EFMA. However, it had its own problems and the domination and alleged financial impropriety of Dr. Carl McIntire and the International Council of Christian Churches made it difficult for many of its agencies to continue their membership in good faith. A number of the missions left The Association of Missions and formed Fellowship of Missions. Eight mission agencies, including several large Baptist agencies, were the original founding member agencies as FOM was constituted on September 25, 1969.[32]

Another concern of many Evangelical/Fundamentalist believers was an obvious trend within once evangelistic Bible-based missionary societies to shift their emphasis to meeting the social and political challenges faced by cultures here and abroad. Charles Ryrie in his book *Social Responsibility* noted that "In the late 1940s when the movement known as New Evangelicalism set forth its manifesto, one of its main concerns was to do something about the social implications of the Gospel."[33] Although all should recognize the social implications of the Gospel in any society, keeping the balance is a challenge. Properly contextualizing the Gospel avoids the pitfall of syncretism. Incorporating unbiblical practices and beliefs into The Faith makes adjustments to the Gospel necessary, and fatally corrupts biblical Christianity. This was ably illustrated in the last century by theological liberalism's attempt to create a Faith more compatible with secular society and the "modern mind."

While the Gospel must confront the unbiblical dimensions of modern society in any culture, it must do so without forsaking the declaration of the holiness of God and His purposes. The power of the Gospel to liberate a person from the guilt of sin and transform a believer to reflect the character of the Lord Jesus Christ must remain the primary emphasis in its declaration. Ryrie later pointed out that the next generation of New Evangelicals known as the young evangelicals felt that the "establishment evangelicals" had only given lip service to genuine social concern. He quoted Richard Quebedeaux's book *The Young Evangelicals*:

> We found social concern among Establishment Evangelicals to be often merely an offering of pious words rather than a demonstration of prophetic action. Hence, if we are looking for a powerful expression of spiritual renewal in Orthodox Christianity — one genuinely committed to reconciliation and active faith in a secular society, we shall have to search elsewhere.[34]

The young Evangelicals, later to develop into the Worldly Evangelicals, had a profound effect upon the missionary endeavor as the Establishment Evangelical leaders retired. They succeeded in including an entire article dedicated to social responsibility in the covenant of The International Congress on World Evangelism held in Lausanne in 1974. While this in itself did not alarm most Evangelicals, the intent was to include social responsibility as part of evangelism and therefore an integral part of the Gospel. When this became apparent, many became alarmed: the Gospel was being adjusted to meet the desire of these influential evangelicals to become socially relevant. This passion began to infect many within the missionary movement in the 1980s.

The resultant dumbing down of doctrinal purity manifested itself in a new ecumenism among Evangelicals. This would blend the worldliness of the Worldly Evangelicals, the emotionalism of the Charismatics, the pragmatism of the Neo-Fundamentalists and the anthropocentricism of the contemporary worship movement.

What can we learn from the past abuses that resulted in doctrinal division and splintered relationships? The lessons are diverse and multileveled. There are genuine biblical reasons to limit relationships within the Body of Christ. But the attitude with which the limitation is pursued makes all the difference in the world. I once read a little book *The One Minute Manager* in which the author noted that the positive approach of helping people to reach their potential can be accomplished by "Catching people doing something right."[35] Unfortunately, many divisions in the past have been caused by strong leaders looking to catch others doing something wrong, so that they could solidify their leadership.

Warren Weirsbe in his book *Integrity* notes that many local churches are so enamored with being "Independent" that their members catch a warped spirit of "doing their own thing." Taking the wonder of the doctrine of the priesthood of the believer, they twist its intent to justify their prideful actions. Weirsbe writes:

> The church member who doesn't like the pastor simply gathers together a group of fellow dissidents and starts a new church or else invades another church and tries to take over. Did anybody search the Scriptures to see what the Spirit might want to say to the churches? Did anybody call for a prayer meeting? Did anybody ask under whose authority they were starting a new church? Did anybody ask other churches to pray and give counsel? No! It's easier to follow a leader with charisma and be independent.[36]

PARTNERS IN COOPERATION

Local Churches

Local churches become the ideal arena where interdependent relationships can thrive, reflecting the light of the Gospel. We can learn from many ministry organizations that started out well but ended on a slippery slope, brought to a place of compromise. Many were oblivious to the primacy of the local church in God's program. It is in local churches where cooperative relationships are most effectively forged. Individual believers can learn valuable lessons on how to evaluate their own participation in ministries by observing those who are the servant leaders of their local churches. Ministries that look to local churches for their board members, for counsel, for personnel and financial support will foster a spirit of interdependence. They will avoid following a model in which they are merely using the church to gain their own ends.

True cooperative relationships on the level we have called "Light" demand an integration of para-church ministries within the ministries of the local church. Local churches need to carefully evaluate para-church organizations with this in mind. Many of the tensions in the body could have been avoided if evangelistic efforts, Bible conferences, and mission agencies had been concerned with the local churches they sought to serve, seeking compatibility with their doctrines and practices. This may mean some para-church organizations and local churches would discover they are not free to work together on this particular level of relationship. Both should seek to find those with whom they can whole-heartedly become involved in cooperative ministry.

Approaching the establishment of a cooperative relationship between local churches should be pursued with a positive attitude, first seeking agreement rather than seeking to establish areas of disagreement. In this endeavor catching a ministry doing something right is important. The great tendency is to so restrict the parameters that you look to establish a cooperative relationship only with the church that is a mirror image of oneself. Some churches have adopted a spirit of independence that asks the question: "Why do we need any other church? What can fellowship with other churches do for us?"

IFCA International exemplifies cooperative relationships that are possible on the "Light" level. Churches and Christian workers have to seek membership in this Fellowship. In fact, the Fellowship states: "We envision ourselves as the Fellowship of choice for independent churches and organizations, desiring to prayerfully work together in the spirit of interdependence."[37] When I became the Executive Director of IFCA International, I soon learned that within our Fellowship there was great diversity among the churches. Traditions and cultural differences became very evident. I was taken back after I spoke in one of our larger Hispanic churches in Southern California. The congregation all stood and applauded my message. I was not sure if they were applauding my message or were grateful that I was finally finished. This just was not done in our suburban Philadelphia churches. I found a variety of worship methods, styles of music and versions of Bible translations being used. Yet all these churches had established a cooperative relationship based upon commitment to a common doctrinal statement and ministry causes.

Another fine example of this kind of cooperative endeavor is found in the churches working together with Slavic Gospel Association through "The Antioch Initiative." This approach provides an opportunity for a number of local churches of different fellowships in America to cooperate by adopting a targeted area in Russia where there is a sound and thriving church reaching an entire region in Russia. The Russian Evangelical Union of Christians-Baptists designates that strong church as an "Antioch Church." It then becomes a point of outreach in that region and the American churches help by providing training and resources for the church planting efforts. This partnership between American and Russian churches seeks to advance the Gospel in an entire region, made possible by the highly cooperative spirit of the sponsoring churches. Through this initiative, positive unity and commitment are enhanced while the light of the Gospel penetrates even further in Russia. The Antioch Initiative provides an arena in which many local churches discover how much they have in common, both with each other and with their brothers in the other country.

The terrible tragedy of the Asian Tsunami on December 26, 2004 provides another example of believers banding together to show the love of Christ. The people affected by this catastrophe were overwhelmed. Believers from a variety of churches gave abundantly through various Christian agencies to underwrite supplies and teams of helpers that went in the name of the Lord. I spoke with one missionary who told me the Muslims could not understand why Christians were willing to help them when Buddhists all around ignored them. This relief effort in the name of the Lord is opening doors for the message of the Gospel.

I remember the cataclysmic Hurricane Andrew that devastated South Florida on August 24-26, 1992. Believers responded quickly with funds and personnel to provide water and plastic tarps to cover damaged roofs. One pastor told of a group of believers going into a neighborhood to offer help. The people there said they could not afford to pay for the materials, let alone the labor. Needless to say, when the believers responded that they did not want any money but they came only to help, the people were overwhelmed. The pastor recounted that several on that street were willing to listen to the Gospel and a number trusted Jesus Christ as Savior.

It is incumbent upon churches and their members to seek opportunities to enter arenas where they can participate interdependently with others in the common cause of advancing biblically authentic, dynamic, compassionate Christianity both at home and abroad. When establishing these relationships, one should always be characterized by a desire to find common ground in maintaining the integrity and purity of the Gospel message. In addition to this desire, there must be an understanding that there are certain essentials to be truly of one mind and one heart. If a church is not comfortable with the degree to which the integrity of the Gospel is being maintained and the authority of the Word is being emphasized and followed in the life of the church, it should avoid that cooperative relationship to reach souls for Christ. When common ground and unity of the bond of the Spirit are found, then a cooperative relationship can be established. A paraphrase of Amos 3:3 illustrates this: "*Do two walk together unless they have agreed to do so.*"

Mission Organizations

One of the most frustrating experiences I had as a pastor was to have a student come home from college and announce that he/she had decided to go to the mission field with a particular mission that our church had not approved as a partner in ministry. Family and friends were involved and many times the church found itself in the dilemma of keeping the peace or refusing to support the missionary. This problem often occurred because of two failures. First, the church had not established the ground rules for approving missionary organizations. And second, the missionary organizations recruited missionaries without including the local church in the initial stages of contact. If one regards the missionary organization as a servant of the local church, then it only seems logical that the church should carefully select those mission boards which reflect its doctrine, missionary philosophy and goals.

Sometimes there may be doctrinal agreement, but certain other characteristics may hinder establishing a relationship as partners. Many times I received calls from missionaries from a particular group of mission boards asking to come and present their work in the church I pastored. I would ask them the following question: "If one of our young people felt led of the Lord to join you in ministry with your mission board, would he/she have to leave our church and join a church in your Fellowship in order to be accepted by your mission?" If there was a deep silence, I knew that this was an issue with their mission. Needless to say, we would not invite a missionary to come to our church and recruit our young people if it would lead them to sever affiliation with our church. Fortunately, several of the mission boards that once made this a requirement have changed this particular demand. Now they only ask that the recruit and his church be in doctrinal harmony with the mission.

Other Para-Church Organizations

There are numerous other Para-Church organizations which should be considered when establishing partnership relationships. Some of them would be on the "Salt" level such as crisis pregnancy centers and local food banks. But others such as rescue missions, Gideons International, Christian camps, Bible Conferences, evangelistic associations, institutional chaplains, just to mention a few, require individual evaluation. You need to see if partnering with them will enable your local church to more effectually fulfill your God-given commission to reach the world for Christ without doctrinal compromise. The challenge for the Church is to remain true to its teaching concerning the integrity of the Gospel and the authority and sufficiency of the Word of God while at the same time serving as "Light" in the world.

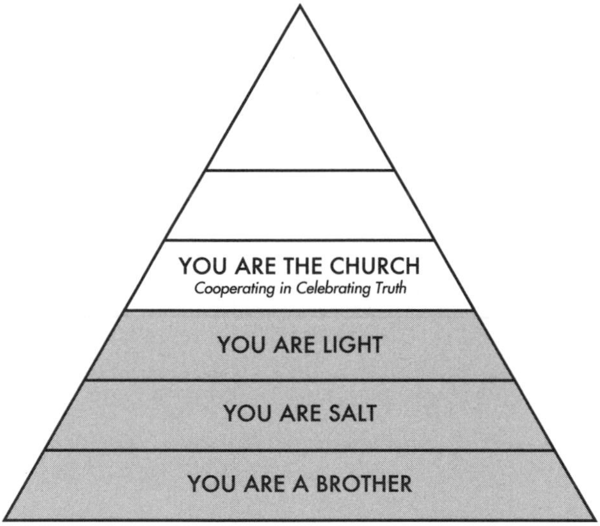

PYRAMID OF RESPONSIBILITY

The mandates of biblical relationships

CHAPTER FOUR

YOU ARE THE CHURCH

Cooperating in Celebrating Truth

The Lord Jesus Christ revealed the preeminent role of the Church in His plan He declared: "*I will build My church; and the gates of Hades will not overpower it*" (Matthew 16:18). The special and intimate relationships that He intends within the context of the local church are part of the means He will use to accomplish this. The loving, preferring, supporting, sacrificing, and encouraging that characterize these relationships are all demonstrations of the presence of God's Spirit. These bring vitality to the Body of Christ. The joy of the Lord present in the celebratory assembly becomes a sustaining blessing for the believers who gather to form the church.

The word "church" is used to translate the Greek word *ekklesia* meaning to "call out" for the purpose of assembly. However, the English word seems to have evolved from a German word, *kirche*. This word is derived from the Greek word *kuriokon* which means "belonging to the Lord." "Its application to the church stems from its use by early Christians for the place where they met together, denoting it as a place belonging to God, or God's house."[38] By extension, it has been used to translate the term *ekklesia* given that the assembly of believers likewise belongs to the Lord (Acts 20:28).

The Apostle Paul invested himself with great passion in the process of establishing local assemblies wherever he preached the Gospel. His great burden was for the health, edification and growth of these local churches. At times, his burden was so great that he was "weighted down" with care, for he understood the threats that faced each local church. Despite the patient endurance of personal hardships, Paul tenderly says: "*Apart from such external things, there is the daily pressure on me of concern for all the churches*" (2 Corinthians 11:28). Commenting on this verse, Charles Hodge writes:

> The solitude which the apostle felt for the church which he had founded is apparent from all his epistles; and it may be easily imagined how various and constant must have been the causes and occasions of anxiety and trouble on their account.[39]

Certainly these concerns sprang out of a love and devotion for the Lord Jesus Christ. As an apostle of Christ Jesus, he felt responsible to maintain within local churches the interests of the Master. He obligated the spiritual leadership of the Ephesian church with this same intense sense of stewardship. This is demonstrated in his instructions in Acts 20:25-31:

> "And now, behold, I know that all of you, among whom I went about preaching the kingdom, will no longer see my face. Therefore, I testify to you this day that I am innocent of the blood of all men. For I did not shrink from declaring to you the whole purpose of God. *Be on guard* for yourselves and for all the flock, among which the Holy Spirit has made you overseers, to *shepherd the church of God* which He purchased with His own blood. I know that after my departure savage wolves will come in among you, not sparing the flock; and from among your own selves men will arise, speaking perverse things, to draw away the disciples after them. Therefore *be on the alert*, remembering that night and day for a period of three years I did not cease to admonish each one with tears." (Emphasis mine)

Therefore, from the very first days of the Church, God expressed through the apostles a tremendous priority on biblically responsible relationships within the local church. The expressed concern was that the people in these relationships in the local church must be even more vigilant and focused than on any of the other levels previously discussed.

THE PROBLEM

A Mixed Multitude

Applying biblically responsible relationships on the local church level is tremendously difficult. It is hard to draw the lines where they need to be drawn because it involves people - friends, family, neighbors - that may fall on the other side of these lines. No one wants to offend people they care about. Consequently, the temptation is to apply the cooperative responsibilities that exist on the broader levels of fellowship to the level of the church. This often results in accommodation where lines ought to be drawn, rather than overlooking the more focused responsibilities the Scripture calls for on the level of the local church.

The Pressures of Inclusivism

The nature of inclusivism is a major threat to the church. This is the tendency within the church to remove whatever barriers exist in order to build relationships with people. Doctrine is often perceived as the great divider and so it is minimized in order to appeal to people and maintain relationships.

I learned this early in my ministry, for I had not been in the pastorate too long before this pressure became apparent. I was called to pastor in a small Midwestern farm town. I found people friendly and everyone seemed to know everyone else. They worked, played, educated, and worshiped in close proximity and relationship to one another. Whether folks were members of the Reformed Church of America, Christian Reformed, Protestant Reformed, United Methodist, Baptist, Roman Catholic, or Bible Church, they were all neighbors and friends. On occasion, for the purpose of celebrating this strong sense of community, churches would cancel their evening services and gather for a community worship service. I knew that this was going to present a problem for me. Some of the folks in our church had not yet refined their understanding of the levels of fellowship. They saw little wrong with cooperating with this occasional ecumenism.

I had already begun to teach the biblical responsibilities for relationships on the local church level. This resulted in our decision to no longer participate in these community worship services. Although our church's leadership agreed, it was difficult for some of the people of our church. Several couples came to the parsonage to make an appeal not to divide the community. They noted that the churches of our community did not really represent the various heresies present in their respective denominations. The local Reformed Churches of America and United Methodist churches were represented in the World Council of Churches / National Council of Churches. The local Christian Reformed churches were associated as members of the National Association of Evangelicals. Yet many of these people in our community were true believers who believed the Bible, even among some of the Roman Catholics.

It was clear from the argument presented to me in my living room by those people from our church that the responsibilities for the level in Chapter One (*You are My Brother*) were being applied to the relationships of the local church. The *You are My Brother* level of relationship allowed us to enjoy individual fellowship with the Christian members of our community. Responsibilities on the *You are Salt* level enabled us to join together with them in various attempts to restrain moral decay[40] and provide for the needs of the poor and destitute through the food pantry in town. However, responsibilities on the *You are Light* and *You are the Church* levels were more limited when it came to assembly and corporate worship. Genuine worship demands a unity that the ecumenical community service did not provide. While it included believers, at best it was a "mixed multitude" which provided an opportunity to undermine teaching concerning genuine biblical worship and the more focused relationships in the local church.

Satan's Strategy to Corrupt the Church

Satan's strategy from the beginning of his great campaign against God has been to attempt to undermine the integrity of the people of God. Satan seeks to dilute and defeat God's people. This is seen in the inducement of the sons of God (the descendents of the godly line from Seth and Enosh) to marry the daughters of men (the ungodly line of those who had not yet begun "*to call upon the name of the Lord*" Genesis 4:26). This was found in Genesis 6:1-2: "*Now it came about, when men began to multiply on the face of the land, and daughters were born to them, that the sons of God saw that the daughters of men were beautiful; and they took wives for themselves, whomever they chose.*" In other words, they made no discrimination between the righteous and the unrighteous.

Satan attempted this again when Israel was leaving Egypt. Many went with them who were not God-fearing. This created a "mixed multitude" of complainers and grumblers (Exodus 12:38). While in the wilderness, Satan once again resorted to what became known as the Doctrine of Balaam as the enemies of God were instructed how to defeat Israel. The way to defeat God's people was to get them to compromise their purity by establishing inappropriate spiritual relationships with the ungodly (Numbers 31:16-17; Jude 11). In the Old Testament this repeated attempt to mix the truth of God with idolatry was called syncretism and it led to Israel's ultimate judgment by God.

This remains the favored strategy of Satan to defeat the church: bring defeat by diluting the church. As the local church fails to discern spiritual differences in the more intense responsibilities for relationships, Satan has churches where he wants them. For this reason, the Apostle Paul admonished the Church by echoing Old Testament instructions given to Israel: there is to be no "fellowship" between believers and unbelievers in the context of the people of God. Although these verses do not exclusively apply to the local church, it is within the context of the local church where they are most destructively ignored:

> *Do not be bound together with unbelievers; for what partnership have righteousness and lawlessness, or what fellowship has light with darkness? Or what harmony has Christ with Belial, or what has a believer in common with an unbeliever? Or what agreement has the temple of God with idols? For we are the temple of the living God; just as God said*, 'I will dwell in them and walk among them; and I will be their God, and they shall be My people. Therefore, come out from their midst and be separate,' says the Lord. 'And do not touch what is unclean; and I will welcome you And I will be a father to you, and you shall be sons and daughters to Me,' *says the Lord Almighty* (2 Corinthians 6:14-18).

In his epistle, Jude the brother of our Lord takes up this very issue as he bares his heart with those who are:

> *the called, beloved in God the Father, and kept for Jesus Christ: May mercy and peace and love be multiplied to you. Beloved, while I was making every effort to write you about our common salvation, I felt the necessity to write to you appealing that you contend earnestly for the faith which was once for all handed down to the saints. For certain persons have crept in unnoticed, those who were long beforehand marked out for this condemnation, ungodly persons who turn the grace of our God into licentiousness and deny our only Master and Lord, Jesus Christ* (Jude 1-4).

In this text, God provided us a clear expression of Jude's concern:

- **Calling for the Protection of the Faith** - Jude's intention was to write about the unity of their faith. But God redirected him to address His concern for the preservation of the "*faith which was once for all handed down to the saints*" by means of the "strenuous struggle" against false teaching. Thus, a prime directive to the church is to make sure that the identical faith they received is passed on to those coming behind them.

- **Certifying the Permanence of the Faith** - There is propositional truth that must be acknowledged. It is defined as "the faith" and it is not open to personal agenda or definition. The "apostles' doctrine" must remain that to which the church is continually devoting itself (Acts 2:42). It will never be annulled, amended, or rewritten. It does not need to be updated, softened, or corrected politically. The verb "*handed down*" to the saints is an Aorist passive participle – an action completed in the past. At the completion of the Scriptures, God's revelation was to be considered a unit, completed, unalterable, and fixed for all time. It is forever settled (Psalm 119:89).

- **Condemning the Polluters of the Faith** - The reason we have to remain vigilant to contend for the faith is that there are enemies of the truth who will endeavor to undermine it by altering, adding, or amending the revealed truth of the faith. These individuals are not keeping their distance and lobbing their heresies from outside the church. They are "creeping in" unnoticed! Thus, there are false teachers imbedded among us who seek to alter the grace of God and deny the Lord. The implication is that every local assembly of believers must understand that such threats to the integrity of truth may be found among them at any time. Usually the reason they go unnoticed is twofold: 1) there exists an apathy toward the truth by believers who consider doctrine and truth to be boring or difficult to fully comprehend; and, 2) there exists a tactic whereby false teaching is accepted in the church because it is mingled with enough truth to make it palatable to most believers – even the most insidious and dangerous forms of error.

Combating Satan's Strategy

As Jude warns us, it is not a matter of whether Satan will attempt to bring corruption and compromise into the church; it is a matter of *when* and *how*. This is the reason that strong biblical churches must remain vigilant in the defense of the faith. Two important elements in God's design for the church provide "firewalls" in the defense of the faith. History demonstrates those who remain true are churches that remain *independent and interdependent* at the same time. Although some do not like the use of such words in making the point for purity, nevertheless, the concepts are taught in Scripture and must be dealt with in the context of local church relationships.

The Priority of Independence/Autonomy in Local Churches

One of the basic tenets of the Fellowship of IFCA International is our teaching on the local church. We believe that the independence of the local church is to the church what the priesthood of the believer is to the individual. Believers assemble in a given locality under the leadership of biblically qualified spiritual men with purpose. They do so to worship God, to reach out to their community with the message of God's transforming love, to teach the truths of God's Word, and to nurture mutual support among believers. In pursuing this, they establish for themselves an identity distinct from other local churches. This identity must be centered on the careful delineation of biblical doctrine as found in God's Word. As such, each local church must strive to be an accurate representation in a given locality of the greater Body of Christ known as the "universal" or "invisible" Church. Inherent in this is the concept of local church autonomy, that is, the freedom from any external control or authority. Each local church, through its leadership, answers directly to the Lord.

Also inherent in this structure is independence, the idea that each local church is free from reliance on any external organization for its livelihood and vibrancy. Since each church is autonomous, they are free to choose to partner with a variety of para-church organizations in fulfilling their commission. When the independence and autonomy of the local church are ignored, the danger of external authority and control increases.

This control is the basic essence of denominationalism. Remaining autonomous and independent, the local church can exercise its responsibility "*to contend for the faith once and for all delivered to the saints*" (Jude 3) without external denominational influences. It is able to defend against the spread of false doctrine, compromising alliances and the abuse of centralized authority.

In contrast, as local churches align themselves under the authority of denominations, it is much more difficult for them to remain true, for they can be lured, lobbied, and forced to flow with the particular denominational current. This is the historic precedent of denominationalism. Through unbiblical organizational controls, many denominations have dominated local churches through the manipulations of pensions, property, and personnel. The history of the Fundamentalist / Modernist controversy in the last century is a prime example. Churches were forced either to comply with denominational directives or to lose everything associated with the denominational "blessing," including their places of worship. Remaining autonomous and independent of denominational control eliminates such spiritual bullying.

The Biblical Pattern of the Independent Church Movement

It is our position that the independent church movement is an attempt to maintain the biblical pattern of the autonomy and independence of the local church. This biblical pattern is demonstrated in several ways in the independent local church:

- **The Preeminence and Headship of Christ** - this emphasizes the reality that Christ Jesus is in living, vital contact with each biblical local church and there is no mediating authority over the body that stands between Christ and the members. He is the head of the Body (Matthew 18:20; 1 Thessalonians 4:9; Colossians 1:18).

- **The Power of the Indwelling of the Holy Spirit** - this is the means by which the Living Head controls the members of His church, through the Holy Spirit who resides within each true believer (1 Corinthians 3:16; 6:19).

- **The Priesthood of Believers** - this is the focus on the privilege of the believer in light of the Headship of Christ. There is no mediator between the believer and Christ. In addition, there is no mediator between the Lord and the local church (1 Peter 2:5, 9).

- **The Practice of the Church** - this is the common, usual practice of the independent local church regarding church discipline (Matthew 18:15-17), the election of officers and delegates (Acts 6:3-5), and the responsibility for doctrine and practice (Jude 3).

Through the gifting of the Holy Spirit, each local church possesses everything needed to be a vibrant, effective witness for Christ. However, when pride is introduced in the concept of autonomy, churches can develop the "spirit of independence" whereby self-sufficiency and arrogance become a "virtue." When such is the case, the local church loses its perspective regarding how it fits into the broader Body of Christ: "And the eye cannot say to the hand, '*I have no need of you*'; or again the head to the feet, '*I have no need of you*'" (1 Corinthians 12:21). See the discussion on this in Chapter One (*You are My Brother*).

Interdependence

Interdependence within the body means that believers are to rely on each other for encouragement, edification, and greater effectiveness. This also provides the platform upon which churches are able to work together. It is appropriate for local churches of like faith to cooperate with each other to present and propagate the faith. However, each local church, through its leadership and their interpretation and application of Scripture, should determine the extent of and qualifications for such cooperation. The nature of the body of Christ recognizes that all individuals are part of something bigger than themselves. This interdependence begins within the local church, and proceeds to cooperative and interdependent relationships between churches for missions, evangelism, social concerns, military chaplaincy, and such efforts. Realizing that we can do together more than can be done individually is a mark of maturity and selflessness in the cause of Christ. A church's participation in such groups as IFCA International or the General Association of Regular Baptist Churches (GARBC) provides an excellent venue in which this can be accomplished.

The Preamble to the 1930 Constitution and By-Laws of the Independent Fundamental Churches of America (now called IFCA International) declared:

> Whereas, it has always been both an encouragement, and a more effective means whereby to prosecute the work of the Lord, for such ministers and congregations to join in a common bond of fellowship, counsel and cooperation, so strengthening one another in the Lord's work; and, Whereas, in the providence of God, we believe the time has come for an advance movement among these independent churches and groups of Christians to thus unite in a closer fellowship and cooperation in the defense of the faith and in the proclamation of the gospel of God's grace.[41]

The founders of the IFCA perceived the need to cooperate with each other. The language in that Preamble makes it clear. But the founders also recognized the peril of denominational authority and control. As a result, IFCA International requires that its membership be free from any affiliation with denominationalism. This represents balance between independence and interdependence.

OTHER PERILS

Independence and Exclusivity

As mentioned above, a twisted sense of independence will result in a sense of exclusivity. Churches can become so defensive in the name of truth that they build walls of protection to keep themselves "unspotted from the world." In doing so, they neglect the responsibility given to the local church to reach the lost with the Gospel. These churches become so consumed with protecting the truth, that they will develop newer and more precise applications of truth. An application for them becomes a new "interpretation," which begs further application into practical "Christian" living. This cycle begins to feed on itself. It results in a great violation of the divine instruction that we *"learn not to exceed what is written, so that no one of you will become arrogant in behalf of one against the other"* (1 Corinthians 4:6). Congregations and individuals guilty of violating this instruction tend to multiply the "laws of men." This is exactly what happened with the Pharisees of old. Through satisfaction with their own self-righteousness, these people become like the Pharisees. They begin to see the lost as unwelcome intruders who will do nothing but defile them.

Typically, this process continues until these people begin to avoid interaction with anyone whom they believe are less spiritual than they. Since the "unspiritual" will likely attend, they absent themselves from fellowship opportunities, Sunday School, youth outings, and other activities provided within the context of the local church. In addition, they look with suspicion at other local churches and find fault with non-essential differences they think disqualify them from being able to "have fellowship."

Issues and Preferences

Scriptures repeatedly warn the believer concerning the devastation to the Gospel of grace when we run past what is written in the Bible. When the church or individuals attempt to legislate beyond what God has determined to be matters of conscience, the Gospel is not *helped*. Things of this nature ought to be settled by each individual believer before the Lord. Scriptures teach that false teachers will come who endeavor to promote their own positions over Scripture. They will declare that in order to advance true biblical awareness and true godliness, you must agree with their understanding or personal convictions. Examples of such devastating issues which existed in the early church include: festivals or holy days (Romans 14:5-6; Colossians 2:16); vegetarianism (Romans 14:2); eating meat sacrificed to idols (1 Corinthians 8:4ff); apostles traveling with their wives (1 Corinthians 9:5); marriage (1 Corinthians 7:32ff; 1 Timothy 4:3); and eating various condemned foods (1 Timothy 4:3). Matters of conscience before God must be decided by the believer before the Lord alone – not on the basis of imposition by someone else's relationship with Jesus Christ.

The transgression is when men impose themselves on the consciences of others by "*exceeding what is written [so that they] ... become arrogant in behalf of one against the other*" (1 Corinthians 4:6). To do so is to raise oneself as the standard by which all others are judged in areas where God Himself has not definitively ruled (Colossians 2:16-23). When this occurs, one essentially raises himself up against God and insists on what God has not required. If an individual's conscience requires of him a particular prohibition, he ought to comply. However, insisting that others comply causes such a one to "*teach as doctrines the precepts of men*" (Mark 7:7). Through this errant approach, entirely appropriate personal decisions can become "*doctrines of demons*" that we are warned against in 1 Timothy 4:1-5. While it is completely appropriate for an individual to embrace a clear position on any of these issues, they can become "doctrines" that "exceed what is written" and thereby become canons of spirituality, generating arrogance against all who "fail" to adopt them as God's truth. Successful participation in the Kingdom of God is not dependent upon such things. To suggest so is error. Such men are warned against in 1 Timothy 1:5-7: "*But the goal of our instruction is love from a pure heart and a good conscience and a sincere faith. For some men, straying from these things, have turned aside to fruitless discussion, wanting to be teachers of the Law, even though they do not understand either what they are saying or the matters about which they make confident assertions.*"

Again, Scripture does not warn that a person cannot hold to a personal conviction in an area of preference. A position which advocates betrothal, for instance, is well within the parameters of biblical precedent through the cultures (both pagan and believing) of the biblical era. However, observation of a biblical situation such as betrothal should not be elevated to a biblical commandment. Or, to say it another way, what is biblically observed cannot be advanced as a biblical precept. Tradition does not necessarily equate with God's expectation.

Examples of matters of conscience are more fully discussed in Appendix Six, but they would include matters such as:

- Bible Translations
- Styles of worship
- Dress

- Mixed swimming
- Church polity
- Styles of preaching
- Entertainment issues
- Financial policy
- Educational methodology
- Dating vs. courtship vs. betrothal
- Inter-Generational discipleship

These are not the only issues over which Christians fail to agree to disagree. Churches divide over whether they should be Republicans, Democrats, or Independents; whether they should be involved in civil disobedience; whether there is a five mile leeway on speed limits; the requirement of a believer's baptism for membership; whether a widowed elder is still qualified to serve since he is no longer married; whether there should be pews or chairs; whether the multipurpose room should be called a gym or a family center; whether the carpet should be blue or red; whether the pastor should be called by his first name or by his title; whether believers should or should not shop online. For issue-driven people, the list of possibilities goes on and on.

Interests and Cliques

Scriptures warn believers against the haughtiness that accompanies a particular group when it concludes it is the only group that has it right. The church at Corinth is a prime example. The Apostle Paul addressed this when the Corinthians had so haughtily segregated into their "partisan preferences." Disunity was threatening the church. Paul says: "*For I have been informed concerning you, my brethren, by Chloe's people, that there are quarrels among you. Now I mean this, that each one of you is saying, 'I am of Paul,' and 'I of Apollos,' and 'I of Cephas,' and 'I of Christ.' Has Christ been divided? Paul was not crucified for you, was he? Or were you baptized in the name of Paul?*" (1 Corinthians 1:11-13). The Corinthian church had divided along the lines of special interests and cliques. Some preferred the powerful, legal presentations of Paul. Others preferred the eloquent oratory of Apollos. Still others related to the common, down-to-earth practicality of Cephas (Peter). Finally, there were those who were so arrogant that they declared that they would listen to nobody but the Lord Himself. Some ancient commentators supposed that the Apostle had substituted the names of eminent men for the obscure names of the real party leaders to show how unjustifiable such rivalries are.[42] But the basic diagnosis for such partisanship was provided by Paul just a few chapters later: "*For since there is jealousy and strife among you, are you not fleshly, and are you not walking like mere men? For when one says, 'I am of Paul,' and another, 'I am of Apollos,' are you not mere men? What then is Apollos? And what is Paul? Servants through whom you believed, even as the Lord gave opportunity to each one*" (1 Corinthians 3:3-5).

Such exclusivity can exist as people favor the personalities of various spiritual leaders such as John MacArthur, Adrian Rogers, Bob Jones, Chuck Swindoll, David Jeremiah or Charles Stanley. It can also exist over other issues such as home schooling, Christian education, or public education. It can exist over colleges, social issues or even ethnicity. Should a church say it is exclusively a Black, Hispanic or Asian church? Should a church designate itself as a White church? Should a church call itself a blue collar or white collar church? I understand that these terms are often used to describe the predominate race or social status of its members, but do we do the Church of Jesus Christ a disservice by using such "partisan" terms?

These same kinds of cliques can exist within a single assembly of believers as well. There are some who are part of a clique existing among a group of upper middle class believers. Another might exist among those who are blue collar workers, or union members. There can be the cliques among graduates of a particular school or college. Such division within the body does not promote the unity of the body called for by our Lord. When such divisions exist within the body, believers need to approach the issue "*with all humility and gentleness, with patience, showing tolerance for one another in love, being diligent to preserve the unity of the Spirit in the bond of peace*" (Ephesians 4:2-3).

Pragmatism

The command to reach out with the Gospel is an inherent part of our responsibility as believers. But unless the church remains, at the same time, defensive for the truth and offensive with the truth, Satan will succeed in bringing defeat and neutralizing the church.

Many churches choose to maintain either an offensive or a defensive vigilance. One church may do its best to take the Gospel to the lost. But in doing so, they may begin to neglect the necessity of defending the faith. With great desire to reach the lost, they do "whatever it takes" to see them come to Church. Instead of viewing the Gospel as a stewardship that must be kept pure because it belongs to the Master, they seek to make the church a venue where the world has an equal sense of priority as the believer. For some, this perspective goes so far that assemblies are developed with a priority of attracting the unchurched using pragmatic methods that find no precedent in Scripture. When warned about worldliness in the church, a typical response from these churches is: "methods don't matter – it's only the message that matters." However, they also say that old methods (preaching, praying, fellowship, and hymns sung to piano and organ) will not work in this new generation. *Apparently methods do matter*! The question becomes: What methods produce what result? Worldly methods attract worldly people and the "assembly of the worldly" is not the "Body of Christ."

This was demonstrated tragically at a missionary commissioning service where I was asked to give a charge to the candidates. In my ten minute exhortation, I encouraged the couple to beware of Satan's desire to draw our energies away from biblically based methods of ministry such as the preaching of the apostles' doctrine, fellowship, breaking of bread, and prayer (Acts 2:46-47). I challenged them to avoid the pitfalls of being culturally driven by the popular yet inordinate desire for "relevance" that turns to less offensive methods. I charged them to remain true to a confidence in the sufficiency of the Savior and the Scriptures as the basis for the assembly of believers. As soon as I sat down, the next speaker began to blatantly countermand my challenge, calling for a methodologically relevant approach to ministry. He declared: "We don't advocate the purposeful pursuit of cultural irrelevance." He stated that we need to figure out what "works," and use that. He then diminished my previous emphasis on prayer by stating (and I quote): "*we've done everything that we can for you and now you're on your own*" (as if our ongoing prayers were of no value!) My soul was grieved all the way home as I envisioned the cloud hovering over that church, accompanied by ill winds of dilution and defeat. Unfortunately, it was only a matter of months before the methods being taught and the manner in which they were employed, decimated the church. Today it is only a skeleton of what it was, or, for that matter, could have been.

Indifference

Another threat to biblically responsible relationships within the church is the problem of indifference. Whether due to busy schedules, the depersonalization of our culture through technology, or some other reason, people too often lack concern for one another. Jesus stated that one of the foremost ways that people know we are His disciples is through the nature of our relationships with one another. He said: "*By this all men will know that you are My disciples, if you have love for one another*" (John 13:35). When believers fail to possess the desire to meet together (Hebrew 10:25), to pray together (James 5:16), to share meals together (Acts 2:46), to talk together (Ephesians 4:25), to avoid judging one another (Romans 14:13), to help bear one another's burdens (Galatians 6:2), to comfort one another (1 Thessalonians 4:18), to accept one another (Romans 15:7), there is a lack of evidence that we share Christ.

Another peril of indifference is with reference to the lost. Believers are surrounded by people who are going to face the horrible judgment of God. We have the good news that will deliver their souls. How indictable is the indifference that maintains a silence while these Hell-bound sinners interact with us from day to day. This ought to shake the thoughtful Christian to his very soul – understanding that such indifference signals a serious lack of harmony and connectedness with the Savior. He Himself declared: "*Follow Me, and I will make you fishers of men.*" (Matthew 4:19). Further, Jesus promised that when the Holy Spirit would come, we would receive power, and the consequence would be Spirit-filled believers who would "*be My witnesses both in Jerusalem, and in all Judea and Samaria, and even to the remotest part of the earth*" (Acts 1:8).

If reaching the world for Christ is the "mission" of the church, how can the individual believer escape his involvement in that mission? What is the ramification of his failure to do so? If a believer is not seeking to bring men to Christ for salvation by means of personally sharing the Gospel and involving himself in the missionary endeavor of fishing for men, it is only logical to conclude that he: 1) is not following Christ; and/or 2) is not filled with the Spirit. The only alternative is that Jesus Christ was wrong! These things are not commonly expressed because they whittle away at the comfort believers give to themselves saying they do not have the spiritual "gift" of evangelism, despite the fact that every believer is charged to "*do the work of an evangelist*" (2 Timothy 4:5). Apparently, to many professing believers, the Great Commission given by our Lord is not intended for them, but for some other "class" of Christian. But Jesus said, "*Go therefore and make disciples of all the nations, baptizing them in the name of the Father and the Son and the Holy Spirit, teaching them to observe all that I commanded you; and lo, I am with you always, even to the end of the age*" (Matthew 28:19-20). Failure to obey brings a tragic emptiness to the focus of the church. It ultimately results in the very spiritual narcissism that prevails in the church today.

The Partners

With whom then is the believer able to partner when it comes to biblically responsible relationships on the level of the local church? Again, the Church is defined in two different spheres. First, the term *Church* refers to all believers who have been saved through faith in Jesus Christ from the Day of Pentecost (Acts 2) through the Rapture of the Church (described in 1 Thessalonians 4:8-13). Other equivalent terms are "Universal Church" and "Invisible Church" since it includes every believer from every place in every epoch of the Christian era. Second, the term *Church* refers not merely to the buildings where the Christian assembly meets, but to believers

- assembling in a given locality
- under the leadership of biblically qualified men
- for the purpose of worshiping God
- reaching out to their community with the message of God's transforming love
- teaching the truths of God's Word
- and nurturing mutual support among believers.

This is called the "local church" or the "visible church." The various elements of the local church help to clarify who can participate properly on this level.

Location *(believers assembling in a given locality)*

The local church is the manifestation of the universal church in a given location. Thus, it is proper for a believer to assemble together with a church as close to his community as possible. With the advent of modern travel, people are able to choose from a far greater variety of churches. Consequently, many people have developed a "consumer" mentality to which churches have begun to appeal. Instead of having to work together in their community, solving tensions, correcting theological errors, exercising church discipline for sin, and diligently preserving unity, people are free to uproot and move on to other churches. They will shop for the one that "best suits" what are often their unbiblical ideals. Many churches will cater to these "needs" instead of motivating believers toward greater sanctification and selfless investment in seeking to reach the lost and contributing to building up the local Body of Christ through their giftedness (Ephesians 4:15-16).

Leadership *(under the leadership of biblically qualified men)*

The local church is not merely an informal gathering of believers. Indeed, it is true that when two or three are gathered in the name of Christ, He is in their midst (Matthew 18:20). However, the local church is the specific representation of the Body of Christ and depends upon the leadership of men who have been given to the church for protection, guidance, and provision. Sheep having no shepherd induce the compassion and pity of the Lord, which is not a desirable state (Matthew 9:36). Thus, Christ has provided "under-shepherds" whom the sheep are to follow. These godly men are to provide Christ-honoring and biblically sound leadership. This is what is described by Peter when he said: "*Shepherd the flock of God among you, exercising oversight not under compulsion, but voluntarily, according to the will of God … nor yet as lording it over those allotted to your charge, but proving to be examples to the flock. And when the Chief Shepherd appears, you will receive the unfading crown of glory*" (1 Peter 5:2-4). This is anticipated in the Old Testament where the prophet Jeremiah declares on behalf of the Lord: "*Then I will give you shepherds, after My own heart, who will feed you on knowledge and understanding*" (Jeremiah 3:15). Individual believers are commanded to yield to this leadership. They are informed that they are to "*Obey your leaders and submit to them, for they keep watch over your souls as those who will give an account. Let them do this with joy and not with grief, for this would be unprofitable for you*" (Hebrews 13:17). Spiritual leaders are commanded not to lord over the sheep. Believers are commanded to obey the leaders God supplies. God's provision of leadership is part of the essential characteristics of a local church (Ephesians 4:11; Acts 14:23; 1 Timothy 3:1-13). This argument reaches a crescendo in Titus 1:5 where we learn that things are not "in order" until such leadership exists in every church.

The Scriptures teach that the Holy Spirit is the One who establishes those who are the "overseers" (Acts 20:28). However, the principle of "two witnesses" (Deuteronomy 17:6; 19:15; Matthew 18:15-17; 2 Corinthians 13:1) becomes applicable, as they are also recognized by the believers in a local assembly and are thus "appointed." Believers need to carefully evaluate spiritual leadership for authentic yieldedness to the Holy Spirit. This enables spiritual leadership to protect the church adequately from false doctrine, provide them with nourishment from the Word, and correct and discipline willful, sustained sin.

Believers should expect that the spiritual leadership in their churches would possess clear qualification to be spiritual leaders (as prescribed in 1 Timothy 3:1-7). Too often congregations are interested in having pastors who demonstrate the same weaknesses and struggles as they possess. Instead of being comforted by the fact that the man God has placed in leadership of their assembly is a man of strong spiritual integrity and blamelessness, they celebrate when a man fails. They often refuse resignations when there have been moral failures or when children consistently display rebellion and lack of responsiveness to his leadership or when there has been a divorce. These are clear compromises of the standards for leadership that the Lord Himself has established in His Word. Believers have the responsibility to preserve the directives of the Lord as authoritative, not merely passive suggestions!

Worship *(for the purpose of worshipping God)*

The local church is the venue where the people of God are to gather for worship. Although believers who fail to worship the Lord privately throughout the week will merely feign worship when they gather in public occasions, there is the direct expectation that when the church gathers, it is for the purpose of genuine worship. A.W. Tozer wrote: "I can offer no worship wholly pleasing to God if I know that I am harboring elements in my life that are displeasing to Him. I cannot truly and joyfully worship God on Sunday and not worship Him on Monday. I cannot worship God with a glad song on Sunday and then knowingly displease Him in my business dealings on Monday and Tuesday." [43]

Worship is so tremendously varied in our churches today, and there are many reasons for this. One reason is we have developed designer worship for the pleasure of the one "offering" it instead of seeking to conform to the God for whom worship is designed. Believers are under obligation to seek a church where the clear audience during worship is the God of glory, for whom our awed awareness of His central attribute of holiness is displayed. It is for His enjoyment that His truth is thoroughly embraced and celebrated by the ones worshiping. Thus, a central theme in worship, as sought by the Lord, is humility. Humility is not seen in the arrogant assertions of morally compromised "singing stars," who with contorted faces crank out ballads of affection for their "significant spiritual other." The hype engendered by popular Christian "worship" today is often indistinguishable from that which is generated by an assembly of the worldly listening to a popular secular diva. But to the common Christian today, such "fun" in church is the essence of a desirable "worship" experience.

Genuine worship stirs contrition not conceit, contentment with God not the satisfaction of cultural impulses. It motivates us toward maturity. True worship does not affirm the sinner in his mediocrity. It's about humility, not hype! Tozer said it best when he declared that: "libidinous impulses and the sweet, deep moving of the Holy Spirit are diametrically opposed to one another."[44] Believers who encounter the entertainment model of worship (where God is perceived as somewhere in heaven prompting teams of worship to bless and please a congregation best described as a "mixed multitude") ought to run from such a place. Instead, we find church after church jumping on the "bandwagon" and designing their worship to strike chords of pleasure in the ungodly, immature, and unspiritual. Ron Owens, in his excellent book *Return to Worship*, shares an experience that illustrates this.

> We recently held an *Experiencing God in Revival* conference in a large church in the south. The minister of music phoned me prior to the first meeting to see what our needs would be. He described the "stage." He asked whether I would like the piano located on stage left or stage right. It had been so long since I had done any theater that I wasn't sure what I wanted. He then asked what kind of lighting I would like to have high light us as we sang. I said that I wanted it to be just like a church service. He said that they always dimmed the lights in the "auditorium" and spot lighted whoever was "performing" on the stage. I said that I really didn't want any dimming or spot lighting, but would rather leave all the lights up. There was then the choice of microphones, whether we wanted reverb added to the voice and so on. I was soon to discover that the choir rehearsal room was called the music theater. I had the feeling that we were going to a concert hall. What was supposed to be a church sanctuary or worship center was more like a huge theater.[45]

We have come to believe the twisted logic that God can be pleased with a form of worship that attracts the ungodly. Either God will be lifted up in worship and sinners brought to humility and repentance, or sinners will be cuddled and affirmed while God is slighted. When unbelievers enter the assembly of believers, the desire of the church must be to receive them with love and consideration. However, when God is the focus of worship, the result will be the presentation of the truth in such a way that an unbeliever can be "*convicted by all, he is called to account by all; the secrets of his heart are disclosed; and so he will fall on his face and worship God, declaring that God is certainly among you*" (1 Corinthians 14:24-25). Believers must seek churches where God is the clear object of worship and where spiritual leaders prompt the congregation of redeemed sinners to humbly exalt the One who is both Lord and Christ (Acts 2:36).

Evangelism *(reaching out with the message of God's transforming love)*

Someone once said: "The church gathers for worship and scatters to evangelize." Some churches have banners above their exit doors saying: "You are now entering the mission field." This emphasis must be regained by all local churches. The great hindrance (traceable to mass evangelism strategy) is that many individual saints have concluded they are not adequate to evangelize. Many believe in order to evangelize they have to bring the unsaved to an "event" so the "professionals" can present the Gospel. This mistake is carried further by churches that design their assemblies for the unsaved, stirring their members to bring in the unchurched. Although evangelism needs to remain a priority of the church assembled, it is not the objective. Evangelism must become the objective of a church when it scatters throughout the week.

In order to participate in evangelism on the local church level, there must be unity regarding the essentials of the Gospel. In the latter part of the Twentieth Century, a fiery debate arose among Evangelicals as to the nature of the Gospel. Was repentance an inevitable partner with faith? What was the nature of "saving" faith?

IFCA International wrestled with the issues and came together with tremendous unity in defining the nature of saving faith. (For a further discussion, see Appendix Seven: *Salvation by Grace through Faith.*) We observed that saving faith consists of two indispensable elements: the intellectual (an awareness of the facts of the Gospel particularly about Christ's sacrificial death for sins and His physical resurrection, a persuasion that these facts are true); and the volitional (total personal reliance upon Christ and the power inherent in His death to provide forgiveness of sins and everlasting life, engaging a person's mind and will). "The intellectual apprehension of orthodox doctrine alone will avail nothing (James 2:19). A volitional act of faith in the wrong object (e.g., John 2:23-24; 6:26-27;

8:31, 44) is useless. To save, faith must be directed toward the person and work of the Lord Jesus Christ" (Romans 3:22).46 Churches that teach salvation is an uncertain matter because it depends on the quality of a sinner's faith must be avoided. It is not the quality of faith that saves, but the object of faith. Likewise, churches that teach personal faith is unnecessary because of participation in the Covenant (via family connection and infant baptism) are also to be avoided. Confidence, or faith, in the wrong thing does nothing but make sinners the two-fold children of hell (Matthew 23:15). Agreement on the nature of the Gospel is essential for fellowship and participation by responsible believers.

Doctrine *(teaching the truths of God's Word)*

Perhaps more than any other issue, doctrine needs to serve as the determining factor in participation in fellowship on the local church level. Tragically, doctrine is often dismissed as that which "divides." It is often greatly deemphasized when choosing a church home.

Not too long ago, I had a discussion with a person in a Reformed Church of America who was seeking to change churches because they had moved into a new area. He told me he was trying a local Nazarene church. I expressed some surprise that his family could make such a huge doctrinal swing with ease. He responded: "I know, but we really like the style of worship." Doctrine did not seem to matter!

To many, the church's location, worship style, attractiveness of the building, nursery facilities, and other issues are given priority over doctrine when selecting which church to attend. A firm commitment to sound, biblical doctrine needs to be the single most important factor when selecting a church. If a church does not embrace sound doctrine, it cannot be a church of choice. Yet some believers are so naïve that they make such a choice without hesitation.

Some time ago, a church began in our area. It grew by leaps and bounds. Believers from churches all over the area left their churches to attend. The pastor had a charismatic personality. However, it became evident there were very important doctrinal issues, even aberrations. But it did not seem to make any difference. Attendance still grew. An interview in *Christianity Today* confirmed these doctrinal problems. In this article the pastor shared, "This is not the same old message with new methods. We're rediscovering Christianity as an Eastern religion, as a way of life."[47] The interview noted that this pastor started questioning the assumptions about the Bible itself and shared that he is "discovering the Bible as a human product" not the product of divine fiat. This is very similar to the basic approach liberal theology has to the Word of God. Yet believers have been attracted by the "freedom" that this "culturally relevant church offers.

Certainly, the most critical issues of doctrine are what have become known as the "fundamentals of the faith." They include: 1) the inspiration and inerrancy of the Scriptures (including miracles); 2) the Virgin Birth; 3) the substitutionary Atonement; 4) Christ's Bodily Resurrection; and 5) the physical Second Coming of Christ. These basic teachings provide the objective, essential and necessary beliefs to determine whether or not a person is in the true Christian faith. (For a fuller discussion see Appendix One: *A Brief History of the Conservative/Liberal Theological Controversy*.)

The local church needs to formulate and codify other major Scriptural doctrines since they are also part of God's revealed truth. In a recent discussion with a Reformed Church of America pastor, he stated that if he were to regularly emphasize doctrine it would greatly hinder fellowship in his church. This same pastor informed me that he believed that the Reformation was the single-most tragic event in Church History. In his opinion, it fractured the church and multiplied denominations, convincing the world that Christians do not love. He identified doctrinal distinctives as unwarranted obstacles to love.

A local church must state what it believes to be sound doctrine and agree to these doctrines as a test of fellowship within the local church. This defines the more limited relationships present on the local church level. These matters would include:

- the Godhead (Trinity)
- the Person and Work of Christ
- the Person and Work of the Holy Spirit
- Creation
- the Total Depravity of Man
- Salvation (Justification, Sanctification, and Regeneration)
- Eternal Security and Assurance of Salvation
- the New Nature of the Believer
- Spiritual Gifts
- the Nature of the Church (identity, establishment, autonomy, ordinances)
- the Personality of Satan
- The Second Advent of Christ (including the Rapture)

- the Eternal State
- Biblical Separation
- Movements contrary to the Faith (ecumenism, ecumenical evangelism, Neo-Orthodoxy, New Evangelicalism)

All of these should be delineated and subscribed to by those who will be part of the membership of the local church. For the preservation of doctrinal integrity, anyone who does not agree to the doctrinal statement ought not to be admitted to the membership of a local church. Failure to secure unity on stated doctrines is a formula for division and unrest.

Fellowship *(nurturing mutual support among believers)*

This is the area of involvement in the church which highlights the relevance of life in Christ. When believers gather for the purpose of encouraging one another with the news of what Christ is doing in their lives (ways in which they have discovered the beauty of Christ to be more stupendous, or prayers that have been answered), they are enjoying the true kind of fellowship that needs to occur between believers. The Christian assembly is designed to encourage one another (Hebrews 10:25). Believers need to look purposefully for ways they can enjoy what is called in many churches "Body Life". This is the practical family relationship that needs to exist where we enjoy participation as children of God within the context of the church. In the very beginning of the Church, this is described: "*all those who had believed were together and had all things in common, and they began selling their property and possessions and were sharing them with all, as anyone might have need. ... they were taking their meals together with gladness and sincerity of heart, praising God and having favor with all the people*" (Acts 2:44-47a).

The word "fellowship" comes from the Greek word that means "common, something shared in common." Obviously, what is most importantly shared is the one Lord who is over all and is Redeemer and Master. The more believers are able to share things of a common spiritual nature, the deeper the level of relationship becomes. Those with whom we are able to enjoy the richest fellowship within the Body of Christ are those with whom we are able to share the most significant, common spiritual experiences:

- **A Common Holiness** - This refers to the consummation of God's purpose for the believer. His expressed plan for our lives is to produce in us

Christlikeness through which we are transformed into His image from glory to glory (2 Corinthians 4:18; 1 John 3:1-3). As believers are progressively sanctified through this transformation process, they share common experiences of growth in holiness. Instead of a church becoming increasingly secularized and compromised, believers should be able to enjoy more fully the holiness of God as they celebrate together His worthiness.

- **A Common Heritage** - This refers to the reality that every believer in the Body of Christ has the same story. All believers were once lost in sin, were brought under the influence of the Gospel, were convicted by the Spirit of God, repented of sin, called on Christ to forgive them, and were regenerated by the power of God's Holy Spirit. There is not a single Christian without the experience of the same new birth. With God as our Father, the Lord Jesus Christ as our Master, and the Spirit of God as our guide, we celebrate the work of God in our lives. Despite individualized testimonies of God's work in our lives, we all have the same heritage.

- **A Common Hope** - This refers to the greatly anticipated deliverance that every true Christian possesses. We are instructed to be "*looking for the blessed hope and the appearing of the glory of our great God and Savior, Jesus Christ, who gave Himself for us to redeem us from every lawless deed, and to purify for Himself a people for His own*" (Titus 2:13-14). As we anticipate His coming, everyone with this hope "*purifies himself just as he is pure*" (1 John 3:3). As we await His coming, we are to encourage one another "*all the more as you see the day drawing near*" (Hebrews 10:25). The hope of the glorious assembly in Heaven stirs the assembly here on earth as we wait. It is an encouraging time as we anticipate the perfect fellowship we will enjoy in glory.

- **A Common Honor**- This refers to the opportunity to celebrate the honor we receive as part of the Bride of Christ. God is at work in us through His Spirit to prepare us "*so that He might sanctify [the church], having cleansed her by the washing of water with the word, that He might present to Himself the church in all her glory, having no spot or wrinkle or any such thing; but that she would be holy and blameless*" (Ephesians 5:26-27). The distinct honor of being the Bride of Christ and looking forward to the day when we are presented as His Bride is an honor beyond compare. This is celebrated by those in such an honorable position.

Believers who agree in the above areas are those with whom we can have biblically responsible relationships on the level of the local church.

THE PURSUIT

The Practice of the Church (Acts 2:42)

We live in a day when the church is attempting to become all things to all people. The leadership of local churches feels the pressure to provide for whatever is perceived as a need, or lose people to churches that are willing to do so. However, the church must maintain its focus on what the Scriptures identify as the core values of the church's ministry. There are some objective instructions whereby any pursuit within the church must be evaluated. The essential activities of the early church from the very beginning are found in Acts 2:42: "*They were continually devoting themselves to the apostles' teaching and to fellowship, to the breaking of bread and to prayer.*" These four activities serve as the blueprint for the ministries of the church. Every initiative within the church assembled needs to be traced back to the foundation of these four activities. Understanding that we are addressing the assembly of the church and not the scattering of the church for the sake of evangelism, let us look briefly at each of these activities.

- **Apostles' Doctrine** - Continual devotion to the Apostles' doctrine demonstrates the way that the early church celebrated the truths regarding Jesus Christ. Today, it depicts concentrating on and celebrating the truth of God's Word, the inspired text which preserves what was taught by the apostles. This demonstrates the centrality of the preaching and teaching of the Scriptures and the central role God's Word must have in the life of the church. Devotion to the Apostles' doctrine is today accomplished through preaching, teaching, memorizing, meditating, and applying God's Word. Whenever the church assembles, a devotion to the Word of God must prevail. Again, this is the celebration of the complete picture of Jesus Christ as God's Son and our Savior.

- **Fellowship** - Continual devotion to fellowship demonstrates how important it is for believers to celebrate the present work of Christ in their lives. Fellowship is not merely having dinner together, talking about the latest sports scores, or sitting in a pew at the same time (although those things can provide a venue in which fellowship can happen). Fellowship is the ability to share with other believers what Christ is currently doing in one's life. It involves rejoicing when prayers are answered, lessons are learned, sins are confessed, burdens are lifted, and joys are trumpeted. It sees the current relevancy of walking by faith in the Son of God. It is the instigation of joy in others and the inspiration to joy by others over the wonder of the power of Christ in our daily living. This is the celebration of the current work of Christ in believers' lives. Getting together for a meal without sharing the wonder of the work of Christ is not genuine spiritual fellowship.

- **Breaking of Bread** - Continual devotion to the breaking of bread shows how important the consideration of sin is to be in the local church. The "breaking of bread" is a descriptive way of referring to the celebration of the Lord's Table, symbols of the finished work of Christ. As believers ate together, they consistently concluded their meals in the same way the Lord did at the Last Supper – they would break bread. On that great day of joy, on the road to Emmaus, Cleopas and the other disciple discovered that their traveling companion was actually the Lord only after He broke the bread and gave it to them (Luke 24:30-31). Believers continually remembered the sacrifice of Christ as they shared communion together (1 Corinthians 11:24-25). As they did so, they were commanded to carefully examine themselves and then eat of the bread and drink of the cup. In so doing, the early Church repeatedly examined their lives for sin and celebrated the provision of the body and blood of Christ as the propitiation for their sin. When a church downplays the relevance of sin it minimizes the impact of the atonement provided in Christ. The more a sinner comprehends of what he has been forgiven, the greater the motivation to bless the Lord. Therefore, this activity in Acts 2:42 refers to the celebration of the past (finished) work of Christ on behalf of sinners.

- **Prayer** - Continual devotion to prayer depicts the early church's confidence in the power of God regarding the future. Matters that required the application of God's power were taken to Him and supplication, intercession, and petition were made. Believers called on God to act in glory. This displayed a confidence that God would indeed act in the future to bring Himself glory. To pray as a church is to demonstrate a dependency upon the Lord for His continued grace. Essentially, it celebrates the potential work of Christ in our lives.

In these four activities, the centrality of Christ is seen. The assemblies of the early believers were consumed with seeing Christ magnified as Lord of the church. They celebrated the complete picture of Christ in the Apostles' teaching, the current work of Christ through fellowship, the finished work of Christ through breaking of bread, and the future work of Christ in prayer. Thus, everything to which the Church was devoted was Christocentric. We need to be able to say the same thing about our churches if we expect to know the power of Christ in transforming us into the vessels of honor designed by God.

THE PRIORITIES OF THE CHURCH

The Integrity of Spiritual Leadership

As discussed above, the local assembly of believers is responsible to maintain the biblical qualifications for those who serve as their leaders. I have heard some argue that these qualifications are nearly impossible to find in men today. Therefore, many churches have designated these divinely imposed standards "ideals that serve as a goal but are impossible to attain".

Years ago I was in a discussion with several local pastors concerning the process of nomination for spiritual leadership in their denominational churches. It was interesting to hear them state that their men merely "take their turns." As I listened, I was amazed at the lack of concern about the qualifications listed in the New Testament for elders and deacons. I asked, "What about the requirements that Paul listed in 1 Timothy 3 and Titus 1?" They looked at me with amazement and disbelief and one man responded: "You've got to be kidding! Do you honestly believe that meeting those qualifications is possible? If we expected our board members to measure up to those standards, we wouldn't have any eligible men." Sadly, this attitude often prevails in Evangelical churches as well as in the liberal denominational churches.

There is a growing perspective that the biblical standards for leadership are nothing more than recommendations – not requirements.[48] As we see our culture slouching and shifting morally, it becomes all the more important that we preserve these standards. Certainly, if there were ever an occasion for the mitigation of such high "ideals" for leadership it would have been in places with the moral decadence of cities like Corinth and Ephesus. Nevertheless, Paul gave these instructions for the qualifications of leadership to Timothy while he was at Ephesus (1 Timothy 1:3). One of the greatest responsibilities for local assemblies is to value the spiritual leadership God has given them, granting them honor as the servants of Christ and holding them accountable for exemplary living (1 Timothy 5:17-20).

Some have suggested that Leadership might be an additional level of relationship within the body of Christ on The Pyramid of Responsibility. Certainly, it is a great responsibility for leaders to relate properly to one another in a way that promotes the unity of the Spirit in the bond of peace. When the hand of the Lord rests upon a man and he is chosen for the ministry of deacon or elder, it is assumed that he and others recognize the character qualities for leadership (given in 1 Timothy 3 and Titus 1) are obviously present in him. Unless actions or attitudes by a leader call into question his spiritual qualification, his ability to lead should not be stifled by petty criticisms and personal preferences on the part of others. The sphere of influence godly leaders possess should be the arena where their unity of heart and spirit should be most observable. It is therefore incumbent upon leaders to communicate, pray, and openly share their hearts with one another. Board meetings, committee meetings and congregational meetings can be a joy when leadership seeks the mind of God in a concerted effort to preserve the unity of the Spirit in the bond of peace. When leaders properly relate to one another in a godly way, the church prospers, and God's blessing rests upon all who benefit from their oversight.

The Preservation of the Unity of the Spirit

Unity is one characteristic of a church that is Spirit-filled. However, true biblical unity is not the sentimentality so commonly in vogue in our modern ecumenical context. Often we hear theological liberals declaring unity to be the greatest good and anything that brings division needs to be de-prioritized. Essentially to them, the issue that needs de-prioritization is doctrine and they immediately quote John 17:22 where Jesus prays: "*The glory which You have given Me I have given to them, that they may be one, just as We are one.*"

In the previous section of John 17, Jesus indicates that with reference to unity, the Word of God will provide His followers with the ability to remain together despite being in the world. They would not only be preserved and protected by the power of God through the Word, they would also be able to be witnesses as they take the Gospel to the world. Jesus indicates that He is sending them "into the world" armed with the truth that sanctifies men, with the expectation that the Word would not return "void" (Isaiah 55:11). Here is the proof. Jesus is confident in the success of those He sends out: "*I do not ask on behalf of these alone, but for those also who believe in Me through their word*" (v. 20). His work of redemption would extend farther than the mere handful of men listening to His prayer. They would go as they have been sent and they would see converts. Therefore, Jesus is praying for us, those who would come to faith after having the opportunity to hear the Gospel message delivered through the Apostles. They are to adhere to His Word which would be communicated through them: "*... those who believe in Me through their word.*" This describes the basis of the faith for all Christians, the message delivered through the ministry of the inspired authors of Scripture. Everyone who comes to faith will do so as they have opportunity to hear the Word of God which was communicated through the ministry of those sent forth by God beginning with the Apostles (Romans 10:14-17).

The Apostles wrote the Scriptures and served as the conduit through which the Word of God was delivered (2 Peter 1:21). It is obvious that God intended men to be saved through individuals taking the truth of the Gospel to other individuals (1 Corinthians 1:18-21). When the Word of God is delivered, the result is that men will believe. The means by which all people are brought to God is the Spirit of God applying the Word of God to a person's heart and that person obtains faith unto salvation. This faith is in the person of Jesus Christ and in the facts of redemption which center on Him (Acts 4:4)

The impact of the Word in the hearts of men will conform them to a new image. This image is not arbitrary nor individualized. It is singular and universal. It is the image of Christ ("*that they may all be one*"). Jesus is not praying about unity that focuses on incidentals or externals, but on an essential unity (John 17:11). The Word of God calls all men to have fulfilled in them that which God has predestined for the believer: the absolute and total conformity to the Person of Jesus Christ (Romans 8:29). The more a person grows into Christlikeness, the more comprehensive the unity is with others in whom Christ is likewise being formed (Ephesians 4:13). The sanctifying power of God's Word will work out this unity of essence in believers' lives so that this unity will be found in perfect conformity to Christ, even as the unity between the Father and Son exists due to perfect conformity ("*even as You, Father, are in Me and I in You*" John 17:21).

Clearly then, the unity to which Jesus refers in John 17 is not attained at the expense of truth. It is the result of truth bringing diverse men into conformity with God ("... *that they also may be in us*" John 17:21). This is synonymous with the truth in Peter's epistle whereby, through the agency of God's Word, we are made partakers of the Divine nature (2 Peter 1:3-4). When the Word has had this impact in our lives, the world takes note of it ("*so that the world may believe that You sent Me*" John 17:23). The impact of the unity caused by believers being conformed to the image of Jesus Christ will convince the world of Christ's integrity. He is indeed who He says He is. Every deviation in doctrine, life, and practice from the Word mars, disrupts, and hinders our oneness and, therefore, damages the credibility of Christ.

As believers seek to be conformed to Christ, they are made more powerful in their ability to be used as witnesses and they can convince the world of its need. Notice that the emphasis is not on the attempt to project a particular image, nor is it to conform to another group or person. Christ's emphasis is on the careful progression toward Christlikeness that will provide the testimony which will make the difference. Essentially, the image of Christ given to us through the Word causes one's conformity to Him ("*The glory which You have given Me I have given them, that they may be one, just as We are one*" John17:22).

Whenever believers concentrate on horizontal relationships in their attempt to establish a testimony, they will always know disaster. When they compare themselves to themselves, they will become proud, or feel as if they do not quite make it. Believers need to simply yield to the Word of God in their lives and focus on the glory of Christ. This transforms them into conformity to Jesus Christ (2 Corinthians 3:18). Christians who have no impact on the world around them need to evaluate the degree to which they are truly being conformed to Christ through the power of the Word.

This process of yielding and being fashioned into Christlikeness is ongoing and ever-increasing: "*I in them and You in Me, that they may be perfected in unity*" (John 17:23). What Christ prays for is that we will manifest externally in practice, experience, and daily living what is being accomplished in us internally. Again, this unity is not *despite the truth* as varying groups down-play the importance of doctrine for the sake of putting up a façade of unity. Rather, it is unity *because of the truth*, genuine unity around the Person of Christ Jesus as revealed throughout the doctrines of Scripture.

The Expression of the Love of Christ

The love of Christ is manifested through a variety of cooperative efforts of the local church. These efforts are designed to demonstrate the practicality of Christ's compassion for us. Essentially, these efforts allow the light of the Gospel to be displayed brilliantly for all to see. Jesus instructed us to "*Let your light shine before men in such a way that they may see your good works, and glorify your Father who is in heaven*" (Matthew 5:16). These efforts to display the compassion of God's love are seen in efforts to minister through the local church to widows, sick, spiritually weak, single-parents, the wayward and backslidden, orphans, and the poor.

Conclusion

The priority of biblically responsible relationships within the level of the local church is more intense and focused than on any of the previous levels. Cooperation between believers on this level depends upon the ability to assemble for the purpose of celebrating the truth about who Jesus Christ is and what He has done. This celebration of Christ as the Living Word is dependent upon God's revelation of Him in the written Word. Thus, when the church assembles it is for devotion to the Lord Jesus Christ as He is revealed in Scriptures. The deeper one goes in doctrine and truth, the greater the capacity for genuine unity and fellowship in Christ Jesus. The more shallow one remains with reference to doctrine, the more superficial the unity will be.

On an individual level, a believer must assemble with other believers of like precious faith for the purpose of rejoicing in the truth. Devoting oneself to the "apostles' doctrine, fellowship, breaking of bread, and prayer" must dominate the assembly that is chosen. If there is a compromise in any of these areas, a believer finds a limited capacity for cooperation. Matters of style, denomination, location, family, and other lesser points of interest must never supersede the principal priority of doctrinal truth. Having found such an assembly, a believer must invest himself in strengthening that assembly through the exercise of spiritual giftedness to the glory of Christ.

On a corporate level, doctrine remains a priority for the church. There are four different issues that contribute to the preservation of the truth. While remaining responsive to the changing societies of the world, the church must be constantly reminded that the spiritual nature of the world does not change. It remains constant in its estrangement and alienation from God. Thus, the church must not fall prey to the attempt to see it conformed to the world. It must continue to seek the transformation of those that are in Christ. In order to do this, the church must first protect itself from those within and without that would seek to do it harm through false teaching or carnal behavior. Second, it must be engaged in interdependent relationships with other churches to help preserve its devotion and maximize its impact on the world. Third, it must function independently as an autonomous body of believers answering directly to the Lord for its faithfulness. Finally, it must concern itself with the spiritual condition of those participating in the assembly.

Given the tremendous value of the church to God, it must be highly prized by those who are in Christ Jesus. It is something to be cherished and nourished as the Bride of Christ. This priority cannot be over emphasized.

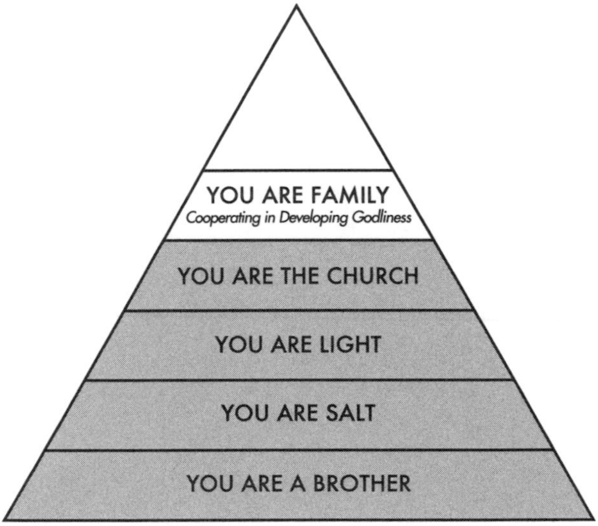

PYRAMID OF RESPONSIBILITY

The mandates of biblical relationships

CHAPTER FIVE

THE FAMILY

Cooperating in developing Godliness

Relationships within the family should be intimate, personal and responsible. They must be maintained while other relationships may be biblically limited. In fact, family relationships are so important that maintaining them often supersedes other considerations. This is why family relationships are near the top level of the Pyramid of Responsibility.

I remember a circumstance when it became necessary to discipline a church member who failed to respond properly to the church's attempts to appeal to him to confess his open sin and return to the Lord. Great care was given to follow the biblical procedures in the matter of the discipline. Finally, it became necessary to involve the congregation in the appeal to repent and return to the Lord. In the final step of discipline, our elders shared with the congregation the responsibility each member had to respond biblically to this individual in their personal relationship with him. It was important that people not hinder the biblical intent of the discipline nor provide the individual with a false sense of security by relating to him as if nothing had happened.

Family members in the congregation came to me and asked how these instructions applied to them. I immediately responded they should convey they could not support him in his sin; but no matter what, they should also communicate that their love for their brother and son was as strong as ever. They should be careful to maintain their personal social relationships within the family. But spiritually, their relationship was of necessity limited, for the Scriptures indicate he should be regarded as an unsaved member of the family. The spiritual fellowship they once enjoyed was interrupted by his refusal to respond to their attempts and those of the church to call him to repentance. This made true spiritual fellowship impossible.

Unfortunately, some cannot see the priority of family relationships and they endeavor to impose on these relationships the same limitations given to believers in general. I had a dear friend who was raised in an Amish family. He came to know the Lord and began to attend a Bible Church. Consequently, he was placed under discipline by his former Amish church. When he and his family went back to his parents for holidays or a Sunday dinner, they were required to sit at a separate table because of the discipline. His Amish family had imposed upon their relationship the Apostle Paul's instruction "*not to even eat with such a one*" (1 Corinthians 5:11). They failed to recognize that this admonition had been written to the Corinthians to instruct them in how to respond to an immoral person, or covetous person, or an idolater, or a reviler, or a drunkard or a swindler who called himself a believer.

Basic Family Relationships

The family is by God's design one of the basic building blocks of society. The Scriptures address family relationships specifically. God has given to us a clear blueprint for godly relationships in the family. The family begins to disintegrate when the biblical relational principles are ignored. These relationships include:

- The elder members of the family: grandparents
- The marriage partners: husband and wife
- The mother and father: parents
- The children: brothers and sisters.
- The extended family: aunts, uncles and cousins

These are the most focused cooperative relationships of all we have examined so far in The Pyramid of Responsibility. They carry with them the intimate expression of mutual responsibility. They call for family members to submit to one another, love one another as Christ loved the church, raise children in the nurture and admonition of the Lord, and be obedient and respectful children in the Lord. Paul carefully discussed the responsible relationships of a wife to her husband, a husband to his wife, children to their parents and fathers to their children in his teaching on the family in Ephesians 5:22-6:4. Additionally, grandparents are urged to encourage their grandchildren to successfully live out their personal faith. Proverbs 17:6 points out that "*Grandchildren are the crown of old men, and the glory of children are their fathers.*"

Family relationships extend beyond the immediate family. There are illustrations in the New Testament of this. Paul and his nephew must have been close because Paul's nephew ran right to his uncle Paul who was in jail and told him he overheard a plot to assassinate him (Acts 23:16). John Mark, Barnabas's nephew, accompanied Barnabas and Paul on their first missionary journey. When he left the team and returned home, it was his uncle Barnabas who later interceded with Paul on his behalf. When unsuccessful, Barnabas took John Mark and went to Cyprus to minister with him. Extended family relationships can be deep and loyal.

Marriage, a Foundational Relationship

When each member of the family is a believer, the potential for maintaining biblical relationships is enhanced. Therefore, it is crucial when initiating a foundational relationship like marriage not to ignore the biblical principle of the unequal yoke (2 Corinthians 6:14). Paul illustrates this in 1 Corinthians 7:39 by pointing out: "*A wife is bound as long as her husband lives; but if her husband is dead, she is free to be married to whom she wishes, only in the Lord.*" The principle here is that marriage is designed by God to be life long and within the boundaries of belief. It is designed to reflect the relationship between Christ and His Church.

A marriage that reflects the character of Christ's love for His Church and lives out the biblically designed roles for the partners will set the tone for all other relationships in the family. When a husband loves his wife as Christ loves His Church, he brings out the best in her. And it is far easier for her to fulfill her role of a help-mate who brings out the best in her husband. Undermining these key roles is the demand for individual rights, which results in a marriage that has been designed by society's priorities or by a male dominated bigotry. It is Satan's program to frustrate the marriage relationship by subtly corrupting how the family is understood and designed.

Marriage: Contract or Covenant?

Marriage is a covenant between a man and a woman, made with God and witnessed by people (especially the church). As a covenant, it makes the couple accountable to God and accountable to the church before whom their covenant was made. Being a covenant and not a contract, it must not be easily dissolved. Yet in today's world, marriage is often viewed as a contract with provision made for one or both to terminate the contact if either feels the promises of the contract are not being kept. Divorce is the legal result.

Is this what God designed? Jesus addressed divorce in Matthew 19 when the Pharisees were testing him: "*Why then did Moses command to give her a certificate of divorce and send her away*?" (Matthew 19:7) Jesus' answered their question: "*Because of your hardness of heart Moses permitted you to divorce your wives; but from the beginning it has not been this way*" (Matthew 19:8). He was making the point that divorce is contrary to the plan of God for His children.

Historically, Fundamentalists did not readily accept the concept of marriage as a contract. In recent years the church has been invaded by the divorce culture, and divorce has grown more prevalent among God's people, even among some of the Church's leadership. A recent study by George Barna showed the percentage of born-again Christians who have been divorced (27%) is above the national average by two points. "While it may be alarming to discover that born-again Christians are more likely than others to experience a divorce," says Barna, "that pattern has been in place for quite some time."[49] How could this be? Should not the Christian family be discernibly different from the secular society? One would think so. But the underlying biblical principles that made the American family strong in the past have been subtly eroded by an increasing compartmentalization in believers' thinking. The Christian life was formerly understood to affect every area of a believer's life. Today, many have relegated it to the realm of the "spiritual" which produces a marked contrast between professed belief and behavior. This often leads to a scenario where behavior alters belief. Thus, relationships that are clearly regulated by the Word of God become subject to circumstances and are broken because of an unwillingness to alter behavior and conform to the teaching of the Scriptures. There is great danger in dividing life into the "sacred" and the "secular."

Another dimension of divorce among Christians might be due to the Church not consistently labeling divorce as sin. A *Christianity Today* editorial made this point. "But there's no getting around it: whether we define sin as a transgression of Christ's commands, missing the mark, or the breaking of relationships, divorce is a sin. To be sure, divorce is sometimes the lesser of two evils, but it nonetheless nullifies God's intent. God joins people together; he doesn't pull them apart."[50] There are perceivable consequences when you lose the understanding that God's design in marriage is a sacred covenant between a man and a woman and you accept divorce as the termination of a contract. This has produced an atmosphere where the Sexual Revolution of the 1960s separated sex from marriage and fostered acceptance of the aberrant behavior of homosexuality. Now the legal advantages of the "marriage contract" are sought by those who advocate same sex marriage. Satan's desire to corrupt and destroy the building block of the family is systematically being accomplished in a secular society that has relegated "religion" to its own compartment.

The Effects of Divorce on Children

Those most drastically affected by the breakdown of family relationships are often the children. I have observed teenage and adult females whose parents' divorce affected them in such ways as lower self esteem, promiscuity and greater delinquent behavior, as well as difficulty maintaining long-term relationships. Girls seem to experience the emotional loss of the father directly and personally. Many believe it is a direct rejection of them: they are not pretty enough, affectionate enough, athletic enough, or smart enough. I saw one long-term study of the effects of divorce up to twenty-five years later. It showed that when the parents first were divorced, the children reported feeling lonely, ashamed, or terrified of abandonment. In teens, half of the children became involved in alcohol and drugs. In their twenties and thirties, the women in the study had less education, decreased socio-economic status and difficulty with long-term relationships. Children asked questions like:

- "What did I do wrong?"
- "What will happen to me if they both leave?"
- "Was it my fault?"[51]

Barbara Dafoe Whitehead notes in *The Divorce Culture* that divorce is not just a therapeutic problem but a moral one in which, to use biblical language, the commandment to love is thwarted: "Divorce has brought a steady weakening of the primary human relationships and bonds," says Whitehead. "Men's and women's relationships are becoming more fleeting and unreliable. Children are losing ties to their fathers. Even a mother's love is not forever." [52]

Susan Orr made this observation, "Children of divorce do worse academically, are more prone to delinquency, are more vulnerable to the appeal of substance abuse, are more likely to bear a child out of wedlock, and are less equipped to enter marriage themselves."[53]

Single Parent Households

Children are not the only ones who suffer because of divorce. The single parent, whether man or woman, is emotionally and often financially impacted by the breakup of a marriage. The spiritual devastation that occurs when a marriage fails to reflect the mystical union that is between Christ and his Church causes one or both of the parties in a divorce to seek to punish the other.

I remember counseling with a woman who had been married to her husband for over twenty-five years. The husband had an affair and the marriage ended in a divorce. This woman was devastated by the demand to sell their house and its contents so that she could pay her ex-husband his half. Up to that point, her husband had been a "model" Christian and even at one time studied to prepare for the ministry. But his sin clouded his concern for his wife and this caused her great emotional and financial pain. Even though their children were grown, the divorce divided the family and induced anger and deep resentment on the part of the children that will undoubtedly be passed on to the next generation (if God's grace does not intervene). It is incumbent on family members and the ministry of churches to seek to defuse the carnal reactions which inevitably follow divorce. This is accomplished as they carefully and prayerfully minister to those who feel the stinging hurt of a failed marriage.

Here are some of the ways that churches can assist single parents (as outlined by Crown Ministries):

> The following needs were identified as a result of our research. We are developing a coordinating manual and video on each identified need to show churches how they can meet these needs through simple ministries or full-scale ministries. Spiritual and emotional support is listed last but is a vital component of each type of ministry.
>
> - Obtaining affordable, quality child care.
> - Obtaining an affordable, safe car; caring for the car.
> - Affordable, safe housing options.
> - Support for welfare-to-work parents.
> - Help with budgeting and money management.
> - Education, job training, and career options.
> - Affordable, quality professional services and medical care.
> - Mentoring for parents and children.

- Food and clothing resources.
- Spiritual and emotional support.[54]

Child Abuse

One would think the Christian family would not be subjected to the horrible effects of child abuse. But in my years as a pastor there were numerous occasions where I dealt with believers horribly scarred by abuse. I encountered everything from a step father who had sexually abused his teenage stepdaughter, to children in our school having severe bruises on their bodies. One teenage girl from a fine Christian family went off the deep end and became very promiscuous. Her parents were frantic and would not let her out of their sight. My wife sought to counsel her but seemed to get nowhere. One day in a counseling session my wife asked, "Honey, have you ever been sexually abused?" The girl was startled, and then began to sob. It took some time to get the whole story out of her, but responding to my wife's tenderness and love this girl was finally delivered from the deep, dark secret. The most amazing thing was she had a searing sense of guilt that it was her fault. When my wife told her she should share this with her parents, she looked wild eyed and said "I can't. I'm so ashamed." A meeting with her parents was arranged and she shared how her uncle, who used to baby sit for her, had abused her from the time she was nine until she was thirteen. The parents were shocked, but the "dirty secret" was out. And they could do something to help her recover her self respect. She eagerly sought help from a Biblical Counselor. Soon the young lady enrolled in a Bible College and eventually married. Some time ago my wife and I saw her. She rushed up to my wife and threw her arms around her and just cried tears of gratitude. But, those terrible scars will always remain.

Sexual abuse is not the only kind of abuse possible in Christian families. There are many situations that can result in other kinds of abuse.

> Abuse can happen in any family, regardless of any special characteristics. However, in dealing with parents, be aware of characteristics of families in which abuse may be more likely:
>
> - Families who are isolated and have no friends, relatives, church or other support systems.
> - Parents who tell you they were abused as children.
> - Families who are often in crisis (have money problems, move often).

- Parents who abuse drugs or alcohol.
- Parents who are very critical of their child.
- Parents who are very rigid in disciplining their child.
- Parents who show too much or too little concern for their child.
- Parents who feel they have a difficult child.
- Parents who are under a lot of stress.[55]

Domestic Violence

Avoiding domestic violence begins with training our children that "hitting" is not tolerated and is never a solution. I never saw my father strike my mother, nor have our children ever seen me hit their mother. To hit your spouse is an expression of selfishness and disrespect. Our children were not allowed to hit each other. Spankings were the last resort in discipline and impulsive slaps were never used to show frustration. We taught these ground rules and then modeled them for our children.

Unfortunately, some do not teach or model physical restraint in their relationships. Children are beaten in frustration. Partners in marriage are battered in anger. Siblings fight one another with anything they can get their hands on. It is a natural expression of the flesh to strike back. I remember talking to my grandson about his temper when he was little. After his older brother and sister would tease him, he would come at them with arms flailing. I shared with him that the Lord was not pleased with "hitting" and told him he should pray when he became angry and ask the Lord to help him. I advised him to count to ten and give the Lord the opportunity to help him "turn the other cheek." I reminded him Jesus had given instruction in Matthew 5:39: "*Do not resist an evil person; but whosoever slaps you on your right cheek, turn the other to him also.*" He looked at me and asked, "After he hits me twice, can I hit him back?" I think he missed the point Jesus made: by turning the other cheek my grandson would be doing something unnatural. The response Jesus called for signifies one is controlled not by natural reaction but by the power of the indwelling Holy Spirit.

God is not pleased with physical violence. One of the characteristics of a spiritual leader in 1 Timothy 3:3 and repeated in Titus 1:7 is that his disposition should be "*gentle and peaceable.*" He is not to be "*pugnacious.*" A brawler, or one who resorts to physical fighting to solve problems, is not a man to be lifted up before others as a spiritual leader.

Parents and grandparents must first guard their own souls as a primary prevention against abusing their children. Loving relationships that are taught and modeled protect our children. Men and women who are growing in the grace and admonition of the Lord do not abuse their children in any way. They understand: "*Children are a gift of the Lord, the fruit of the womb is a reward. Like arrows in the hand of a warrior, so are the children of one's youth. How blessed is the man whose quiver is full of them*" (Psalm 127:3-5).

PARTNERS

The Family as a Team

Some time ago, my wife and I and our youngest daughter were having Sunday dinner with the pastor and wife of a church where I had previously served as pastor for over seventeen years. The pastor's wife asked my daughter what our children had done to be so loved by the congregation. She replied, "This morning when we came in the church I was faced with a decision. On one side of the foyer were my friends I had not seen for over five years. On the other side were a number of widows sitting on the deacon's bench. While growing up it had been a part of my ministry as a member of our family ministering team, to visit with these widows each Sunday. So, before going over to visit my friends, I went and gave each of these ladies a big hug. Dad and Mom always emphasized all of us were at the church by design and not by default. Dad was the pastor, but each of us was a part of the family ministering team."

Building a family ministering team requires careful communication and proper leadership. Serving the Lord together is a basic requirement. Fathers and sons can help widows by spending a Saturday raking their leaves or mowing their lawns. Mother and daughters can prepare meals for new mothers or people who have been in the hospital. There are so many ways a family can build relationships through common interests and serving the Lord together.

Just before Christmas one year, I set aside an evening to take the children Christmas shopping. We finished supper and were getting ready to leave when the phone rang. It was a young father whose infant son had been born with his heart outside his chest. His wife had been staying at the hospital for over a week and was exhausted. He wanted me to drive to Philadelphia with him to help him convince his wife to come home and get a good night's rest. I asked him if I could call him back in a few minutes. I had to make some arrangements concerning a previous engagement. I sat all four of my children down on the steps and explained to them what was happening. I then asked,

"What do you think I should tell Jim?" They all agreed I had to go. My youngest said, "Daddy, you know I can be selfish. But I say go."

I left my children that night feeling they were part of the ministry I was undertaking for that struggling family. What made it all the more wonderful was, that night we had a snowstorm and the next morning school was canceled. I was able to take them to the mall for the whole day. And as an added blessing, they found a $10 bill in the snow which enabled them to do a little more shopping. But best of all, they learned a valuable lesson about ministering together as a family.

The Family as the Center of Mentoring

Where can a son learn how to be a godly man and a loving husband? Where can a daughter learn how to be a godly woman and a devoted wife? God intended these qualities should be learned through precept and example within the family structure. Solomon writes in Proverbs 2:1-2, "*My son, if you will receive my words and treasure my commandments within you, make your ear attentive to wisdom, incline your heart to understanding.*" These admonitions are repeated at the beginning of Chapters 3, 4, 5 and 7 where he writes:

- "*My son, do not forget my teaching, but let your heart keep my commandments.*" (3:1)

- "*Hear, O sons, the instruction of a father and give attention that you may gain understanding.*" (4:1)

- "*My son, give attention to my wisdom, incline your ear to understanding, that you may observe discretion and your lips may reserve knowledge.*" (5:1-2)

- "*My son, keep my words and treasure my commandments within you. Keep my commandments and live, and my teaching as the apple of your eye. Bind them on your fingers; write them on the tablet of your heart.*" (7:1-3)

These chapters are full of instructions of a father to his son, with this observation being made in Proverbs 10:1, "*A wise son makes his father glad, but a foolish son is a grief to his mother.*" All these precepts are very important to follow in the mentoring process.

However, Solomon failed to live out his own instructions. This resulted in a foolish son, Rehoboam, who did not have the wisdom and understanding needed to follow the counsel of the elders who had served his father. Rehoboam opted to follow the foolish counsel of his peers (2 Chronicles 10:6-11). As a consequence, the kingdom was divided.

Mentoring requires more than teaching by precept. It requires learning from example. When a father, mother and older brothers and sisters become mentors, the family is strengthened, loyalty is developed and leaders emerge all of which encourages the growth of family unity.

The Family as a Support Group

When I graduated from college, I was called as pastor of a small church in a resort community in northern New Jersey. During the summer months our attendance would run around two hundred people. But from the fall through spring, there were about 30 souls (including children) that made up our congregation. Needless to say, my salary was only enough to cover the cost of renting a house. Someone told me that a local school district needed teachers and suggested I apply, which I did. In the interview I mentioned that my degree was in philosophy, but they replied the teacher shortage was so great all that was required was a college degree. I was hired as a Fifth Grade teacher.

I came from a very close-knit Christian family in a rural community. Therefore, my knowledge of the "real world" was rather limited. I soon learned that not all families were like mine. Many of the students were from broken homes. Others had working parents and were what some refer to as "latch-key kids." Many fathers worked in New York City and left early in the morning and did not return home until seven or eight o'clock in the evening.

When I attempted to schedule parent/teacher conferences, I saw the lack of understanding that a family is a support group. These conferences were opportunities to discuss the strengths and weaknesses of students with their parents and map out ways we could work together in their children's education. Sometimes, parents would just not show up. At other times, parents would convey the attitude that they thought their children's education was the school's responsibility. One father even said to me "We hire you to teach our kids. Why are you asking for my help?"

Years later, I was involved in establishing a Christian academy at the church where I was the pastor. I wanted it understood from the first day that the school was a partner with families. If parents would not agree with the partnering concept and its corresponding responsibilities, then we could not work together in preparing their children for life. Parents are responsible for their children's education. They can delegate the authority to assist them to a school, but they cannot delegate the responsibility.

A support group is most successful when the people within it share similar experiences, organized to help people with similar problems. A family can adopt that concept for themselves and enlarge it to include experiencing similar interests. If a child is involved in sports, music, art, drama, reading or photography, it is important for others in the family to show an interest in their activities. Just as strong marriages are enhanced by common interests, so strong families are built by mutual support. A family must make it a point to attend and take photographs at games, concerts, plays and other school and church activities to emphasize that the family is a meaningful support group. It is important that all members of the family perceive the other members have a genuine interest in each other. This will cement family unity, loyalty and love. It also models the interdependent relationships so necessary for strong families.

STRENGTHENING THE FAMILY

Families today are constantly challenged by the schedules of parents, teenagers and younger children. In talking to families, I hear that many even have a hard time finding time to eat meals together. Children go to different schools and leave home at different times in the morning. Sports practices, church events, homework and music lessons are among those activities that fracture our days and scatter the various members of the family. When the family is home the television, boom boxes, videos, computer and so many other voices call for their attention. When is there time to talk, counsel, pray and study the Word of God together?

Worshipping Together

I remember hearing the song "Sunday Morning" about a family's hectic preparations for church. It was rather comical because it was so true to life. At the same time, it was tragic because all the frustration, arguing and posturing of the family members ceased when they arrived at the church parking lot. The family then dispersed into various interest groups until it was time to go home, forgetting that modeling to children the nature and quality of worship demanded parental involvement.

When I became the pastor of a church in suburban Philadelphia, I noticed the families were fragmented. Most of the teens sat together in the back, some thirty pews from the front. I remember an usher came to me complaining about the conduct of the teens. I began to emphasize from the pulpit that families needed to sit together in church. I pointed out that the worship service is not a social time to be spent with friends. Our family modeled sitting together, and gradually more and more of our families followed suit. This afforded parents an opportunity to observe their children's deportment as well as provided an opportunity to share with them in the worship experience. Even today our children, along with our grandchildren, enjoy sitting together when we worship the Lord.

Family Night

Some families schedule a Family Night and guard this time carefully. Everyone understands on the night of the week designated as Family Night, that all must be there. Others have scheduled special events as family activities, like attending a sports event. Vacations and special weekends make for wonderful family memories. I made it a point to schedule a "date" with my children at some point in time around their birthday. I would take them to a restaurant or attend a special event of their choice. I began this when they were five years old. It became a very important event to our children. When she was just a little girl, my youngest daughter came to my office at church and asked my secretary to see my appointment calendar. She wanted to make sure I had reserved a time for our "special date." My secretary informed me that my daughter jumped with glee when she saw her name there.

My eldest daughter's birthday is in October. When she was away at college on her birthday for the first time, she called me in tears reminding me that this was the first year she could remember that we were going to miss our "date." People would often ask my wife why she did not go along. My wife felt strongly that our children should have my undivided attention on these "dates." If she were to go along, it would not be the special time with daddy that we both wanted it to be. All of our children still talk about the places we went and the things we did on our birthday "dates." I am grateful to see my son and sons-in-law continue the practice with their children.

Parental Date Nights

Romance should not stop as years pass in a marriage. Some couples have scheduled regular date nights when they dress up and go some place special. Creative planning on a husband's part will provide some pleasant surprises for his wife. These nights should cater to the personal tastes of the couples.

Family Vacations

There are several vacations that stand out in the minds of our children. We took a trip across country to visit friends in California when the children were small. Later, when they were teenagers, we took that trip again. On both of these trips, lasting memories were created in our family experiences.

Another meaningful vacation occurred in New England. I had a pastor friend who had a cottage on Penobscot Bay in Maine. We spent a week there, eating clams, reading, listening to Red Sox games, fishing, hiking and just being together. Although there was a radio, there was no television. Our children still talk about that as being such a fun vacation when we just spent our time together.

Time with Grandparents

Living close to nine of our fifteen grandchildren provided the opportunity to establish some very close relationships with them. It is very important that special relationships with grandchildren be maintained. Our eldest daughter does not live near us, so we arranged to spend a three week vacation with her family on a trip out west. Seven of us lived together in a motor home as we toured the Dakotas to Arizona. We played games and told stories while traveling. The grandchildren wanted especially to hear stories about when we were growing up. It afforded us an opportunity to share some of the family stories that had been passed down through the years. There were relationships that were cemented on that trip that provide a special closeness with our grandchildren even today.

Our daughter who is a busy pastor's wife in North Carolina makes sure that her three girls come to Florida to spend time with us. Since they are home schooled, they are able to get away to spend a week with their Grandma and Grandpa. What a joy it is for us to have them all to ourselves.

My wife and I have made sure that we have attended all of the graduations of our grandchildren. That has included graduations from kindergarten, high school and college. My wife maintains a special communication with our grandchildren in college and sends them money every month along with an encouraging note. Maintaining meaningful relationships is a two-way street.

Conclusion

The importance of these intimate, personal relationships cannot be overstated in developing a strong family that can endure the pressures of a godless, secular society. This is why the family level of relationship is so high on The Pyramid of Responsibility. Yet how often the tensions between husband and wife and the resentments of sibling rivalry create an atmosphere in family relationships that breeds rebellion and hatred! Instead of strong family relationships, a fractured family disperses and has little desire to relate to one another. David Semands in a *Christianity Today* editorial writes:

> Restoring Christian ideals of marriage and family within our present pagan American culture will require a unique combination of grace, adherence to biblical standards, and pastoral realism. The church must continue to teach, preach, model, and nurture the highest scriptural values of sexual morality, marriage, and family life. Because of the deadly and demonic effects of TV and other entertainment media, this will have to begin with the very young and continue at all age levels. We must underscore commitment to these ideals as an integral part of life in Christ. In this sense, we will create a moral and marital counterculture for the coming generation.[56]

The Church must establish biblical standards of conduct and adhere to scriptural values. In this process it needs the encouragement of the family leadership. But when a family contradicts what is being taught at church and allows or promotes something different in family life, children are confused and lose confidence in their pastor and church leadership. It is therefore incumbent upon family leadership to choose a church which can be trusted to establish its standards of conduct from sound exegesis of the Word of God and which teaches biblically authentic values. If the church is merely a reflection of the culture, it will be difficult to establish any consistent standard of conduct or to identify clear biblical values. The church needs to serve as an anchor for the family so that it does not drift freely, driven by the winds of secular culture.

A family must avoid looking for a church that simply mirrors its own weaknesses or affirms it in the mediocrity derived from the context of its culture. Attempting to live godly by being culturally relevant seems like an oxymoron.

The qualities of the relationships in a family reflect the spiritual maturity of its leadership. When family is important to all its members, it is far easier to understand the various levels of relationship that exist in God's family, His church.

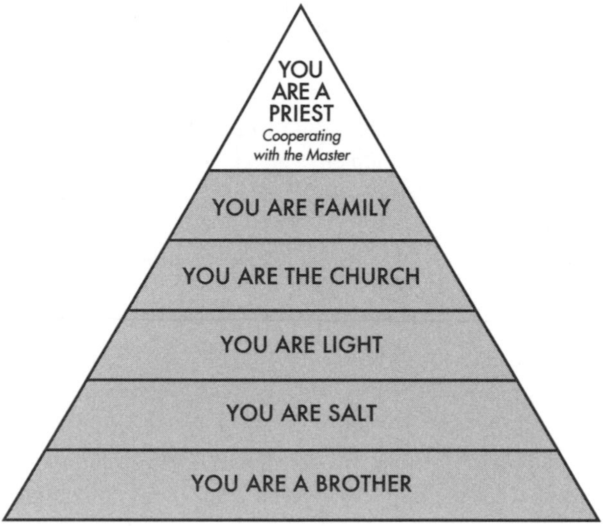

PYRAMID OF RESPONSIBILITY

The mandates of biblical relationships

CHAPTER SIX

THE PRIESTHOOD OF THE BELIEVER

Cooperating with the Master

The ultimate level of biblical relationships is the relationship that exists between the individual believer and the Lord Jesus Christ. On this level of relationship, no one else is permitted. When one stands before God on the day of reckoning, the only question that will be relevant will be whether or not a sinner has an intimate relationship with God through Jesus Christ. It is not whether one has knowledge about God, or whether a person has served God, or whether a person has worshipped God, or even whether a person has lived a life trying to please God. Sincerity, devotion, and deprivation – normally associated with "religious zeal" – will make no difference when a person stands before the Lord. Neither will a person's other relationships. Having enjoyed a good relationship with a pastor, priest, parent, or other godly peers will provide no value in one's personal accountability on the day when such an account is called for by God.

THE PROBLEM, THE SOLUTION, THE PRIVILEGE

One of the most terrifying passages of Scripture for people who are "religious" is found in Matthew 7:21-23:

> *"Not everyone who says to Me, 'Lord, Lord,' will enter the kingdom of heaven, but he who does the will of My Father who is in heaven will enter. Many will say to Me on that day, 'Lord, Lord, did we not prophesy in Your name, and in Your name cast out demons, and in Your name perform many miracles?' And then I will declare to them, 'I never knew you; depart from Me, you who practice lawlessness'."*

The claims of these people were never contested by the Lord in this passage. He did not dispute that they had preached, cast out demons, or performed miracles. He merely stated "*I never knew you.*" This clear statement of rejection is evidence that neither religious activity nor passion will provide advantage on the Day of Judgment. In fact, the issue of personal sin is the only consideration of the Lord in judgment. What we tend to minimize, He elevates to the principal concern. Since sin is not cared for independently of a relationship with Jesus Christ, the only proper designation of a person without a relationship with Christ is "*one who practices lawlessness*" (1 John 3:4).

When a person is reconciled to God through faith in Jesus Christ, the sinner is brought near to God (Ephesians 2:11-13). Jesus described the special honor that a repentant sinner gains when he comes by faith alone in Christ alone for the forgiveness of his sin: "*All that the Father gives Me will come to Me, and the one who comes to Me I will certainly not cast out*" (John 6:37). Jesus Christ declares that He personally knows each of the little sheep that the Father gives to Him as the Good Shepherd: "*I am the good shepherd, and I know My own and My own know Me*" (John 10:14). Taking personal responsibility for each of those given to Him by the Father, Jesus testifies that the essence of eternal life is the ability to enjoy an intimate relationship with God: "*... even as You gave Him authority over all flesh, that to all whom You have given Him, He may give eternal life. This is eternal life, that they may know You, the only true God, and Jesus Christ whom You have sent*" (John 17:2-3).

In this relationship with God, the believer is honored to be adopted into the very family of God. This adoption is through the power of the Holy Spirit who brings about a new birth called regeneration (Titus 3:5; 1 Peter 1:3). "*For you have not received a spirit of slavery leading to fear again, but you have received a spirit of adoption as sons by which we cry out, 'Abba! Father!' The spirit Himself testifies with our spirit that we are children of God, and if children, heirs also, heirs of God and fellow heirs with Christ*" (Romans 8:15-17).

However, the relationship enjoyed by sinners who have been saved through the power and grace of God also places upon them a particular responsibility. We do not merely enjoy the privilege as sons of God. We also must fulfill God's purpose for those He has so redeemed. We are told by the Apostle Peter that as the children of God we are part of a "*chosen race, a royal priesthood, a holy nation, a people for God's own possession, so that you may proclaim the excellencies of Him who has called you out of darkness into His marvelous light*" (1 Peter 2:9). In this text, the children of God, by virtue of their relationship to God, possess a racial distinction, a royal duty, a national character, and a future inheritance. The royal duty of priesthood becomes the occupation of every believer.

The Old Testament Priesthood

From its establishment in the Old Testament, the priesthood was composed of those chosen by God from among men who were set apart as holy (Numbers 16:5). Their primary function was to offer acceptable sacrifices to God on behalf of the people of God. They were ceremonially cleansed, dressed in prescribed clothing, and anointed with oil to signify they were set apart for service unto the Lord. The lives of priests were regimented and prescribed through stringent standards and protocols required of those who would stand before God on behalf of the people. They could possess no uncleanness, defect, or moral impurity. To enjoy the privilege of service in the Temple, they had to be at least thirty years old and could not exceed the age of fifty years. They stood before God in behalf of the people and therefore were judged by the Lord with particular attention. Consequently, they had to offer sacrifices for their own sins before they were able to offer sacrifices for the people.

The book of Hebrews looks back at the function of the priesthood and their work in the sacrifices and views them as engaging in a repetitive work that brought no permanent solution to the problem of sin. Rather, the priestly sacrifices served as "*a shadow of the good things to come and not the very form of things*" (Hebrews 10:1). These anticipated the final sacrifice of the High Priest who would come and put an end to the sacrifices which were nothing more than a "*reminder of sins year by year*" (Hebrews 10:3). The work of the priest focused on performing divine worship, while the work of the High Priest focused on the atonement for the sins of the people. "*Now when these things have been so prepared, the priests are continually entering the outer tabernacle performing the divine worship, but into the second, only the high priest enters once a year, not without taking blood, which he offers for himself and for the sins of the people committed in ignorance*" (Hebrews 9:6-7).

Today, God remains interested in the daily performance of divine worship. He has provided, through the Lord Jesus Christ, the ultimate solution for the removal of the sins of the people. "*Every priest stands daily ministering and offering time after time the same sacrifices, which can never take away sins; but He, having offered one sacrifice for sins for all time, sat down at the right hand of God, waiting from that time onward until His enemies be made a footstool for His feet. For by one offering He has perfected for all time those who are sanctified*" (Hebrews 10:11-14).

Thus, the way has been cleared by Jesus Christ, the Great High Priest, who has opened the way for us to enter into the very presence of God. "*Therefore, brethren, since we have confidence to enter the holy place by the blood of Jesus, by a new and living way which He inaugurated for us through the veil, that is, His flesh, and since we have a great priest over the house of God, let us draw near with a sincere heart in full assurance of faith, having our hearts sprinkled clean from an evil conscience and our bodies washed with pure water*" (Hebrews 10:19-22).

The believer is enabled, through the work of Jesus Christ, to come into the very presence of God in worship. This was demonstrated when the veil in the Holy of Holies in the Temple was torn in two at the death of Christ Jesus (Luke 23:45). There now remains no barrier for the children of God to enjoy free access into the presence of God in the performance of divine worship!

THE PARTNERS

The New Testament Priesthood

God's great delight for His children is that they serve as individual priests, coming before Him in performance of divine worship. He has qualified us as "*a holy priesthood, to offer up spiritual sacrifices acceptable to God through Jesus Christ*" (1 Peter 2:5). He has cleansed us through the "*washing of water with the word*" (Ephesians 5:26; Titus 3:5). He has robed us in the righteousness of Christ Jesus (Romans 13:14). He has anointed us with the Holy Spirit Himself (1 John 2:20, 27). He has chosen us and set us apart as holy, ordaining us into the ministry of offering divine worship as priests! Every believer is equally privileged to enjoy the direct ministry of bringing sacrifices to God the Father through the Lord Jesus Christ.

"Under the old covenant, God's people *had* a priesthood; but in the new covenant, God's people *are* a priesthood."57 There is no hierarchy of spiritual positioning before the Father. Jesus Christ serves as the Great High Priest (Hebrews 4:14). Every believer has the freedom to come directly to God through the High Priest. Wiersbe states this has been the historical conviction of the church as emphasized by Luther:

> Therefore all Christians are priests," said Martin Luther, "and accursed be the statement that a priest is something different from a Christian." In fact,

> Luther, like most of the Reformers, disapproved when people called the ministers of the church priests. He made it clear that "those who serve people with the Word and Sacraments may and must not be called priests.... According to the evangelical writings [the New Testament epistles] they should be called ministers, deacons, bishops and stewards."
>
> His point is simply that *all believers are priests*, and no Christian should allow any other Christian to come between him and his Lord. All Christians are invited to come boldly into God's presence to worship him and present their needs (Heb. 4:14-16; 10:19-22). Jesus Christ today is our High Priest in heaven, and there he represents us and intercedes for us before the Father (Heb. 8:1ff.)[58]

The essential point is that there is no one who can stand between Jesus Christ and the believer. There are no multiple mediators. There is no hierarchical structure. There are no channels through which the individual believer must go to offer acceptable sacrifices of praise to God. God declares that each true Christian has personal and direct access and that each is able to come directly to Him through Christ Jesus. "*For we do not have a high priest who cannot sympathize with our weaknesses, but One who has been tempted in all things as we are, yet without sin. Therefore let us draw near with confidence to the throne of grace, so that we may receive mercy and find grace to help in time of need*" (Hebrews 4:15-16). The attempt to look to another sinner (a peer in the experience of salvation) for access to God is demeaning to the work of Christ who alone serves as the mediator: "*For there is one God, and one mediator also between God and men, the man Christ Jesus*" (1 Timothy 2:5). Believers come directly to God regardless of the tremendous defilement that used to disqualify them from access to God. Through Christ, this defilement has been cleansed and believers are called "saints," sanctified ones who have been set apart for the purpose of serving God in worship (1 Corinthians 1:2; 6:11; and Colossians 1:12).

The corporate worship of the church occurs when we gather and join together with others before God for worship. The priesthood of the believer occurs when the believer comes personally, individually, and privately into fellowship with God Himself. In fact, the integrity of corporate worship depends upon the quality of the personal worship of individual priests. Therefore, this level of relationship on The Pyramid of Responsibility involves Jesus Christ alone as the partner. The fellowship is with Him alone.

All others are to be excluded from this most personal, exclusive, and intimate relationship known to the believer. Attempting to include others, even one's spouse or family, in the highest level of relationship will result in a lack of personal intimacy and singular focus on the Lord. This private intimacy serves as the heart and depth of this principal relationship.

The lack of solitude in one's relationship with Christ Jesus results in the lack of power in spirit that plagues many believers today. Some have no sense of personal relationship. They have a diminished awareness of the awe that the believer-priest should enjoy in the Holy Place as he communes in the presence of the glorified Christ Jesus. Instead of keeping the lamp of intimacy with God trimmed by means of regular priestly sacrifices of praise in the presence of God, believers often let the fire die through neglect. In Leviticus 6:12-13 the Lord said to Moses: "*The fire on the altar shall be kept burning on it. It shall not go out, but the priest shall burn wood on it every morning; and he shall lay out the burnt offering on it, and offer up in smoke the fat portions of the peace offerings on it. Fire shall be kept burning continually on the altar; it is not to go out.*" The priest had the responsibility to keep the fires of sacrifice on the altar perpetually burning. Without this fire, nothing could be offered to the Lord. Should the fire go out through the neglect of the priest, it was a crisis. Two careless priests failed to keep this fire a priority and instead of using it to light the fires of incense, they offered "strange fire" to the Lord. He responded with judgment (Leviticus 10:1-3).

The altar of the Lord today exists in the heart of the believer priest. The believer-priest today has the joy of having within his own body the temple, the dwelling place of God (1 Corinthians 6:19). As such, the fires of sacrifice offered to the Lord must burn within our souls. This passion for the Lord is the place where our worship of God is ignited. One's ability to worship God is affected when the fires of passion grow cold. Jesus said, "*And because lawlessness is increased, most people's love will grow cold*" (Matthew 24:12).

In addition, God is particularly displeased when the hearts of His priests are lukewarm. The Lord's message to the church at Laodicea warned them. "*I know your deeds, that you are neither cold nor hot; I wish that you were cold or hot. So because you are lukewarm, and neither hot nor cold, I will spit you out of My mouth*" (Revelation 3:15-16). When the fire of passion for the Lord is not in a believer's heart, neither is there sincere praise nor adoration of Him. The result is that the believer-priest is unable to offer the sacrifices that God calls upon him to bring.

Spiritual Sacrifices: Our Priestly Pursuit

Since the role of a priest is essentially to "*offer up spiritual sacrifices acceptable to God through Jesus Christ*" (1 Peter 2:5), the pursuit of the believer must be to offer worship to the Lord. In Romans 12:1, the Apostle Paul declares: "*Therefore I urge you, brethren, by the mercies of God, to present your bodies a living and holy sacrifice, acceptable to God, which is your spiritual service of worship.*" The believer's life is to be spent seeking ways in which he can bring glory to God. The Westminster Shorter Catechism succinctly states: "Man's chief end is to glorify God" (Psalm 86; Isaiah 60:21; 1 Corinthians 6:20, 31; Romans 11:36; Revelation 4:11) "and to enjoy Him forever" (Psalm 16:5-11; Psalm 144:15; Isaiah 12:2; Luke 2:10; Philippians 4:4; Revelation 21:3-4).[59] The specific way in which the believer brings glory to God and enjoys Him in the role of priest focuses on spiritual sacrifices he performs (1 Peter 2:5).

The Sacrifice of Consecration (Romans 12:1)

Believer-priests must concern themselves with the obligation to maintain the shrine of the Holy Spirit (1 Corinthians 6:19). In the Old Testament, the place of God's dwelling was considered "holy ground" (Exodus 3:5; Joshua 5:15). The priests of God were barred from entering the Holy Place except after having gone through various purifications and cleansing. They were totally barred from the Holy of Holies, except for one representative (the High Priest) who entered once a year for the purpose of bringing the blood of atonement to the Mercy Seat. This gives evidence of the personal responsibilities of the priests in light of God's presence and it provides the believer-priest with the awareness that the temple of God is a particularly significant stewardship. Today, this temple of the Holy Spirit is the body of the believer.

Thus, believer-priests are charged with the responsibility to worship God by means of maintaining their bodies. In 1 Corinthians 6:20 it declares: "*your body is a temple of the Holy Spirit who is in you … therefore glorify God in your body.*" This involves a variety of responsibilities:

- **Keeping it Pure** -"*Or do you not know that the one who joins himself to a prostitute is one body with her? For He says, 'The two shall become one flesh.' But the one who joins himself to the Lord is one spirit with Him. Flee immorality. Every other sin that a man commits is outside the body, but the immoral man sins against his own body*" (1 Corinthians 6:16-18). Understanding the great proneness to immorality, God's design is for every man to have his own wife, and each woman is to have her own husband (1 Corinthians 7:2). Enjoying sexual delight with your spouse is one way God has designed for a person to enjoy the blessings of marriage (Proverbs 5:18-19). As a believer-priest, the responsibility to avoid immorality will cause me to give my most ardent efforts to keep the Temple pure. This will include avoiding: pornography (Job 31:1); sensuality in movies, television, video games and books (Psalm 101:3); self-gratification (1 Corinthians 7:3-4); and adultery (Hebrews 13:4). A believer's body must remain pure as the sacred dwelling place of God. This is not for the purpose of self-deprivation, but is an act of worship and service to the Lord who dwells within.

- **Keeping It Nourished** -"*For no one ever hated his own flesh, but nourishes and cherishes it, just as Christ also does the church*" (Ephesians 5:29). The stewardship of the body with reference to nourishment has two dimensions. First, it requires a person makes sure that he eats food that is healthy, providing adequate nutrition. The other dimension is making sure that excess is not present. Gluttony is an indictment against the believer-priest who must maintain the temple of God with responsibility and restraint. Scripture declares: "*Do not be with heavy drinkers of wine, or with gluttonous eaters of meat; for the heavy drinker and the glutton will come to poverty, and drowsiness will clothe one with rags*" (Proverbs 23:20-21). One of the most ostentatious demonstrations of a person being a "*lover of pleasure rather than [a] lover of God*" (2 Timothy 3:4) is overindulgence in food and drink. Paul warned that the believer-priest must avoid allowing these things to replace the priority of the Holy Spirit in the temple when he said: "*And do not get drunk with wine, for that is dissipation, but be filled with the Spirit*" (Ephesians 5:18). We are wise to abstain from the use of what intoxicates, but we cannot abstain from the use of food. Rather, we must strive to exercise great stewardship in the way that we eat so that we do not over-indulge.

- **Keeping It Disciplined** -"*But I discipline by body and make it my slave, so that after I have preached to others, I myself will not be disqualified*" (1 Corinthians 9:27). This relates to what has already been already written above regarding morality, as well as eating and drinking. Merely because the body craves something does not mean that indulging in that craving is appropriate. Rather, Scripture teaches us that "*the flesh sets its desire* *against the Spirit, and the Spirit against the flesh; for these are in opposition to one another, so that you may not do the things that you please*" (Galatians 5:17). Therefore, we must exercise great self-restraint in maintaining the body as the temple of God. Self-discipline is taught in the context of the exercise used by athletes in the training of their bodies to function optimally. We, too, ought to see the body as something that should not be neglected, and allow it to deteriorate needlessly. Deterioration of the body is inevitable with the aging process. However, faithful stewardship of the body requires that one exercise the body to preserve the optimal health of the body. Although we are told in Scripture that "*bodily discipline is only of little profit, but godliness is profitable for all things, since it holds promise for the present life and also for the life to come*" (1 Timothy 4:8), bodily discipline is not dismissed as unimportant. In comparison with godliness, bodily discipline is focused on the present life alone. Nevertheless, it is in this present life that our bodies serve as the temple of God and they must be cared for properly. The imbalance of making exercise a "god" to be served is short-sighted. But the body must be cared for as an act of worshiping the true God given that He inhabits it. "Caring for one's body is much more than showing good sense or even practicing good health. It is an act of worship and service to the Lord who lives within (Romans. 12:1-2)."[60]

- **Keeping It Clean** -"*Jesus said to him, 'He who has bathed needs only to wash his feet, but is completely clean'*" (John 13:10). The Old Testament priest had to go through a thorough procedure of washing before entering the presence of the Lord. We are told that "*when they enter the tent of meeting, they shall wash with water, so that they will not die; or when they approach the altar to minister, by offering up in smoke a fire sacrifice to the Lord*" (Exodus 30:20). Although priests were washed ceremonially at ordination (Exodus 29:4), this regular washing depicted the daily maintaining of cleanliness before the Lord. Since the believer's body is the temple of the Lord, it is incumbent on him to keep it clean in honor of the Lord. Thus, personal hygiene is a priority for the believer-priest. A body that offends through sight or smell is unworthy of the Lord.

- **Keeping It Rested** -"*And He said to them, 'Come away by yourselves to a secluded place and rest a while*" (Mark 6:31). God feels so strongly about the fact that we need rest that He modeled it for us at Creation: "*By the seventh day God completed His work which He had done, and He rested on the* *seventh day from all His work which He had done*" (Genesis 2:2). This rest was not taken because God had grown tired. In fact, Scripture teaches us that God never grows weary nor does He sleep (Psalm 121). He was modeling for humans the need and propriety of rest. Perhaps He designed the body to need rest in order to help men remain aware of their frailty and dependence. Once a day, for an extended portion of the day, the body must lie down to sleep. In this condition of sleep, a man is totally oblivious to his own welfare; he cannot protect himself, feed himself, or in any other way control his life. In fact, nightly sleep reminds a person of the fact that one day permanent sleep will come upon him in death. Thus, sleeping is a way God's superiority over humanity is displayed on a daily basis. Accepting this dependency and acknowledging God's design is an important way a believer-priest honors the Lord. Studies demonstrate that the average person needs between 6.9 and 7.5 hours of sleep per night. In a recent survey, "Americans were asked to describe their general moods and attitudes on a typical day. The responses suggest a direct link between more sleep and positive feelings — a sense of peace, satisfaction with life, and being full of energy. Too-little sleep was linked with daytime sleepiness, negative moods, and fatigue."[61] Among the findings:

- Those who got fewer than six hours of sleep on weekdays were more likely to describe themselves as "stressed, sad, and angry."

- People who reported being sleepy often during the day were more likely to describe themselves as "dissatisfied with life and angry."

- Those who reported fewer insomnia symptoms were more likely to describe themselves as "full of energy," relaxed, and "happy."

- Those who did not get enough sleep were more likely to get impatient or aggravated with such common annoyances as waiting in line or sitting in traffic. They were also more likely to make mistakes and have difficulty getting along with others.

It is important to recognize that the health of the body is dependent, in part, on the rest gained from proper sleep habits. This is not merely for the energy and strength gained thereby, but is a sacrifice of worship offered to God as He inhabits the temple of the believer-priest's body.

The activities above (Sacrifices of Consecration) should not be pursued because of an attempt on the part of the priest to gain God's favor. Such a perspective is the essence of legalism (the attempt to gain the favor of God because of performance). Instead, they are the responsible ministries of priestly duty because of the high calling and privilege the believer has been given to present his body as a "*living and holy sacrifice, acceptable to God*" (Romans 12:1). Belittling those priests who have taken ownership of this stewardship of the temple by calling them legalists is to judge improperly faithful servants of God, to the detriment of God's glory (Romans 14:10-12).

The Sacrifice of Praise (Hebrews 13:15)

Believer-priests have the distinct privilege of "*continually offering up a sacrifice of praise to God, that is, the fruit of lips that give thanks to His name*" (Hebrews 13:15). As believers relish the delights of God's blessing in their lives, they naturally bring to Him those expressions of honor and praise that are due His name. In the Old Testament, the priests presented various offerings designed to express to God the thanksgiving for fellowship with Him. Perhaps most closely associated with the "*sacrifice of praise to God*" are the fellowship offerings delineated in Leviticus 1-3. They included:

- **The Burnt Offering** - the expression of a grateful heart to the Lord and an expression of devotion and consecration to Him (Leviticus 1:1-17)

- **The Grain Offering** - the expression of a grateful heart to the Lord for His faithful provision of their physical needs (Leviticus 2:1-16)

- **The Peace Offering**- the expression of a grateful heart to the Lord for the provision of forgiveness of sin through the blood sacrifice (Leviticus 3:1-17)

None of these offerings was designed to restore fellowship with God. All were designed to celebrate the relationship existing between the individual and God. However, for each of these sacrifices, the believer had to come to the priest for the offering of these sacrifices.

The believer-priest has the joy and privilege of offering the sacrifices of praise to the Lord at any time, any place. The emphasis in Hebrews 13:15 is on the constancy of our thanksgiving: "*let us continually offer up sacrifices.*" Repeatedly, throughout the Old Testament, believers offered the sacrifices of thanksgiving to the Lord: *"Offer to God a sacrifice of thanksgiving and pay your vows to the Most High"* (Psalm 50:14). Another example is Hosea 14:2: *"Take words with you and return to the Lord. Say to Him, 'Take away all iniquity and receive us graciously, that we may present the fruit of our lips.'"*

This worship, offered by means of thanksgiving to the Lord, is to be on the lips of the believer-priest continually. Because of the fellowship with God the Father through the work of Christ Jesus, our High Priest, we now offer worship designed to celebrate our relationship with Him. He has been good to us. He has showered us with His goodness. He has forgiven our sins, provided for our physical needs, and responded to our requests. He answers prayer, protects from harm, strengthens for service, and gives us every good gift. We worship Him not only for who He is, but also for what He has done for us. Thus, our worship must be intense and constant. What a tragedy it is to see believers who relegate worship to an event to be performed once or twice a week within the boundaries of "church." "Worship is not something you reserve for certain times. It is not just for your quiet time or when you attend a worship service. Worship is a lifestyle. I am writing to remind you that we were created to worship God. We are worshipers, and the inward response of worshiping hearts to any encounter with our Lord, no matter where we may find ourselves, is to fall on our faces and worship."[62]

What this worship needs to excite passion and fire is not any external stimuli similar to those found at political rallies or rock concerts. This worship needs to see God, in all His glory, girded with truth, elevated in majesty and lauded with reverence. The worship of the believer-priest must focus on God alone. Tozer said it well: "Christian believers and Christian congregations must be thoroughly consecrated to Christ's glory alone. This means absolutely turning their backs on the contemporary insistence on human glory and recognition … I am confident our Lord never meant for the Christian church to provide a kind of religious stage where performers proudly take their bows, seeking personal recognition."[63] The God of glory refuses to share His glory and is jealous for that glory. He declared: *"I am the Lord, that is My name; I will not give My glory to another, nor My praise to graven images"* (Isaiah 42:8). One of the sacrifices that the believer-priest offers up to the Lord is a "sacrifice of praise to God" in the quietness of his own temple. As the sweet incense ascends to the throne of God through the prayers of adoration uttered by the lips of the priests of God, God is sanctified and honored. Such is *"the fruit of lips that give thanks to His name.*" In light of God's grace, this is the "*spiritual service of worship*" reasonably offered by every believer-priest.

The Sacrifice of Good Works (Hebrews 13:16; Philippians 4:18)

The role that good works play in the life of a believer is an important issue. There are those who have failed to understand the impact of man's depravity. Such people believe God can be pleased with what man can offer to Him and thereby gain His favor. However, from the very first recorded act of worship, God has made Himself clear: He will not accept good works as a means of appeasing His wrath toward sin (Genesis 4:3-7). In fact, God completely rejects the good works of sinners. He views the best deeds that sinful man offers as despicable: "*For all of us have become like one who is unclean, and all our righteous deeds are like a filthy garment* [a reference to a woman's soiled menstrual cloth]" (Isaiah 64:6). This is the essential reason God proclaimed in Romans 3:20 that "*by the works of the Law no flesh will be justified in His sight; for through the Law comes the knowledge of sin.*" In order to clarify this issue, God further declares: "*He saved us, not on the basis of deeds which we have done in righteousness, but according to His mercy, by the washing of regeneration and renewing by the Holy Spirit*" (Titus 3:5). Thus, the believer-priest does not offer up good works to God for the purpose of attempting to gain His favor. Rather, they are offered because God's favor has already provided the cleansing from sin through the blood of Christ Jesus, our Great High Priest.

The Scripture therefore instructs those who have gained the calling as a priest of God not to "*neglect doing good and sharing, for with such sacrifices God is pleased*" (Hebrews 13:16). Good works performed by the believer are to be personal expressions of adoration to God. Jesus takes doing good to others very personally: He taught that on the Day of Judgment, those who have performed good works to others as an expression of worship and adoration of God will be acclaimed for their personal treatment of Him. He said: "*Truly I say to you, to the extent that you did it to one of these brothers of Mine, even the least of them, you did it to Me*" (Matthew 25:40). Again, in Luke 9:48 He said: "*Whoever receives this child in My name receives Me, and whoever receives Me receives Him who sent Me.*"

In much the same way, we understand those who persecute and abuse the church will face a personally insulted, offended and vengeful God. When He confronted Saul of Tarsus on the road to Damascus for his persecution of the Church, Jesus said to him: "*Saul, Saul, why are you persecuting Me? … I am Jesus whom you are persecuting*" (Acts 9:4-5).

Capitalizing on the analogy of the Body of Christ as a "Temple," those who damage that temple through persecution or false doctrine will have to answer to God: "*If any man destroys the temple of God, God will destroy him, for the temple of God is holy, and that is what you are*" (1 Corinthians 3:17).

It is clear that the only good works God receives are those good works offered to Him by those who have been brought into His family through faith in the work of Jesus Christ. These holy ones are the priests ordained by God for the purpose of offering Him sacrifices of praise. Such sacrifices are offered in the Temple of God – the Holy of Holies – within the very heart of the believer. Personal worship and the praise of God are undetected by people. In this most restricted level of relationship with God, no one exists except the individual believer-priest and God. No one can see the motive of the heart. However, as people observe the sincere sacrifices of good works, they observe the glory of God in those works. Jesus stated that believers are to allow the Light of the glory of God to "*shine before men in such a way that they may see your good works, and glorify your Father who is in heaven*" (Matthew 5:16). Thus, as the believer performs good works motivated out of a desire to worship God and offer Him an acceptable sacrifice, God's glory is observed by others who will then glorify God.

The good works that bring God pleasure include, but are not limited to, the following:

- Benevolence for the poor
- Visiting the orphan and widow
- Admonishing the unruly
- Encouraging the fainthearted
- Helping the weak
- Being patient with everyone
- Blessing those who curse you
- Praying for those who mistreat you
- Lending expecting nothing in return
- Being at peace with all men
- Forgiving those who offend you
- Loving enemies
- Giving to the Lord cheerfully

Essentially, good works can be defined as: "any activity of a moral agent which proceeds from a right motive (love), is in accord with a proper moral standard (law), and aims at the glory of a worthy object (God)." [64] This helps to explain why some good works are dismissed by God as unworthy. When a believer-priest offers the sacrifice of good works to something other than the worthy object of God's glory, God dismisses the good work. At the Judgment Seat of Christ, when the deeds of believers are evaluated, each believer will "*be recompensed for his deeds in the body, according to what he has done, whether good or bad*" (1 Corinthians 5:10). Those works that have been performed in the flesh for a purpose other than the glory of God will become evident: "*each man's work will become evident; for the day will show it because it is to be revealed with fire, and the fire itself will test the quality of each man's work*" (1 Corinthians 3:13). There are believers who perform good works, but not as sacrifices of praise to God. A person who does the right thing with the wrong motive has diminished reward. Such works are burned up as "*wood, hay, and straw*" (1 Corinthians 3:12). The believer-priest in his personal worship of God must "*offer up spiritual sacrifices to God through Jesus Christ*" (Hebrews 13:15-16). Only then is God pleased and the relationship with Him enhanced.

The Sacrifice of New Converts (Romans 15:16)

The final area of sacrifice offered to God in worship by the believer-priest is that of new converts. Paul stated in Romans 15:16: "*... because of the grace that was given me from God, to be a minister of Christ Jesus to the Gentiles, ministering as a priest the gospel of God, so that my offering of the Gentiles may become acceptable, sanctified by the Holy Spirit.*" The greatest sacrifice presented to God is that of sinners who have turned to God from idols to serve Him. The term used in this passage for "*ministering as a priest*," is a term which refers to the preparations for a sacrifice to be offered. In extra-biblical literature, the term is used commonly of the cultic practice of consecrating a sacrifice to the gods. To "*minister as a priest*," in this context, means to prepare a sacrifice of souls to be offered to God. In Romans 15:16, Gentiles are the sacrifice being offered to God. The means by which they are prepared is through the power of the Holy Spirit and through the agency of the Gospel, which is the "*power of God for salvation*" (Romans 1:16).

The Scriptures tell us that the deliverance of souls through the Gospel stirs Heaven's joy. Luke 15:7 records that "*there will be more joy in heaven over one sinner who repents than over ninety nine righteous persons who need no repentance.*" The joy of men is made an object of glory for the Savior.

When sinners turn by faith to God, they are offered to the Lord as a sacrifice of worship by the believer-priest who shared the Gospel, and there will be little more glorious in the life of the believer than to be able to present them to the Savior. The Apostle Paul declared to the Thessalonian believers: "*For who is our hope of joy or crown of exultation? Is it not even you, in the presence of our Lord Jesus at His coming? For you are our glory and joy*" (1 Thessalonians 2:19-20).

Clearly, the believer-priest should desire to offer to the Lord this type of sacrifice for the glory of God. It has been wisely observed that the only thing you can take from this world into the next is the souls of those who have been won to Christ. In addition, once a person gets to glory, it will be too late to prepare such a sacrifice of worship to the Lord. This ministry of the priesthood is limited to this side of glory. If there will be any presentation of souls to the Savior, it will occur on the other side of glory. Evangelism is bound to this earthly existence. Thus, one of the most intimate sacrifices the believer-priest can make to the Lord is the souls of men, saved through the Gospel which he personally shared with them.

Conclusion

Throughout this chapter, we have observed the fact that the most separated level of biblically responsible relationships is the level of the believer-priest. Having been redeemed and reconciled to God through the work of Jesus Christ, the believer's highest calling and duty is to bring glory to God through "*offering up spiritual sacrifices acceptable to God through Jesus Christ*" (1 Peter 2:5). This is not done in some flashy, ostentatious demonstration of pageantry in the eyes of others. The "spiritual sacrifices" are personal expressions of adoration and worship offered to the Lord from the heart of each believer. This communion with the Lord will occur in personal times of ministry to God. Personal worship, prayer, obedience, and sacrifice will characterize the believer-priest who diligently pursues the duties of his or her priesthood.

A very great danger is for the church to be filled with saints who know nothing of this most intimate level of fellowship with God. The Apostle John clarified that fellowship with God on this level serves as the basis for entering into fellowship with others. He says: "*God is Light, and in Him there is no darkness at all. If we say that we have fellowship with Him and yet walk in the darkness, we lie and do not practice the truth; but if we walk in the Light as He Himself is in the Light, we have fellowship with one another, and the blood of*

Jesus His son cleanses us from all sin" (1 John 1:5-7). Thus, integrity on this level serves as the qualification for inclusion on the lowest level of biblical relationships, that of our brotherhood in Christ Jesus. It serves as the catalyst which empowers the believer as the salt of the earth. It provides the righteousness to serve the Lord as the light of the world. It provides legitimacy to a believer's involvement in the church. It is the basis for the intimacies of a godly family. It enables a person to enjoy the presence of God Himself as believer-priest.

Failure to fulfill one's duty as a believer-priest necessarily renders the other levels powerless. It causes people to exist in the church who are "*holding to a form of godliness, although they have denied its power*" (2 Timothy 3:5). Allowing others to enter into this most intimate level disables the primary relationship that needs to exist for a believer to have integrity in the other levels. How can we share Christ if one of the brothers is estranged from Him? How can we stand together against sin if there is no seasoning through the power of the Holy Spirit? How can we serve as Light while personally in darkness? How can we join together with other believers to worship God when there is no integrity to our worship through personal interaction with God? Yet, many believe that their relationship with God is adequate when it is never intimate or personal. Can one pray in public who never prays in private? Can we worship God in the presence of others if there is no worship of Him in private?

The most separated, intimate level of biblically responsible relationships is the level of the believer-priest. Failure to fulfill one's duty as a believer-priest necessarily renders the other levels powerless.

CHAPTER SEVEN

CONCLUSION

Now let us hear the conclusion of the whole matter. In this book, we have united two concepts: vigilance (necessary to contend for the faith once delivered unto the saints) with deep compassion and concern (which the Scripture demands we show other believers with whom we differ). It is so easy to overlook the spiritual welfare of those who have been deceived and captivated by false doctrine and ungodly attitudes. In addition, there are many who live within the parameters of sound doctrine yet harbor spiritually bankrupt attitudes toward others within the Body of Christ. Rightly relating to genuine brothers and sisters in Christ is a key to successfully pursuing the unity of the Spirit in the bond of peace.

When the Apostle Paul gathered the elders from Ephesus together, he shared with them his deep concern. After his departure "*savage wolves will come in among you, not sparing the flock; and among your own selves men will arise, speaking perverse things, to draw away disciples after them*" (Acts 20:29-30). His concern proved to be an accurate assessment of what would happen among those fledgling believers. In Paul's first letter to Timothy, he urged him to remain in Ephesus in order to confront certain men who were teaching "strange doctrines." However, he instructed Timothy to do this, guided by "*love from a pure heart and a good conscience and sincere faith*" (1 Timothy 1:5). Paul recognized there was great potential for the flesh to dominate in a good cause. Argument, division and condemnation often results when error is confronted. Later in his second letter he reminded Timothy "*the Lord's bond-servant must not be quarrelsome, but kind to all, able to teach, patient when wronged, with gentleness correcting those who are in opposition, if perhaps the Lord would grant them repentance leading to the knowledge of the truth, and they may come to their senses and escape from the snare of the devil, having been held captive by him to do his will*"(2 Timothy 2:24-26).

It is our understanding that responsible biblical relationships are not identical when viewed in context of the levels of responsibility within the Body of Christ. This is illustrated by The Pyramid of Responsibility found at the beginning of each chapter.

A believer's opportunity for cooperation with other believers becomes more limited as the levels of responsibility progress toward the ultimate relationship known as the priesthood of the believer. It is the premise of this book to look for areas where believers can demonstrate their mutual respect and love for the brethren. This book is not dominated by seeking ways to identify those from whom we must separate. Nor is it the intent of this book to overlook the importance of separation when the Scripture clearly demands it. We maintain that implementing separation is not for the primary benefit of the one separating. Rather its ultimate purpose is to provide a platform for ministry to those with whom you differ. Paul placed great emphasis on this when he wrote to the Thessalonian believers: "*If anyone obeys not our instruction in this letter, take special note of that person and do not associate with him, so that he will be put to shame. Yet do not regard him as an enemy, but admonish him as a brother*" (2 Thessalonians 3:14-15). Believers who rightly understand this will never rejoice over the necessity of separating from brothers. They will mourn the breaking of unity that separation always produces. Severance from relationship will be the last resort.

If we properly regard the principles of biblical separation, there will be a marked similarity with the biblical principles of church discipline. Rightly understood, church discipline is exercised: (1) to bring glory to God, (2) to achieve the restoration of the errant believer, (3) to produce purification of the Church, (4) to bring Godly fear to the believers, and (5) to prevent the further chastisement of the Lord. Limiting relationships when the Scripture instructs to do so: (1) brings glory to God, (2) provides the platform for restoration, (3) maintains the purity of relationships, (4) provides a biblical example to other believers, and (5) allows God to continue to bless uninterrupted by wrong attitudes and actions.

The various levels of responsibility help a believer identify the relationships among believers that are appropriate. We have attempted to answer questions such as:

- **With whom may I fellowship as brothers in the Lord?** *You are a Brother* is the broadest of the levels of responsible relationships. If a person is a genuine Christian, he is my brother and I have the biblical responsibility to value him as a member of the Body of Christ. Although I am not necessarily free to have uninhibited relationships with him, on a personal level I can share a common faith and love for the Savior.

- **With whom may I cooperate as the salt of the earth?** On the level of *You are Salt*, we suggested various ways believers are able to band together within our society for the purposes of enhancing flavor, creating thirst, drawing out infection, and preserving from decay. It is on this level where believers can find common ground even though they may have differing views on less essential doctrinal issues. Certainly when it comes to answering the call of the Lord to do good unto all men, there is room for brothers to respond commonly from a diversity of positions. He is the Lord of all, and each believer has the duty to respond in His name. Engaging in social issues on a variety of levels is necessary in order for the people of God to fulfill their role as "*the salt of the earth.*" Yet social reform is not the solution to the problems caused by sin in a culture. The danger of striving to serve as "*the salt of the earth*" is to become so consumed with the effort of preserving morality that it becomes an end in itself. Efforts that fall short of presenting the Gospel as the solution are deficient. Lack of balance in this endeavor leads either to a Social Gospel (which is the error of the liberals) or to an isolationism that abandons the social process (which has been the error of the Fundamentalists.) Both of these errors disable the purposes of God for the believer's impact in the world.

- **With whom may I reach out with the light of the Gospel?** It is on the *You are Light* level that the limitation of responsible relationships begins to be more evident, for the preaching and preservation of the Gospel is a sacred trust. Faithful Christians must be extremely careful about entering into any relationship that would compromise the integrity of the Gospel. We outlined certain hindrances to cooperative relationships in proclaiming the light of the glorious gospel of Jesus Christ. But we also took great care to suggest partners with whom cooperative relationships may be established in the effort to reach the world with a genuine biblical declaration of the Gospel.

- **With whom may I worship within the context of the local church?** From the very first days of the Church, God expressed through the apostles a tremendous priority on biblically responsible relationships within the local church. On the *You are the Church* level, the expressed concern was that the responsibilities for responsible relationships must be even more vigilant and focused than on any of the other levels previously discussed. However, we noted the tendency within the church to remove existing barriers in order to build relationships with people. Doctrine is often perceived as the great divider, and so it is frequently minimized in order to appeal to people and maintain relationships. We also discussed interdependence within the body, emphasizing that believers are to rely on each other for encouragement, edification, and greater effectiveness. Interdependence also provides the platform upon which churches are able to work together. It is appropriate for local churches of like faith to cooperate with each other for the presentation and propagation of the Gospel. However, each local church, through its leadership and their interpretation and application of Scripture, should determine the extent of and qualifications for such cooperation.

- **With whom may I enjoy a true family relationship?** We saw on the *You are Family* level that relationships within families should be intimate, personal and responsible. They must be maintained even when other relationships are biblically limited. In fact, family relationships are so important that maintaining them often supersedes other considerations. The family is, by God's design, one of the basic building blocks of society and the Scriptures address family relationships specifically. The family begins to disintegrate when the biblical relational principles are ignored. We discussed the strengths and weaknesses of today's family and suggested ways in which strong marriages and lasting relationships within the family may be enhanced.

- **Are there any relationships that include no one except the Lord and me?** The ultimate level of biblical relationships is the personal relationship that exists between the individual believer and the Lord Jesus Christ. On the *You Are a Priest* level of relationship no one else is permitted. When one stands before God on the day of reckoning, the only question that will be relevant is whether or not a sinner has an intimate relationship with God through Jesus Christ.

It has been our intent to provoke careful thought and evaluation regarding the levels of responsibility and how they apply to proper biblical relationships. The answers to each of the above questions sharpen the understanding of possible relationships and conclude that each level requires a more limited level of responsibility in establishing and maintaining them.

Seeking to apply the freedoms intended for a "lower" level to a level designed to be more limited produces inclusivism and compromise. Seeking to impose the restrictions intended for an "upper" level to a level designed to be broader brings exclusivism and unwarranted schism. It is our prayer that the material presented in this book will provoke thought and cause evaluation of the levels of responsibility in the approaches to and implementation of the biblical doctrine of separation.

As The Pyramid of Responsibility of biblically mandated relationships is understood and applied, may believers seek to emulate our holy and loving God. And may He alone receive all the glory!

APPENDIX ONE

A BRIEF HISTORY OF THE CONSERVATIVE/LIBERAL THEOLOGICAL CONTROVERSY

Philip Schaff in the introduction to his *History of the Christian Church* notes, "the present is the fruit of the past and the germ of the future."[65] It has been said that those who do not learn lessons from history are doomed to repeat its mistakes. Today's believers would do well to heed the lessons of history. Understanding the complexities Christians face in relating to one another requires knowledge of the events and ideas that produced their Christian culture and impacted the life of the Church. It helps to perceive how today's ideas and actions are intricately involved in affecting the Church of tomorrow.

Believers live in a changing world whose ideas and philosophies constantly assault their values. Francis Schaeffer, in his book *The Great Evangelical Disaster*, identified two things that profoundly influenced God's people during the Twentieth Century.

Cultural Relativism

Schaeffer observed, "There hardly could be a more fitting description of our culture today. Bent on pursuit of autonomous freedom – freedom from any restraint and especially from God's truth and moral absolutes – our culture has set itself on a course of self destruction."[66] This autonomous freedom expresses itself in a rebellion against moral authority and declares that nothing is right or wrong in itself. Its development through the centuries produced a worldview known today as Postmodernism. Dennis McCallum, in his book *The Death of Truth*, defines Postmodernism as "a *mood* - a view of the world characterized by a deep distrust of reason, not to mention a disdain for the knowledge Christians believe the Bible provides. It is a *methodology* - a completely new way of analyzing ideas … it is a *movement* - a fresh onslaught on truth that brings a more or less cohesive approach to literature, history, politics, education, sociology, linguistics and virtually every other discipline including science."[67] This world view can be seen in almost every arena of our culture today with its "political correctness" and "moral relativism." The seedlings of this worldview can be found in the drift of Protestant churches in the first forty years of the Twentieth Century. It was a drift that laid the basis for cultural, social, moral, legal and governmental changes in society. The shifts in society cannot be separated from the theological trends within the Church. It is interesting to note there was a span of approximately eighty years from the time when the Higher Critical methods originated and became widely accepted in Germany, to the disintegration of German culture and the rise of totalitarianism under Hitler[68]

Theological Liberalism

Theological liberalism in America was born in Europe where ideas of The Enlightenment had a profound influence on theologians. The Enlightenment represented a movement of thought which began to appear in the mid-Seventeenth Century and reached its most definitive form in Eighteenth Century Germany. In general, it was an intellectual movement that emphasized the sufficiency of human reason and skepticism concerning the validity of traditional authority.[69] Its influence was pervasive by the late Nineteenth Century. The resultant attacks on the Bible centered on its inerrancy and inspiration. Orthodox theologians responded in many ways, including a series of articles by several faculty members at Princeton Seminary. They defended the accuracy of the Scriptures and the ministry of the Holy Spirit who supernaturally guided its authors and content. Their position was condensed into the statement issued by A.A. Hodge and B.B. Warfield: "We rest in the joyful and unshaken certainty that we possess a Bible written by the hands of men indeed, but also graven with the finger of God."[70] In his introduction to the writings of B.B. Warfield, D. Martyn Lloyd Jones made this observation concerning the encroachment of liberalism into the American church when he described those times as:

> the age of the 'liberal Jesus' and 'the Jesus of history,' who was contrasted with the 'Christ of Paul.' The Bible had been subjected to such drastic criticism that not only was its divine inspiration and unique authority denied but the whole idea of revelation was in question. The Lord Jesus was but a man, 'the greatest religious genius of all time,' miracles had never happened because miracles cannot happen, our Lord's mission was a failure, and his death on the cross but a tragedy. The great truths proclaimed in the historic Creeds of the Church, and especially in the great Confessions

of Faith drawn up after the Protestant Reformation, concerning the Bible as the Word of God and the person and work of the Lord Jesus Christ were being questioned and rejected by the vast majority of 'scholars.'"[71]

Dr. Allan MacRae, President of Faith Theological Seminary in Elkins Park, Pennsylvania, stated in a seminary lecture in 1960, "that there is not a seminary in America over forty years old that does not teach the higher critical Graf-Welhausen Developmental Hypothesis concerning the authorship of the Pentateuch."[72] This humanistic hypothesis denies the Mosaic authorship of the first five books of the Bible and explains their origin as an evolutionary process in which many writings and legends were brought together by a redactor using the names of God as criteria to determine from which document various verses and passages originated. MacRae's observation illustrated the invasive influence of liberal theology. It was motivated by Darwinian Evolution, the Higher Critical approach to the Scriptures and the development of America's own brand of liberalism through New England Unitarianism and the humanistic Social Gospel.

This expression of liberalism was taught in most seminaries. It engendered questions as well as liberal convictions in the minds and hearts of the ministerial students who would become the pastors in the main denominations across America. Their liberal orientation provided the framework for controversy in denominations and divided churches all across America from the turn of the century to the early 1930s. Laymen felt estranged from their denominations as they came into conflict with the liberal teachings of their pastors.

Publication of the Fundamentals

The occasions for conflict were heightened when a committee of strong Christians organized the Testimony Publishing Company in the early years of the Twentieth Century. The committee was funded by American oilmen, Lyman and Milton Stewart, and led by Pastor A. C. Dixon. They commissioned the writing of a series of ninety articles by sixty-four outstanding scholars defining and explaining the historic doctrines of the faith. Once completed, there were twelve paper back books published under the title, *The Fundamentals*. David O. Beale in his book *The Pursuit of Purity* notes:

The focus of *The Fundamentals* was the defense of the orthodox view of

> Scripture, so several articles were devoted to the doctrine of inspiration. Another group dealt with higher criticism and specific points under attack (the unity of Isaiah, the authorship of the Fourth Gospel the accuracy of Daniel, etc.). Another group, perhaps the most permanent in value, supported particular doctrines that liberals had disputed, as the deity of Christ, the atonement, and future retribution. Volume twelve was entirely devoted to evangelism and missions. Other groups of articles covered cults, specific peripheral disciplines affecting the Bible and personal holiness.[73]

Copies of *The Fundamentals* were sent free of charge to ministers and laymen all across America. Though the authors were widely respected scholars, it should be noted that the subjects were consistently written on a laymen's level. The wide distribution of the articles (over three hundred thousand sets), in an era when reading was very much a part of people's lives, proved to have a profound effect. It crystallized public understanding of the differences between those committed to liberal theology and those who came to be known as "Fundamentalists." And it galvanized the defenders of the faith.

Denominational Conflicts

Prior to 1930, Fundamentalists endeavored to keep the Church pure by attempting to purge theological liberals from the main line denominations. Men who denied basic Christian doctrine gradually invaded the Presbyterian Church. Several were brought to trial for heresy. As a result of the controversy, the General Assembly adopted the famous 1892 Portland Deliverance. This document stated that all ministerial candidates must affirm the church's historic position of belief in inerrancy of the original manuscripts of Scripture, and that if a presbytery discovered any minister teaching otherwise, it should charge him with a violation of his ordination vows. However, the Portland Deliverance did not accomplish its intent. Rather than doctrinally purifying the denomination, the controversy produced several highly publicized trials. These in turn produced three distinct views among the denomination's ministers. There were those who were militant about holding every minister and seminary professor to his orthodox ordination vows. Others had a more liberal theological orientation and wanted freedom to hold variant views. The third group might be considered the tolerant conservatives. They recognized liberal views to be innovative and extreme, but thought the denomination should be broad enough to include such views.

Between 1892 and 1910, the battle in the Presbyterian Church raged. Where there was a distinct liberal presence, presbyteries granted ordination to men who took their vows with mental reservation. Once ordination was granted, men would move to other presbyteries where they began to influence the tolerant conservatives to allow an inclusive approach to the church's ministerial membership.

In an attempt to strengthen the 1892 Portland Deliverance, the General Assembly of 1910 adopted a five point doctrinal declaration that later became known as the five points of Presbyterian Fundamentalism. These points were declared as "essential and necessary":

- The inerrancy of the original manuscripts of Scripture
- The Virgin Birth of Christ
- Christ's Vicarious Atonement
- The Bodily Resurrection of Christ
- The reality of Miracles as recorded in Scripture

Although these five points were read in congregations across America and were reaffirmed in the General Assemblies of 1916 and 1923, they were constantly under attack by both liberal and tolerant conservatives. In 1923, 149 ministers in the New York Presbytery became the original signers of what came to be known as the Auburn Affirmation. During this troubled period in Presbyterian history, a theological pattern of accommodation began to grow. It proved particularly influential in the Synod of New York and among ministers educated at Auburn and Union Seminaries.[74] A clear exposition of its content came from Henry Sloane Coffin during the controversies over the Presbytery of New York and Union Theological Seminary.

The following are excerpts from the Auburn Affirmation, ultimately signed by 1274 Presbyterian ministers, illustrating in writing their heresy:

> While it is constitutional for any General Assembly "to bear testimony against error in doctrine" (Form of Govt. XII, v), yet such testimony is without binding authority, since the constitution of our church provides that its doctrine shall be declared only by concurrent action of the General Assembly and the presbyteries. Thus, the church guards the

statement of its doctrine against hasty or ill-considered action by either General Assemblies or presbyteries. From this provision of our constitution, it is evident that neither in one General Assembly nor in many, without concurrent action of the presbyteries, is there authority to declare what the Presbyterian Church in the United States of America believes and teaches; and that the assumption that any General Assembly has authoritatively declared what the church believes and teaches is groundless. A declaration by a General Assembly that any doctrine is "an essential doctrine" attempts to amend the constitution of the church in an unconstitutional manner."

There is no assertion in the Scriptures that their writers were kept "from error." The Confession of Faith does not make this assertion; and it is significant that this assertion is not to be found in the Apostles' Creed or the Nicene Creed or in any of the great Reformation confessions. The General Assembly of 1923 expressed the opinion concerning five doctrinal statements that each one "is an essential doctrine of the Word of God and our standards of ordination or good standing in the church." It challenged the General Assembly's right to bind the presbyteries without the presbyteries voting on the matter themselves.

On the constitutional grounds which we have before described, we are opposed to any attempt to elevate these five doctrinal statements, or any of them, to the position of test for ordination or for good standing in our church. Furthermore, this opinion of the General Assembly attempts to commit our church to certain theories concerning the inspiration of the Bible, and the Incarnation, the Atonement, the Resurrection, and the Continuing Life and Supernatural Power of our Lord Jesus Christ. We all hold most earnestly to these great facts and doctrines; we all believe from our hearts that the writers of the Bible were inspired of God; that Jesus Christ was God manifest in the flesh; that God was in Christ, reconciling the world unto Himself, and through Him we have our redemption; that having died for our sins He rose from the dead and is our ever-living Savior; that in His earthly ministry He wrought many mighty works, and by His vicarious death and unfailing presence He is able to save to the uttermost. Some of us regard the particular theories contained in the deliverance of the General Assembly of 1923 as satisfactory explanations of these facts and doctrines. But we are united in believing that these are

> not the only theories allowed by the Scriptures and our standards as explanations of these facts and doctrines of our religion, and that all who hold to these facts and doctrines, whatever theories they may employ to explain them, are worthy of all confidence and fellowship.[75]

Those who demanded full compliance with the ordination vows found that they were fighting a losing battle. A new approach was forced upon them after they found themselves being purged, no longer welcome in their own denominations. Several months before the Auburn Affirmation, Dr. J. Gresham Machen of Princeton Seminary published *Christianity and Liberalism*. It clearly exposed the liberal view in contrast to the orthodox Christian Faith. It concluded that liberalism is not Christian at all, but a religion so entirely different as to belong to a distinct category.[76] Francis Schaeffer pointed out: "by 1936 liberals were so in control of the Northern Presbyterian Church that they were able to defrock Dr. J. Gresham Machen. Machen's defrocking and resultant division of the Northern Presbyterian Church was front page news in the secular media in much of the country."[77] Whereas the "Fundamentalist" wing of the Presbyterian Church was unable to preserve doctrinal purity by demanding doctrinal integrity, its proponents were in turn disciplined for their unwillingness to exercise Christian toleration (accommodation of theological diversity). Schaeffer comments that this was the great evangelical disaster - namely the failure of the Evangelical world to stand for truth as truth. The result was that the Evangelical church had accommodated the spirit of the age. It accommodated variant views of the Scripture so that men who called themselves Evangelical no longer affirmed the truth in all of what the Bible teaches, including not only religious matters but matters of science, history and morality.[78]

The tragic result of these events in all major denominations was division among genuine brothers. It is one thing to find oneself out of harmony with those who deny the faith. But it is an entirely different matter to find oneself alienated from genuine brothers over how to relate to each other in the midst of controversy. Unfortunately, believers on both sides of the conflict became severely judgmental and intolerant. The militant conservatives were highly critical of the tolerant conservatives. The tolerant conservatives joined liberals in being judgmental of the militant conservatives and refused to be identified with them. The result was a fragmentation of genuine believers within denominations.

The militant conservatives had fought the good fight of faith over doctrinal fundamentals and found themselves no longer welcome in denominations in which they were attempting to preserve doctrinal purity. Many lost their pulpits, churches, pensions and friends because of their conviction that true unity could only be found in common commitment to biblical truth, not in preserving denominational harmony. They found it necessary for conscience sake to leave their denominations and start anew. Where denominations owned the church buildings, many pastors and like-minded people rented community buildings, schools or met in homes. Where local churches owned their own buildings, congregations voted to leave the denomination and become independent.

A missionary spirit captivated people and pastor alike, and evangelism and a zeal for missions flourished. Radio ministries, Bible Conferences and the emergence of Bible Institutes and Independent Christian Colleges influenced thousands. New denominations and Fellowships came into being. Fundamentalism became a recognizable movement as an enemy of apostate liberalism. But the militant spirit that characterized many was destined to lead to further conflicts among those who identified themselves as Fundamentalists.

The Formation of Breakaway Denominations and Fellowships

The decades of the 1920s and 1930s were the time when several significant breakaway denominations and fellowships were founded. In 1920, conservatives from the Northern Baptist Convention organized the Fundamentalist Fellowship to combat spreading liberalism in their denomination. In 1923, the Baptist Bible Union formed to gather Baptist Fundamentalists from all denominations. In 1929, the Independent Fundamental Churches of America was organized and held their first official convention in 1930. In 1932, Northern Baptist Fundamentalists founded the General Association of Regular Baptists. In 1936, Presbyterian Fundamentalists under the direction of J. Greshem Machen founded the Orthodox Presbyterian Church. And in 1937, disgruntled Orthodox Presbyterians founded the Bible Presbyterian Church.

The Formation of the American Council of Christian Churches

A significant conflict occurred in the early 1940's. In 1941, the American Council of Christian Churches was organized as an alternative to the Federal Council of Churches (which later would be called the National

Council of Churches). The American Council of Christian Churches was meant to be a unified voice for Fundamentalism to:

- Challenge the claim of the Federal Council of Churches to speak for all Protestants.

- Warn Christians of the Ecumenical program for propagation of unbelief and the ultimate objective of a one-world-church.

- Present a true Christian testimony by Fundamental pastors and churches through opportunities the Lord would provide, such as rallies, radio, and in the press.

- Provide Christian fellowship for faithful pastors and laymen in local chapters and national assemblies.

- Do for churches what they could not do for themselves alone.

The officers of the American Council of Christian Churches were:

President: Carl MacIntyre, Pastor Bible Presbyterian Church, Collingswood, New Jersey

Vice-President: Harold S. Laird, Pastor First Independent Church, Wilmington, Delaware

Secretary: Newton Conant, President of the Eastern Conference of the Bible Protestant Church, Camden, New Jersey

Treasurer: W. S. Patrick, Pastor Bible Protestant Church, Lynbrook, Long Island, New York

General Secretary: H. McAllister Griffiths

There were a number of early sponsors for the American Council of Christian Churches. These men included, among others, such leaders as:

Will Houghton, President of Moody Bible Institute, Chicago

William Ward Ayre, Pastor of Calvary Baptist Church, New York City

George Mundell, Pastor of Maranatha Tabernacle, Darby, Pennsylvania

J. Davis Adams, President of Philadelphia Bible Institute

Hobart Greer, President of The Christian Businessmen's Committee

R. R. Fritsch, Professor at Muhlenberg College

Vernon Grounds, Pastor of Conservative Baptist Association Church, Patterson, New Jersey

A. F. Williams, Pastor of First Baptist Church, New York City

A. F. Brumbaught, Pastor of Bible Presbyterian Church, Tacoma, Washington

Allan MacRae, President of Faith Theological Seminary, Wilmington, Delaware

James E. Bennet, Attorney from New York City

J. Oliver Buswell, President of National Bible Institute, New York City [79]

It was obvious that some unified expression of Fundamentalism was needed for the emerging denominations, independent church Fellowships and the numerous para-church organizations. However, there was an awareness that even though all desired to stand for the truth against apostasy, there was a distinct difference of opinion as to how this stance should be pursued. Some who originally were sponsors of the American Council of Christian Churches later became part of an alternative organization that came to be known as the National Association of Evangelicals.

The Formation of the National Association of Evangelicals

Shortly after the formation of the American Council of Christian Churches, a group of men called for an organizational meeting to form an alternative Fellowship. By intention, this fellowship would not be as militant at the American Council of Christian Churches. This group was led by J. Elwin Wright of the New England Fellowship, Harold John Ockenga of Boston, Ralph Davis of Africa Inland Mission and Will Houghton, President of Moody Bible Institute. At the initial meeting, a Temporary Committee for United Action Among Evangelicals was created. Wright was named chairman and a national conference was placed on the calendar in St. Louis for April 1942. The committee opened an office in New York, met several times during the winter to make arrangements, and issued a public invitation to join the National Conference for United Action Among Evangelicals. The invitation was signed by 147 leaders, all of whom agreed that "the time is ripe for frank discussion and exploration" of the possibility of a national organization. The following is a statement from A Brief History of the National Association of Evangelicals.

> Moved to action, the conference drafted a tentative constitution and statement of faith and accepted a report of the policy committee that called for a constitutional convention a year later. As the proposed constitution stated, the group determined "to organize an Association which shall give articulation and united voice to our faith and purpose in Christ Jesus." The only source of tension during the proceedings centered upon a motion presented by the fiery fundamentalist from New Jersey, Carl McIntire. He pleaded with participants to join the American Council of Christian Churches, an organization he had founded, a month before the October 1941 exploratory meeting in Chicago, as a declaration of war against the Federal Council of Churches (FCC). The issue had been placed on the table at the earlier Chicago meeting, but in St. Louis the participants declined McIntire's invitation, believing that a more positive testimony to the gospel was needed. While they all shared serious reservations about the FCC, the participants did not feel that militant opposition and direct confrontation with the well-established Protestant council was the best strategy.[80]

Thus, in 1942 a very basic division occurred within the ranks of American Fundamentalism/Christian Conservatism when the National Association of Evangelicals was founded. Those identifying with the American Council of Christian Churches were more confrontational and were proud to be called Fundamentalists. Those identifying with the National Association of Evangelicals identified more with the tolerant conservatives of earlier decades and preferred to be called Evangelicals. Since the meaning of both terms continued to evolve, both Fundamentalists and Evangelicals often found themselves subject to categorization by popular usage of the terms.

It would not be too many years before the Evangelicals adopted a new expression to identify their approach toward cooperation and philosophy of ministry. Harold Ockenga, at the 1948 Convocation Speech at Fuller Theological Seminary in Pasadena, California, introduced the label "the New Evangelicalism." He set forth three characteristics of Evangelicalism as it was evolving:

1. He noted that Fundamentalism had been wrong in separating from liberal denominations, for in so doing they had lost. He therefore urged men to remain in their denominations and look for areas of agreement and cooperation. Thus, the strategy was one of "infiltration" rather than "separation" in order to recapture denominational influence and leadership.

2. He called for a greater influence in society through greater social consciousness and involvement in apply the Gospel to the sociological, political and economic areas of life.

3. He called for more theological dialogue with liberal theologians.

In that speech at Fuller Theological Seminary, Ockenga also identified four major agencies dedicated to promote this New Evangelical approach:

- The National Association of Evangelicals
- Fuller Theological Seminary
- *Christianity Today* magazine
- The Billy Graham Evangelistic Association

Twenty-eight years later, Ockenga commented on the birth of Neo-evangelicalism when he wrote the Forward for *The Battle for the Bible* (a book written by *Christianity Today* Editor Harold Lindsell). Looking back, Ockenga wrote:

> Neo-evangelicalism was born in connection with a convocation address I gave in the Civic Auditorium in Pasadena, California. While reaffirming the theological view of fundamentalism, this address repudiated its

> ecclesiology and its social theory. The ringing call for repudiation of separatism and the summons to social involvement received a hearty response from many Evangelicals.
>
> Because no individual carried the banner for the New Evangelicalism and no one developed a theology or definitive position, many younger evangelicals joined the movement and claimed the name, but did not confess the doctrinal position of orthodoxy.[81]

Historic Evangelicalism, with its commitment to the orthodox Christian doctrinal position, found itself divided into two distinct expressions. These two expressions, Fundamentalism and Neo-evangelicalism, shared a common doctrinal and historical heritage. Both were born when liberalism succeeded in dividing the Church by questioning and denying significant points of historic orthodox theology. Their common enemy of liberalism helped the many divergent groups focus on the Fundamentals. But deep within the movement existed the seeds of division that flowered into the Fundamentalism/Neo-evangelicalism controversy.

There were three major events that promoted this division:

- **First: The formation of an alternative Church Council to the Federal Council** - the lack of ability to maintain denominational integrity and the overt influence of the Federal Council of Churches dominating organizational American Protestant religious life resulted in the formation of the American Council of Christian Churches.

- **Second: The formation of the National Association of Evangelicals** - the attempt at organizational structure which would commit men and churches to a common doctrinal statement and philosophy of ministry caused some to seek another expression of theological Fundamentalism. While reaffirming a common theological view, there was sharp difference over ecclesiology, social theory, and attitude that led to the formation of the N.A.E.

- **Third: The emergence of Billy Graham's ecumenical evangelism**

The Billy Graham Evangelistic Association

The New York Evangelistic Crusade in 1957 caused further division between Fundamentalists and Neo-Evangelicals when Graham refused the invitation of conservatives led by Jack Wyrtzen. Instead, Graham accepted the invitation of the liberal Protestant Council of New York City to conduct an evangelistic campaign. This blatantly illustrated the Neo-evangelical repudiation of separation and their commitment to find areas of agreement and cooperation with liberals. It also legitimized liberals as genuine Christians and contributed to the theological slippery slide that eventually brought Graham to an inclusive position where he affirmed Roman Catholics as genuine believers and stated that the heathen are not lost.

This view was first articulated by Graham in a January 1978 *McCall's* magazine interview where he stated "I used to believe that pagans in far countries were lost if they did not have the Gospel of Christ preached to them. I no longer believe that." A disclaimer was quickly included in the January 13, 1978 issue of *Christianity Today* in an article entitled "Graham's Beliefs: Still Intact."[82] However, perhaps the *Christianity Today* article was incorrect. In a television interview conducted by Robert Schuller on May 31, 1997, Graham was asked to comment on the future of Christianity. Graham answered by giving his belief about the final make-up of the Body of Christ. That body would be made up, he affirmed

> from all the Christian groups around the world and outside the Christian groups. I think that everybody that loves or knows Christ, whether they are conscious of it or not, they are members of the body of Christ. And I don't think that we are going to see a great sweeping revival that will turn the world to Christ at any time. I think James answered that - the Apostle James in the first Council in Jerusalem - when he said that God's purpose for this age is to call out a people for his name. And that is what he is doing today. He is calling people out of the world for his name, whether they come from the Muslim world, or the Buddhist world or the non-believing world, they are members of the body of Christ because they have been called by God. They may not know the name of Jesus but they know in their hearts that they need something they do not have, and they turn to the only light that they have, and I think that they are saved and they are going to be with us in heaven.[83]

The Ascendancy of Moral Relativism

The decades of the 1960s and 1970s brought further reason for widening the gap between Fundamentalists and Neo-evangelicals. The early Sixties saw the invasion of a distinct musical style and message that targeted the youth (this ultimately came to be exemplified by the Beatles). For the first time in American history, there was a music form that did not cross generational lines. It promoted distrust of anyone over thirty years of age and resulted in a lifestyle called first "Beatnik" and later identified as "Hippie." It was the consummate expression of the quest for freedom. It produced anti-social behavior, the rock culture, anti-war demonstrations, the Sexual Revolution and a general atmosphere of rebellion. It captivated college campuses and spawned radical revolutionary societies. Fundamentalists and Neo-evangelicals found themselves in a hostile society that ridiculed religion and everything traditionally moral. Moral relativism reigned.

The Fundamentalist Fortress Mentality

Fundamentalists, by and large, withdrew and developed a fortress mentality in response to the tumultuous 1960s. Emphasis was placed on personal separation from anything that would identify a believer with the worldly culture. Standards that were once a matter of personal choice became tests of spirituality and conditions of fellowship. Length of hair for men and length of skirts for women became indications of one's commitment to Christ. As the world's musical tastes began to invade the Church, music standards were strictly imposed and worship styles were carefully guarded. The emphasis on personal separation and the pursuit of personal holiness were legitimate concerns in the light of the deteriorating culture. But the tendency to extremes caused some to develop an attitude of superiority. They elevated a list of external standards to become the means of evaluating a person's heart. The problem was that the external standards were often determined by their culture rather than by the Word of God.

This expression of Fundamentalism became tainted with characteristics of legalism. Historic Fundamentalism had been based upon commitment to doctrinal purity. But because of its tendency to react, its future began to be controlled by the errors of others. They gave evidence of the axiom: "whatever you react against controls you." Fundamentalism reacted against the error of liberalism, then Neo-evangelicalism and then culturalism. In doing so, it did not determine its own future, but it became the product of its own reactions. The more they tried to control the situation, the less influence they had. Fundamentalism's tendency to control people's cultural expressions limited its ability to influence, minimizing its impact on American culture.

Following the Scopes Trial in 1925, Fundamentalists withdrew from society and constructed defenses against the world. They lost their opportunities to be salt and light by developing a sectarian isolationism. This fragmented the movement into small, reactionary (and often very ineffective) organizations and churches that were self-sufficient. The American Council of Christian Churches suffered internal personality conflicts that rendered it almost totally ineffective. Fellowships like IFCA International withdrew from the ACCC because of the overt effort to control where men could speak and with whom they could fellowship. Many Fundamentalist mission boards, Christian schools, denominations and fellowships struggled to maintain the status quo. Separation had become a doctrine in itself and took on a new dimension, extending its principles beyond doctrinal purity to include relationships with those with whom one disagreed. Second and third degree separation became tests of fellowship and obedience. Separatism began to implode upon itself until those who were once proud to be called separatists began to avoid the label because of the baggage it carried. Many succumbed to the intimidation of others, and conformity without inner conviction produced a pseudo-spirituality that was fraught with suspicion. As the old Quaker once said, "It's me and thee, Mary. And I'm not too sure about thee."

The Growth of the Charismatic Movement

The decades of the Sixties and Seventies saw a dramatic increase in the influence of Charismatic theology. Fundamentalism developed an issue-oriented response rather than one that was strictly doctrinally based. It fostered a critical attitude toward all whose conduct did not conform to the externalisms that became the plumb line of acceptability. This, coupled with the experience-based philosophy of Existentialism that was captivating America's educational system, provided the formula for the success of the newly popular Charismatic Movement. What had once been fringe Fundamentalism in the Pentecostal churches now became a haven for disenchanted, second-generation Fundamentalists and Neo-evangelicals.

The emphasis on freedom, contemporary secular music, emotional expressions and visual evidences of God's approval (like miraculous healings and speaking in tongues), caused many to gravitate to churches where one could see the "stuff" that Jesus did. Many Fundamentalists quickly opposed the Charismatic Movement with its excesses and expressions of libertarianism. But the National Association of Evangelicals had already opened its arms to the Pentecostals. They were included in 1942 when the N.A.E. was founded. And when the Charismatic Movement gained momentum, it was fully embraced without reservation. (It might be observed that the N.A.E. legitimatized the Charismatics in the 1940s, and the Charismatics dominated the N.A.E by the 1990s.) Fundamentalism's lost devotees became the Charismatic Movement's gain as the importance of doctrine was overshadowed by the Charismatic experiences.

Fundamentalism Redefined

Fundamentalism suffered another setback when it was coupled with radical Islam by CBS television news commentator Dan Rather. In searching for a word to identify radical Iranian Muslims during the hostage crisis that began in Tehran on November 4, 1979, Rather chose the word "*fundamentalism*" to describe Islam's radical, intolerant religious views. The label stuck and Fundamentalism entered another phase in its public perception.

Historic Fundamentalism was a proud, doctrinal word, finding its meaning in adherence to the fundamental doctrines of the faith. It was characterized by its doctrine. Contemporary Fundamentalism became a relativistic word describing relationships. It demanded that all who would be called by the name of Fundamentalist must not cooperate with any whose practices did not conform to its particular form of externalisms and must maintain a relationship with those who are separated from compromise in its many forms. It was characterized by its relationships. Popular Fundamentalism was defined by CBS commentator Dan Rather. He repeatedly used the word *fundamentalist* to identify the attitude of intolerance and bigotry among radical Christians and Muslims. It was characterized by its attitude.

Today many who would be proud to be called a Historic Fundamentalist avoid using the word altogether because it no longer communicates what they are. The general public hears the word *fundamentalist* and immediately thinks of an uneducated, reactionary, intolerant religious bigot. Although unfair, this is the perception with which all who call themselves Fundamentalists have to live. With this in mind, the Independent Fundamental Churches of America changed its name to IFCA International in 1996 in order to avoid the confusion caused by use of the word "Fundamental" in our secular society.

Neo-evangelicalism's Deterioration

Neo-evangelicals also faced cultural deterioration. Ockenga observed that since no standard doctrinal position had been developed, young Evangelicals joined the movement without commitment to orthodox beliefs.[83] This began to have practical implications since it enabled these young Evangelicals to accommodate their commitment to truth to contemporary cultural trends. And soon it was very difficult to distinguish their Christian culture from the world around them. When doctrinal conviction is compromised by practice, conviction is often abandoned and culture dictates belief. Richard Quebedaeux wrote a series of books called *The Young Evangelicals and the Worldly Evangelicals*. In them, he identified the impact contemporary culture had in formulating the practices and life-philosophy of the new generation of Neo-evangelical churchmen and their congregations.

Neo-evangelicalism as a contemporary movement had wandered far from its founders' original intent. It became an expression of extremism where the restraints of historical Christianity were foreign to its progeny. It had come full circle, and what was once an attempt to influence by infiltrating, had been captured to become humanistic liberalism.

The Emergence of Culturally-Driven Christianity

The 1980s and 1990s, spurred on by these developments, birthed a hybrid that enthralled disenchanted Fundamentalists and frustrated Neo-evangelicals. The abuses of radical Separatists and worldly Evangelicals attracted people to churches where standards were not emphasized but their felt needs were considered. In these churches, music and dress styles reflected the trends of the day and worship was dominated by singing and praise. These churches, like the Charismatic movement, tapped into the musical dynamic of the Rock culture so preferred by the Baby Boomer generation. The Christian music industry found its market niche among the younger generation and consequently exerted tremendous influence to integrate the contemporary sound into the church's music program. The Church Growth movement discovered people could be attracted to church if the programming provided them what they enjoyed. Just as politicians had learned to determine their political positions based upon what the polls indicated the public believes and wants, so many churches opted to employ the same methodology. Praise choruses replaced hymns and drama became the medium of communication. Preaching was marginalized. Praise teams took the place of choirs and performance (rather than ministry) characterized much of the special music. Form was elevated over substance. Taste dictated worship style and feeling dictated its substance.

In many cases man became the audience of worship rather than God.

Some Fundamentalists reacted to the contemporary cultural influence on worship and built carefully constructed walls around worship services in order to preserve their traditional worship styles. They refused to use worship teams, taped background music and hand held microphones. They avoided contemporary praise choruses and used only hymn books. Others were more responsive and were willing to make cultural adjustments in music and worship styles without sacrificing the primary place of preaching and worship dignity. Others took a very pragmatic approach and structured both traditional and contemporary services in order to give worshippers a choice.

In the midst of this cultural blitz in the Church, generational division was very evident. Music and dress became major issues in many churches and older people found themselves marginalized in the life of the church because of their reluctance to surrender the old hymns and their worship traditions. Churches that were historically Fundamentalist, found commitment to Fundamentalism questioned by those who believed traditional music and worship styles are part of fidelity to holiness of life. The schism was serious enough that some made music and worship style a relational test.

A New Attempt at Unity

In September 2001, a group of church leaders from many Christian denominations started to work together to create the most inclusive Christian group ever envisioned in the United States. They met:

> to listen and to seek the guidance of God on whether all who confess the Lord Jesus Christ as God and Savior according to the Scriptures can talk together about how to share with the world our common confession of Jesus Christ.[84]

This group ultimately called itself Christian Churches Together and scheduled another meeting in April 2002. Thirty-three church leaders met together in Chicago and produced the following statement:

> Christian Churches Together in the U.S.A. gathers together those churches and Christian communities which acknowledging God's revelation in Christ, confesses the Lord Jesus Christ as God and Savior according to the Scripture, and in obedience to God's will and in the power of the

> Holy Spirit commit themselves to seek a deepening of their communion with Christ and with one another; to fulfill their mission to proclaim the Gospel by common witness and service in the world for the glory of the one God, Father, Son and Holy Spirit. 85

Then forty-six individuals met in January 2003 representing Evangelical/Pentecostal, Historic Protestant, Orthodox, Racial/Ethnic and Roman Catholic communities.

> Present as participants were representatives from the American Baptist Churches, Brethren in Christ, Christian Reformed Church, Episcopal Church, Evangelical Lutheran Church in America, Greek Orthodox, Mennonite Church, Moravian Church, Presbyterian Church, Quakers, Roman Catholic Church, Salvation Army, United Church of Christ, United Methodist Church, and the Worldwide Church of God. The National Council of Churches (NCC) was represented. Notably absent was the National Evangelical Association (NEA). The Southern Baptist Convention was represented by an observer.[86]

Wesley Granburg-Michaelson, General Secretary of the Reformed Church in America acted as chairperson of the steering committee and made the following statement:

> CCT is the best chance that we will have in this decade to really change the ecumenical landscape and to create a body that more fully reflects the life of the churches in the United States. It could be a very powerful tool for the mission of the church.[87]

The Christian Churches Today association represents just one more attempt at ecumenical unity. It remains to be seen how influential they will become.

More Controversial Issues that Divide

There were many other issues that promoted exclusivism within the Body. One test of faith became the use of the King James Version of the Bible. Some Fundamentalists maintain that the text of the King James Version is the only true text of the Word of God and that all other translations are corrupted. Others hold that the King James Version is a beautiful and even preferred text, but contains archaic language and even some interpolations in the text. They hold that only the original text of the Scripture is inerrant. Others prefer the New King Version or the New American Standard Bible and feel that they are the most accurate. The New International Version is preferred by many of the younger generation. The Bible Version controversy is a serious breech in the Fundamentalist camp since the "King James Only" adherents find it necessary to limit relationships with all others, thus promoting factionalism within the body.

The various approaches toward education of children have also divided many churches. Some believers feel very strongly that parents who send their children to the Public School are violating a biblical mandate. Usually these parents choose a Christian school or opt for Home Schooling. Many other believers conclude it is their family's responsibility to serve the Lord by representing Him within the community through participation in public education (by being in the world but not of it). These various educational approaches have become the source of controversy within the body. A full discussion of this issue can be found in Appendix Five: *Educational Choice*.

Conclusion

Although this is a brief overview of the history, trends, events and assorted societal changes that have produced division within the Body, it is clear that many have attempted to do the right thing ... but often in the wrong way. Reaction rather than response many times became the rule of the day within Fundamentalism.

It is also evident that some believers lack an understanding of the various levels of biblically-mandated responsibility to relate to others within the Body of Christ. This failure has produced an atmosphere of suspicion, intimidation and judgmental criticism among the various expressions of the Body of Christ.

APPENDIX TWO

FACING HOMOSEXUALITY IN YOUR COMMUNITY

Reprinted from *VOICE* magazine (May/June, 1996)

The controversy took our community by surprise. No one expected it in our small, conservative community of Byron Center. Just five years ago, the first business opened on Sunday in this community of fifteen churches and twelve thousand people.

One of our public school teachers upon receiving tenure entered into a same-sex union. He had worn a "wedding ring" to school and informed the inquisitive students that he was homosexual. This assault on the moral foundation of our community encountered a confused populace. People could not believe that it had happened here.

I attended a ministerial meeting to discover what the local pastors planned to do. Some feared a public stand would "divide the community." Others wondered whether it was necessary to make it an issue, especially since some "research" suggested homosexuals are "born that way."

It was not that unclear to me. I shared with the pastors that Christians must stand upon the biblical instruction on the issue. If we fail in our calling to be the "*salt of the earth*," then how can morality be preserved? I noted that God's Spirit is clearly the restrainer of lawlessness, and that He often performs this through those He indwells (1 Thessalonians 2:5-7).

I found no pastor willing to accompany me in approaching the teacher. Instead, they asked that I represent them. I called and asked to meet with the teacher. He responded that he already knew what we believed (having attended a local Christian college) and was not interested in talking to me. I shared with him that I had called him out of compassion, for it was more loving to confront someone with the consequences of their sin than to allow them to "*fall into the hands of the living God*" (Hebrews 10:31), and "*knowing the fear of the Lord, we persuade men*" (2 Corinthians 5:11). I ended our conversation with the invitation that if he ever desired help to escape the bondage of his sin that he would remember that I cared enough about him to call him. My door would remain open to help him.

As a consequence of this call, I felt compelled to appeal to the School Board to hold the teacher accountable for his immoral conduct since they were the divinely instituted authority over the situation. Since the appeal was covered by the media, I was thrust into the forefront of the controversy by standing for biblical morality in the face of a culture that is steadily abdicating its loyalty to the biblical principles that made our nation great.

The homosexual community was outraged at our insistence on loyalty to the biblical precepts concerning the abomination of homosexuality. This began a campaign of harassment in the form of thirty to fifty phone calls per day, disruption of our Christmas Eve service by throwing skunk oil through the church door, receiving a package containing the neck and head of a partridge and a death threat splattered with blood. Thankfully, after several months of this, the FBI got involved and the press notified the public of what was happening. The harassment stopped!

The teacher has kept his job because of tenure laws. However, the School Board, presided over by a solid member of our church, courageously condemned homosexuality through this public statement: "The Board does not support or condone, in any manner, homosexuality as an alternative lifestyle. The board firmly believes that homosexuality violates the dominant moral standard of the district's community. Individuals who espouse homosexuality do not constitute proper role models as teachers for students in this district."

As it was read, several hundred homosexual supporters hissed at the School Board. It was chilling. The Board continues to investigate its legal alternatives as parents continue to earnestly pray for the teacher's deliverance from the bondage of his sin.*

Several questions surfaced during this controversy that helps the church understand how to face the issue of homosexuality in the community.

1. "*Doesn't the Bible say: 'Judge not or you will be judged'? Who are you to condemn, a homosexual?*" Jesus forbids the sinner from usurping His role as the judge of men. His point in Matthew 7:1 is that no sinner has the right to hold himself up as the standard by which other men must live. However, a judge both acquits and condemns. Hence, when a sinner condemns what God has not, he is judgmental. In addition, to acquit what God has condemned likewise usurps His role. To call a homosexual to repentance is to defer to the judgment of God and uphold the verdict of God on the matter.

2. "*What causes Christians to react to homosexuality when they do not to other sins? Is homosexuality a 'worse sin' than others*?" All sin is grievous in God's eyes. However, not all sin carries the same consequence and ramification as other sins. Homosexuality is such a serious problem according to Romans 1 in that it results from a defiance of the Creator. One does not naturally develop homosexual desires. In order to be homosexual, one must be characterized by the following:
   a. refusal to honor God as God (Romans 1:21);
   b. a darkened heart that believes it is accountable to no one (Romans 1:22-23);
   c. a removal of restraint through indulgence resulting in greater impurity and dishonoring of the body (Romans 1:24);
   d. being delivered over to degrading passions by God as a form of judgment, whereby both men and women abandon the natural function of sexuality and possess homosexual desire that results in "indecent acts" of sodomy (Romans 1:26-27).

   Hence, homosexuality is the ultimate defiance of God.

3. "*What about the studies that suggest that homosexuality is genetic, and that they are 'born that way*'?" Studies performed provide no credible evidence that there is a genetic cause. One that asserts such findings is considered flawed since it was conducted by "scientists" committed to the homosexual agenda. Such activist "research" conflicts with two other major authorities in the field. First, it conflicts with Scripture that declares homosexuality is within an individual's control and moral will and is an act of unrighteousness that bars people from the Kingdom of Heaven. However, it is also something from which sinners can be "*washed* ... *sanctified* ... [and] *justified in the name of the Lord Jesus Christ*" (1Corinthians 6:9-11). There is extensive clinical research that contradicts the claim that homosexuality is genetic (see "Setting the Record Straight" by Dr. Larry Burtoft, *A Focus on the Family Report*). Perhaps the greatest damage done by the activists "research" is that it maintains a stranglehold on practicing homosexuals who want to be delivered from the bondage. To declare that they were born to be homosexual removes all hope of being delivered.

4. "*Are you not being extremely homophobic and bigoted when you stand up*

against the homosexual agenda?" In Galatians 4:16, Paul asks; "*So have I become your enemy by telling you the truth*?" To "live and let live" is an ungodly response since it displays a lack of concern for the homosexual's well-being. To refuse to take a public stand for biblical morality through a "live and let live" approach is a self-centered attempt to avoid the discomfort of reaching out to the homosexual. Is that not more homophobic than approaching them out of a concern for their souls?

5. "*What is the biggest danger of taking a public stand for morality*?" The greatest danger is surrendering the luxury of speaking for yourself. I desired to be seen as caring about the homosexual and attempting to promote biblical morality in our community. The media, however, accused me of being anti-gay and intolerant. Through it all, it is more important to stand for biblical morality than against immorality. The world has little ability to tell the difference. Also, one must be prepared to encounter harassment from the homosexual community. However, "*God has not given us the spirit of timidity, but of power and love and discipline*" (2 Timothy 1:7).

6. "*Are you not attempting to legislate morality through your call for the preservation of moral restraint*?" It is true that you cannot legislate morality. It has never been the purpose of laws to make people moral, only to restrain immorality. Consider Romans 13:3-5. "*For rulers are not a cause of fear for good behavior, but for evil. Do you want to have no fear of authority? Do what is good and you will have praise from the same; for it is a minister of God to you for good. But if you do what is evil, be afraid; for it does not bear the sword for nothing; for it is a minister of God, an avenger who brings wrath on the one who practices evil.*" Hence, one purpose for legislation and authority is to restrain immorality. Genuine morality comes only through conformity to Jesus Christ, not through a legal system.

It is imperative that our efforts to restrain immorality do not divert us from the immediate responsibility to focus on the Gospel of Jesus Christ. Social activism is not the answer...intense prayer and unashamed declaration of the Gospel of peace are the keys to building a moral society. So help us God.

*** Postscript:**

The following summer, the homosexual teacher resigned his position from the school district. Four months later, he collapsed in a local bar and died. The local media publicized comments from the coroner suggesting that there was a congenital heart weakness that was aggravated by the stress caused by the Religious Right in Byron Center. This caused a resurgence of hostilities by the homosexual community. Ultimately, the ABC television News Magazine "20/20" did a story that contained a clear bias and some very creative editing.

Throughout the ordeal, the greatest blessing came from the contact that I received from the deceased teacher's parents. They would occasionally call to express their tremendous gratitude for the way in which I was attempting to get the message of God's grace to their son. They were thankful for the fact that there were people who were finally standing up and declaring the truth of God's Word to their son. After he died, they asked if it would be OK to come and visit our church and worship with our people. We welcomed them with open arms and were grateful for the fellowship that we were able to share in Christ.

APPENDIX THREE

WITHOUT HANDLES

Reprinted from *VOICE* magazine (May/June, 1999)

Several years ago, I was in a discussion with several local pastors concerning the process of nomination for spiritual leadership of their denominational churches. It was interesting to hear them state that their men "take their turns." As I listened, I was amazed at the lack of concern about the qualifications listed in the New Testament for both elders and deacons. I asked, "what about the requirements that Paul listed in 1 Timothy 3 and Titus 1?" They looked at me with amazement and disbelief and one man responded: "You've got to be kidding! Do you honestly believe that meeting those qualifications is possible? If we expected our board members to measure up to those standards, we wouldn't have any eligible men." Sadly, this attitude is beginning to prevail in evangelical churches as well as in the liberal denominational churches. There is a growing perspective that the biblical standards for leadership are nothing more than recommendations – not requirements.

There is an old proverb that states "a fish rots from the head first." The axiomatic reality is that the kind of leadership that exists at the head of the church will inevitably affect the spiritual quality of the Body. In clear support of this principle, the inspired author of Scripture states that "*it is necessary*" *(dei),* that elders and deacons be qualified according to the standards listed in 1 Timothy 3 and Titus 1. The New American Standard states that "*an overseer, then, must be above reproach* …" Thus, it is not merely recommended or suggested that men placed in spiritual leadership of the church "measure up" – it is required that they do so. Today, the attitude is often portrayed that to disqualify a man from service is to deny his legitimacy and will inevitably discourage him. Or, that a particular culture is so bad that it is impossible to find someone who can meet the qualifications. However, the welfare of the Body of Christ demands that we not mitigate or compromise our obedience to God's will for spiritual leadership. To lower the bar of fitness for spiritual leadership is to place the Body of Christ in the hands of men whom Scripture itself declares to be unqualified.

Once this issue is established, the objection of those resisting the application of Scriptural qualifications presses the point of the degree of qualification. I remember one of the pastors in that small group asking me with incredulity: "Do you believe that you perfectly measure up by possessing each of the qualifications listed by Paul?" I felt somewhat conflicted between an appearance of arrogance and an affirmation of fitness. The sentiment was "Can any of us say that we perfectly measure up, with no lapses in spiritual excellence?" Is any man always "temperate, prudent, respectable, hospitable … gentle, uncontentious, free from the love of money…"? This is the place where the debate concerning the qualifications of spiritual leadership focuses. How is this debate to be settled?

My response was that there are two primary qualifications – one I could honestly assess, the other I needed the help of both spiritual leadership and the church in general. First, the one that can be personally assessed deals with one's desire to serve. 1 Timothy 3:1 states: "*It is a trustworthy statement: if any man aspires to the office of overseer, it is a fine work he desires to do.*" Thus, in order to be spiritually qualified, one must have a desire to serve. No one can assess this but the individual being considered for spiritual leadership. A man who possesses no desire to serve as a spiritual leader in the church is not currently qualified to serve as a spiritual leader. Thus, a man who turns down a nomination ought not be coerced to change his mind through either manipulation or shame by existing spiritual leadership.

The second qualification deals with what others are able to observe about a man's life. The very next statement prevents a person's desire from being the primary qualification, since it is very possible that a man would desire the office, but not be spiritually fit to serve in that position. Paul states in 1 Timothy 3:2ff: "*An overseer, then, must be above reproach.*" This is the general description of a man who will serve as a spiritual leader. This is not a qualification that can be accurately assessed by a man by himself. It is the assessment of other spiritual leaders and by the church at large. The specific qualifications that God says each elder and deacon must possess are clearly catalogued and must be used to define what "*above reproach*" means.

A man who is to be placed in a position of spiritual leadership of the church must be "*blameless*" (KJV). The term "*above reproach*" deals with one's testimony and reputation before the public at large – not merely inside the church. The term addresses the issue of whether or not there are any accusations that can be legitimately hurled at a spiritual leader. In fact, the term itself can be understood as suggesting that there are "no handles" sticking out of a man's life that someone could grasp and use to accuse him of some spiritual deficiency (from *anepilemptos* - *a*, negative, *n*, euphonic, and *epilambano*, "to lay hold of"). Has a man's testimony been such that no one can step forward to denigrate the integrity of the Body of Christ by revealing some violation of spiritual integrity? It is not to suggest that spiritual leaders have to be "without sin," for clearly, no man would qualify. However, it is necessary that a man's life be free from any legitimate accusation that he is other than as described in the Scriptures.

It is as if Paul stated that if a man is going to be placed into leadership of the church, his testimony and reputation must be without any legitimate ability to bring a charge against him; he must not be open to any form of censure. He then explains what he means – no one should be able to step forward and state that, in their personal experiences and interaction, a man being placed into spiritual leadership is known for being dominated by involvement in violating his marital covenant ("*the husband of one wife*"), the lack of control of his temperament ("*temperate*"), unwise decisions ("*prudent*"), disorderliness ("*respectable*"), an unwillingness to extend himself for the sake of others ("*hospitable*"), inability to properly handle God's Word ("*apt to teach*"), a weakness for the use of intoxicants ("*not addicted to wine*"), defiant ("*pugnacious*"), harsh ("*gentle*"), argumentative ("*uncontentious*"), greedy ("*free from the love of money*"), lacking influence and respect in his home ("*one who manages his own household well*"), or newly converted ("*not a new convert*").

The biblical requirements for spiritual leaders do not describe a superhero of the Christian faith, as though being this kind of man is the fantasy of spiritual leaders. These are the rudimentary, basic, and minimal canons to be used in evaluating a man for spiritual leadership. He must at least possess these qualifications of being above reproach. Although no man is perfect, every man who serves in the office of overseer must possess a personal desire to serve, and must be "without handles" in the eyes of others. Let us obey God's Word and expect such leaders to be provided through the power of God's Spirit together with the efforts of spiritual leaders who will disciple younger men toward spiritual maturity.

APPENDIX FOUR

IFCA International 1994 Resolution on

EVANGELICALS & CATHOLICS TOGETHER: A CHRISTIAN MISSION FOR THE 3RD MILLENNIUM

Whereas, on March 29, 1994, an accord bearing the title: "Evangelicals and Catholics Together: The Christian Mission in the Third Millennium," was released by prominent Roman Catholic and Evangelical leaders declaring their "common convictions about Christian faith and mission" which they "believe may signal a [sic] historic realignment of Christian communities in the U.S. and elsewhere..; and,

Whereas, this accord "explains and celebrates a 'pattern of convergence and cooperation' between Evangelicals and Catholics in shared Christian faith, common cultural and social tasks, and evangelistic commitment;" and,

Whereas, this accord is based upon the common cause of social activism, not a genuine unity which is centered on truth as delineated in John 17:21-23; and,

Whereas, this accord teaches that "the cause of Christ" is all that really matters, thereby minimizing theological differences which are essentially irreconcilable, by stating that "we cannot understand completely the transcendent reality of God and his ways...In this search to understand the truth more fully and clearly, we need each other;" and,

Whereas, this accord calls for Evangelicals and Roman Catholics to stop aggressively "proselytizing or sheep stealing," claiming that such recruitment "undermine[s] the Christian mission" as defined in this agreement; and,

Whereas, historically, the Roman Catholic Church has vigorously opposed the biblical teaching of salvation by grace, plus nothing, and has consistently held with the Council of Trent (Sixth Session), as confirmed by the Second Vatican Council, that "no man can know with infallible assurance of faith that he has obtained the grace of God," and in the 1971 St. Peter's Catechism, taught that "to say one is saved and sure of heaven is a sin of presumption;" and,

Whereas, the March 1994 English edition of the Roman Catholic Catechism disparages the historic Reformation and IFCA position on biblical inerrancy and the intelligibility of Scripture by saying that "It invites people to a kind of intellectual suicide. It injects into life a false certitude;"

Be it therefore resolved, that the members and delegates present at the Sixty-fifth Annual National Convention of the Independent Fundamental Churches of America, meeting in Santa Rosa, California, June 23-28, 1994, plead with our brethren, who have signed this accord in an effort to help them see that this is a compromise of biblically authentic Christianity (1 Timothy 6:11-16; 2 Timothy 3:5, 14-17; 4:1-5, 7); and,

Be it therefore resolved, that we call upon IFCA churches and pastors to treat this agreement as one which promotes "another gospel" (Galatians 1:6-8), and to use this opportunity to teach the importance of doctrinal distinctives, the subtle dangers of compromise, and the need for vigorous evangelism of all the unsaved in the world; and,

Be it finally resolved, that a copy of this resolution be sent, with a letter of loving admonition from our National Executive Director to the following individuals whose signatures appear on this accord: Dr. Mark Noll, Wheaton College; Dr. James J. I. Packer, Regent College; Rev. Pat Robertson, Regent University; Dr. Bill Bright, Campus Crusade for Christ; Mr. Charles Colson, Prison Fellowship; Dr. Richard Land, Christian Life Commission of the Southern Baptist Convention; Dr. Larry Lewis, Home Mission Board of the Southern Baptist Convention; and Dr. Os Guinness, Trinity Forum.

APPENDIX FIVE

ONE CHURCH'S POSITION STATEMENT ON EDUCATIONAL CHOICE

Reprinted from *VOICE* magazine (May / June, 2003)

Introduction

The purpose of this position statement is to address the issue of God's individual leading in the families of our congregation with reference to what educational methodology they deem best for their children. We do not advance this statement as a comprehensive treatment of each position. The advantages and disadvantages of each choice exceed what can be addressed here. However, our purpose is to provide demonstration that each position has both advantages and disadvantages with reference to seeing God's purposes fulfilled in our children's lives.

Since children are a blessed stewardship with which parents have been entrusted by God, each set of parents has the individual responsibility before the Lord to fulfill their stewardship in the fear of God. Although God does not require uniformity among His people, He does command that we strive for unity in the midst of our diversities. Thus, regardless of the different choices that individual families make regarding education, there ought to be mutual respect and the diligent preservation of the unity of the Spirit in the bond of peace.

God can use different avenues to adequately prepare His people for their lives of service to Him. Throughout history, He has chosen to bless through a variety of educational methodologies to promote His purpose for individual servants. This statement looks at some of the benefits as well as dangers of each approach and provides a corresponding admonition from the elders as to biblically responsible parenting.

Christian Education

We recognize that there are some believers whose choice of overseeing their children's education will include utilizing the Christian school opportunities afforded by believers who have established evangelical Christian schools. It is the priority of many of these parents to cooperate with the biblical principle taught in Luke: "*A pupil is not above his teacher; but everyone, after he has been fully trained, will be like his teacher*" (Luke 6:40). These parents see the advantages of placing their children under teachers who share their values and convictions and who will promote biblical truth in each discipline being taught. Those who choose to educate their children by using Christian schools must recognize the critical need to be constantly engaged in mentoring their children spiritually. Without such parental mentoring, students in Christian schools can respond to the pressures to conform while failing to internalize the truths that ought to be transforming them. This can contribute to a heart that is hardened to truth. The Bible declares: "*Therefore everyone who hears these words of Mine and acts on them, may be compared to a wise man who built his house on the rock. And the rain fell, and the floods came, and the winds blew and slammed against that house; and yet it did not fall, for it had been founded on the rock. Everyone who hears these words of Mine and does not act on them, will be like a foolish man who built his house on the sand. The rain fell, and the floods came, and the winds blew and slammed against that house; and it fell—and great was its fall.*" (Matthew 7:24-27).

Thus, the elders of Byron Center Bible Church urge parents who feel directed by the Lord to delegate a portion of their children's academic training to the Christian schools to remain aggressive in providing spiritual leadership to their children. We call on them to remain attentive to the potential hardening of their children's hearts to the Holy Spirit by keeping Christ Jesus and His Word central in the home (Deuteronomy 6:4-9). Saul (who later became known as the apostle Paul) is an illustration of a biblical character in whom the value of this particular methodology is modeled. He was reared in the context of the rabbinical training afforded to the children of the Rabbis and Pharisees. God had a particular purpose for Paul to perform and prepared him for that purpose in the institutions of Israel (Acts 22:3).

Home Education

We recognize that there are some believers whose choice of overseeing their children's education will by conviction consolidate the process within their own homes. Many of these parents believe that the biblical principle that teaches that "*you shall teach them diligently to your sons and shall talk of them when you sit in your house and when you walk by the way and when you lie down and when you rise up*" (Deuteronomy 6:7) limits their freedom to outsource their children's education. Those who choose to home educate believe that the responsibility to train their children includes academics as they seek to *"bring them up in the discipline and instruction of the Lord."* (Ephesians 6:4b). However, they must recognize the critical need that exists to preserve a dependency upon the Holy Spirit to do the work of sanctifying their children. The danger of this choice is reliance upon protective care and the absence of peer dependency to insure the spiritual safety of their child. Because of the protection afforded by limiting the influences of peers and the lures of culture, some parents may relax their concerns for their children's spiritual well-being, believing the dangers to be external. However, as God's Word does declare: *"God has not given us a spirit of timidity, but of power and love and discipline"* (2 Timothy 1:7). As will be demonstrated during the Millennial Kingdom of Jesus Christ, even the most desirable settings will not produce genuine godliness.

Thus, the elders of Byron Center Bible Church urge parents who feel directed by the Lord to personally educate their children at home to remain sensitive to the dangers of developing an excess in withdrawing from others in order to protect a child from negative influences. Such excess can lead to a lack of passion in reaching the lost and thereby hinder the child's ability to ultimately fulfill God's purpose for their lives (Matthew 28:19).

Throughout most of the world's history, only the wealthy were able to gain a formal education while the average man gained whatever education was available through friends, parents and self-motivation. Until the modern era, home education was the most common means by which the majority of people were educated.

Public Education

We recognize that there are some believers whose choice of overseeing their children's education will include utilizing the public school opportunities afforded by local communities. It is the priority of many of these parents to cooperate with the biblical principle that their family serves the Lord by representing Him within the community through this educational method.

The Scriptures teach that it is the heart of Christ Jesus that we serve as salt and light; salt – in that we provide a means by which lawlessness is restrained and morality is preserved; and light - as a means by which the Gospel message is clearly seen in the contrasting lifestyles of believers among those who do not believe. Jesus stated in His prayer to the Father just prior to His crucifixion that His followers would be able to properly represent Him in the world – "*I do not ask You to take them out of the world, but to keep them from the evil one. They are not of the world, even as I am not of the world. Sanctify them in the truth; Your word is truth. As You sent Me into the world, I also have sent them into the world.*" (John 17:15-18). Those who choose to educate their children by using the public schools must recognize the critical need to be constantly engaged in mentoring their children spiritually (Deuteronomy 6:4-9).

The danger of this choice is for the child to be overwhelmed by a secular culture that is hostile to the holiness of God. The Bible declares: "*For those who are according to the flesh set their minds on the things of the flesh, but those who are according to the Spirit, the things of the Spirit. For the mind set on the flesh is death, but the mind set on the Spirit is life and peace*" (Romans 8:5-6).

Thus, the elders of Byron Center Bible Church urge parents who feel directed by the Lord to represent Him in the public schools to remain aggressive in providing spiritual leadership to their children, remaining attentive to the encroachments of the world in the worldview of their children, keeping Christ Jesus clearly central in the home. An illustration of a biblical character for whom the value of this particular methodology is demonstrated is Moses who was educated from his earliest days in the secular institutions of Egypt (Acts 7:22). God clearly had a specific purpose for Moses and therefore had him educated in a secular environment in order to prepare him for that purpose.

Conclusion

It is the position of the elders of Byron Center Bible Church that the heart of a child is not shaped primarily by his or her environment. The particular educational choice that is made is not the *deciding* influence in the preparedness of a child to serve the Lord. God can and does lead individual families to pursue any of these methodologies depending on His purposes for that family and the individual child. At times, He may even lead one family to utilize an assortment of these methods depending upon the individual needs of the children. The determining factor in all three methods is the attentiveness of the parent to the spiritual well-being of the children that focuses on the Gospel. Thus, the only genuine parental issue that is indispensable to successful parenting and education of a child is the integrity of the parent relying upon God to produce godliness in the lives of their child by pointing them to Jesus Christ. Any methodology that replaces one's dependency upon God to produce godliness in a child is not of faith and is therefore deficient, regardless of its technical merit. Scripture goes so far to say that "*whatever is not of faith is sin*" (Romans 14:23b). Therefore, if parents are truly relying upon the Lord and providing spiritual leadership to their children, God can and will bless. The Holy Spirit will do the work necessary to produce godliness in the lives of our children regardless of the specific educational methodology used.

Since this is the case, we believe it to be unacceptable for the leading of the Lord in individual families to be called into question by others. If a family feels led by the Lord to utilize Christian education, other families ought to respect God's leading. If a family is led to use home or public education, God's leading in their family should likewise be validated. No one method is a guaranteed success. In addition, no one method is a guaranteed failure. Division among believers that is based on educational choices is unacceptable and will be rebuked. We are to accept one another even as Romans 14:10 declares: "*But you, why do you judge your brother? Or you again, why do you regard your brother with contempt? For we will all stand before the judgment seat of God.*"

It is our prayer that the children in all of the families of Byron Center Bible Church will have the benefit of parents who, regardless of their educational choice, will seek to fulfill the admonitions of Deuteronomy 6:4-9 with faithfulness relying fully upon the grace of God as they point their children to the hope found solely in Jesus Christ.

APPENDIX SIX

CONTROVERSIAL MATTERS OF CONSCIENCE

The following is a list of controversial issues that may cause division within the Body. It is our prayer that the discussion of these matters will "*preserve the unity of the Spirit in the bond of peace*" (Ephesians 4:3).

Bible Translations

There are some who make a particular Bible translation a "litmus test" for fellowship. If a particular assembly does not use the correct translation, then it is deemed a compromising church. Some look upon the King James Version as the only version that is "inspired." Others look upon a King-James-Only church as cultish. Still others view the New International Version as nothing better than the "Nearly Inspired Version" and have little use for it. Some consider any congregation that fails to use the NIV is putting unnecessary obstacles in the way of people learning the truth. This is not to suggest that the issue of Bible translations is not important, or that a person ought not to have a clear understanding of what translation they believe is best. However, it ought not to become a litmus test for fellowship.

Style of Worship

There are some churches that consider the issue of the style of worship to be a moral absolute. To hold a microphone, use taped music, and use "sinful" instruments such as a guitar, drums, or saxophones is to compromise the sacredness of worship. Others determine that certain styles of music are wrong, particularly when based on cultural orientation (such as Hispanic, Caribbean, Indian, etc.). This is not to suggest that we ought to ignore the relevance of biblical standards with reference to sacred music in order to avoid bringing worldliness into the church. However, too often we close the door to fellowship due to preferences and conscience rather than objective truth. We say this with definitive positions on the issue of the propriety of sacred music within the Church, but it is our conclusion that it ought not be a litmus for fellowship.

Dress

Some believe a woman who wears pants is violating the principle that forbids a woman to wear men's clothing. Others believe that shorts are immoral. They hold that if a church fails to take a position on such things, it is compromising or liberal. Others believe that if men do not wear suits and ties to church, they are insulting God. Although, it is true that God looks not on the outward appearance, but on the heart, men cannot see the heart. The Scripture addresses modesty and "showy" apparel (1 Peter 3:3-4) and emphasizes dressing in a way that expresses the heart. Beyond those issues, clothing is largely an issue of preference.

Mixed Swimming

Some believe that because of the lusts of the flesh, men and women ought never to be in a position where they defraud one another in swimming suits. Others believe that to the pure, all things are pure and only those consumed with sexuality are worried about this. Others believe that because of homosexuality issues, it is never appropriate to swim with either gender because of a fear of stirring lusts.

Church Polity

Some believe the Bible teaches there is one elder in a church – the pastor, and that deacons exist to assist him in providing leadership in the church. Others believe in a plurality of elders, among whom the pastor is the principal teacher and the greater among equals. Some believe in a strict congregational form of government, and others believe in elder rule. This can bring such division that one man attending an elder rule church was denied graduation from a seminary that believed in the congregational form of government in the church.

Styles of Preaching

Some believe in a strict expositional methodology of preaching while others believe in the use of topical messages. While various methods can be used, all of which are expositional, division occurs in churches over which particular style is better. Would Jesus promote such division?

Entertainment Issues

Some believe that Christians are able to discern the wheat from the chaff and feel free to involve themselves in movies, music, and literature that depict the classic struggle between good and evil with good triumphing. Others believe that movies, music, and fictional reading distract a person from the ability to concentrate on things that are lovely, virtuous and of good report.

Financial Policy

Some believe there is a difference between a delinquent financial obligation and debt (money borrowed and repaid according to agreement). Others believe that to owe money in any form is disobedient to Scripture, which states that we should owe no man anything but to love one another (Romans 13:8).

Educational Methodology

Some believe there is only one way to educate their children – the way that they have chosen. Whether you home school, send children to a Christian school, or send them to a public school, there needs to be clear biblical reasoning for doing so. However, as believers adopt a view, they will commonly make judgments against whoever chooses a different method than they have. (See Appendix Five: *Educational Choice*.)

Dating vs. Courtship vs. Betrothal

There are those who believe dating causes a young person to "give away a portion of their heart" that they will never be able to give to their future spouse and therefore advocate stringent guidelines of courtship or even betrothal. Others believe that to allow dating provides opportunity to discover character qualities in people that will help develop what they can ultimately appreciate in their future spouse.

Inter-Generational Discipleship

Some believe that to provide departmentalized and age-oriented classes in a local church's Christian Education ministry fosters a peer dependency that frustrates family unity. Others believe teaching truth on the age-level of the student is a proper way of discipling people toward greater levels of maturity. Others believe that both are appropriate and can be used in the proper context.

APPENDIX SEVEN

IFCA International's Position Statement

SALVATION BY GRACE THROUGH FAITH

"We believe that salvation is the gift of God brought to man by grace and received by personal faith in the Lord Jesus Christ, whose precious blood was shed on Calvary for the forgiveness of our sins" (Ephesians 2:8-10; John 1:12; Ephesians 1:7; 1 Peter 1:18, 19). [Constitution of IFCA International, Article IV, Section 1, Paragraph 6]

I. The problem of faith that does not save

Some individuals profess faith in Christ but have failed to trust in the person and work of Christ alone. This kind of faith will show no evidence of spiritual life.

A person must be prepared to believe in Christ. He must be aware of his need of salvation as was the Philippian jailer (Acts 16:30). He must be conscious of his hopeless condition apart from God and the sinfulness that has caused this estrangement (Isaiah 64:6; Romans 3:10, 11, 18, 23; Ephesians 2:12). He must also have had presented to him information about the death of Christ and His resurrection and the sufficiency of Christ's sacrifice in dealing with his sin (1 Corinthians 15:1-4).

True salvation requires the work of God. An unsaved man, who is spiritually dead, must be enabled by the Spirit of God to believe. This involves the convicting work of the Spirit of God concerning sin and unbelief, God's righteousness which can be bestowed on the individual, and that Christ died for the sins of the world (John 16:7-11; 1 John 2:1,2). The unsaved person must receive grace and enablement from God to believe as stated in Ephesians 2:8-10, "*For by grace are ye saved through faith, and that not of yourselves, it is the gift of God.*" That is, that salvation is a work of God, not a human work, "*Not of works lest any man should boast.*" Such salvation is "*unto good works which God has before ordained that we should walk in them*" (Ephesians 2:10).

II. Definition of faith

Saving faith consists of two indispensable elements:

A. The intellectual, an awareness of the facts of the gospel, particularly about Christ's sacrificial death for sins and His physical resurrection, and a persuasion that these facts are true (1 Corinthians 15:3-8), and

B. The volitional, total, personal reliance upon Christ and the power inherent in His death to provide forgiveness of sins and everlasting life (John 3:16; 14:6; Acts 4:12; 16:31; Romans 1:16; 3:21-26). Thus, saving faith in Christ is an act of the person's mind and will.

The absence of either of these elements indicates that the seeker's faith is not of a quality that leads to salvation. The intellectual apprehension of orthodox doctrine alone will avail nothing (James 2:19). A volitional act of faith in the wrong object (e.g., John 2:23-24; 6:26-27; 8:31, 44) is useless. To save, faith must be directed toward the person and work of the Lord Jesus Christ (Romans 3:22).

Some suitable expressions equivalent to the reliance on Christ that brings salvation include "believe in," "trust in," and "depend on." Other terminology that may be misleading in representing this relationship include "submit to," "yield to," "dedicate [oneself] to," and "make Jesus Lord of one's life." These are better reserved for a stage of sanctification that usually comes subsequent to saving faith. Two additional phrases, "make a commitment to" and "become a disciple of," are ambiguous because they could or could not refer to reliance on Christ, depending on how they are defined. "Repent" is not a suitable way to describe saving faith, because it only partially represents what it is to rely on Christ alone.

III. Responsibility of faith

The exercise of saving faith is the responsibility of the sinner in need of salvation. For the one coming to Christ, saving faith (a) is uncomplicated (Acts 16:31). He decides to put his eternal well being into the hands of Christ as his Savior. Subsequent to regeneration, he has a growing awareness of the far-reaching effects of what he has done, but this fuller grasp of the implications of saving faith is not a condition for salvation. (b) Rests squarely on his shoulders. The responsibility for the choice is wholly his. At the time of or subsequent to regeneration, he realizes that the totality of the salvation process is a gift of God, including the grace of

God and his own choice to believe (Ephesians 2:8-9). It is something for which he himself can take no credit.

IV. Implications of faith

Faith that is saving faith carries with it certain implications, that is, characteristics of which the one coming to Christ may or may not be conscious at the point of initial trust in Christ. The one under conviction is persuaded that the finished work of Christ is sufficient and that nothing else is needed. At the time of his decision, he may be so overwhelmed with his dependence on Christ that the implications of such dependence are not his primary focus of attention. The absence of the following implications may indicate that his dependence is not on Christ alone:

A. Christ is God and consequently sovereign Lord over all things and as such is the object of saving faith (Acts 16:31; Romans 10:9; Hebrews 1:8). Few people at the moment of salvation understand fully the implications of Christ's sovereignty for their own lives well enough to comply with the exhortation of Romans 12:1-2.

B. Obedience to the command of the gospel to believe in Christ (Romans 1:5; 10:16) is another way of looking at saving faith, but beyond that initial obedience is implied an absence of rebellion against what Christ stands for (John 3:36). One can hardly place his full trust in Christ while harboring enmity against Him or having a predisposition to oppose Him.

C. Repentance is a change of mind toward sin, self, and the Savior (Acts 2:38; 17:30; 1 Thessalonians 1:9). A person can hardly seek forgiveness for something toward which he has no aversion (Acts 2:36; 11:18; 20:21; 26:20; 1 Peter 2:24).

V. Results of faith

Good Works

At the time of saving faith, a believer is regenerated by the Spirit (cp. Titus 3:5), indwelt by the Spirit (1 Corinthians 6:19), sealed by the Spirit (Ephesians 4:30), and baptized by the Spirit (1 Corinthians 12:13). Always associated with saving faith is the impartation to the believer of a new nature (Romans 6:5-7; Galatians 2:20; Colossians 3:9-10) which displays its presence through good works (1 Corinthians 4:5; James 2:18, 21-26). Good works may not always be immediately discernible by man, but are an inevitable consequence of the new birth which occurs in conjunction with saving faith (John 3:3, 5; Ephesians 2:10; Titus 2:11-12, 14; 3:8; 1 Peter 1:3, 23). Salvation is in no way contingent on good works.

Faith in Christ which does not result in "good works" (Ephesians 2:9-10) is not saving faith, but is dead faith (James 2:17, 20, 26). The missing element in such faith may be intellectual, a failure to grasp or accept the truthfulness of the facts of the gospel, or it may be volitional, a failure to trust Christ wholly for forgiveness of sins. Failure to trust Christ completely may be traceable to attempts to accumulate merit through the performance of human works by attempting to add to the finished work of Christ (Romans 4:5; 2 Corinthians 13:5; Galatians 2:16; 2 Timothy 1:9).

Sanctification

Sanctification in the experience of the believer is the logical continuation of saving faith, namely:

1. The believer is expected to submit to the lordship of Christ over all things in his life (Romans 6:11-13; 12:1-2).

2. The implied obedience to Christ is expected to become an active obedience to Christ's explicit commands (James 4:7-10; 1 John 2:3-10).

3. The implied repentance is expected to become explicit, resulting in a purging of sinful behavior (1 Corinthians 5:7; 6:9-10, 18; 1 Thessalonians 4:1-8; 1 Peter 4:15-16).

The lack of such progress in sanctification is characteristic of a carnal Christian (1 Corinthians 3:1-4). God may tolerate this lack of response to the regenerating work of the Holy Spirit for a time, but will eventually bring chastening against the delinquent saved person. Such delinquency without correction may serve notice that the person's profession was not saving faith (1Corinthians 11:30-32, Titus 1:15-16; Hebrews 12:5-11).

A biblical method of confronting a Christian with his carnality and a pretending Christian with the insufficiency of his faith is through presenting the fact that God judges sin (Matthew 16:24-28; 1 John 3:6, 9; 5:18).

The carnal Christian is faced with the illogical nature of his behavior and forced to reevaluate his spiritual standing, and the pretending Christian is faced with the realization that he was never saved.

Assurance of eternal life is provided by God's written Word (1 John 5:13). Yet, the Scripture brings reminders and tests to cause those who have professed faith in Christ to examine themselves (1 Corinthians 11:28; 15:2; 2 Corinthians 13:5; 2 Peter 1:10). When carnality creeps into the life of a believer, causing him to fail the test of self-examination, he may entertain doubts about whether he has met the biblical criteria of saving faith. The solution for such doubt is for the believer to confess the sin which has broken his fellowship with God (1 John 1:5-10).

The Constitution of the Independent Fundamental Churches of America (Article IV, Section 1, Paragraph 7) states:

> We believe that all the redeemed, once saved, are kept by God's power and are thus secure in Christ forever (cp. John 6:37-40; 10:27-30; Romans 8:1, 38, 39; 1 Corinthians 1:4-8; 1 Peter 1:5).

We believe that it is the privilege of believers to rejoice in the assurance of their salvation through the testimony of God's Word; which, however, clearly forbids the use of Christian liberty as an occasion to the flesh (Romans 13:13, 14; Galatians 5:13; Titus 2:11-15).

IFCA Study Committee on Saving Faith:
Dr. George Harton, Capital Bible Seminary
Dr. Robert Lightner, Dallas Theological Seminary
Dr. Leslie Madison, Calvary Bible College
Dr. Robert Thomas, The Master's Seminary
Dr. John Walvoord, Dallas Theological Seminary
Dr. Lowell Wendt, past president, IFCA International

August 21, 1990
Cicero, Illinois

Adopted by the IFCA Executive Committee, November, 1990

GLOSSARY

Arminianism – This refers to the theological position articulated by Jacobus Arminius (1560-1609). It teaches that God's (conditional) predestination of the destiny of individuals is based on His foreknowledge of the fact that they will freely accept or reject Christ. Another basic tenet of this position is that believers may lose their salvation and be eternally lost if they fail to remain faithful to the Lord.

Calvinism – This refers to the theological position regarding soteriology, articulated by John Calvin (1509-1564), that can be summarized by the acrostic TULIP: Total Depravity, Unconditional Election, Limited Atonement, Irresistible Grace, and the Perseverance of the Saints.

Dominion Theology (Theonomy/Reconstructionism) – This identifies the belief that the laws of God revealed in the Old Testament represent the keys to a godly society. Thus, it is asserted that civil governments of the world need to be brought back under these laws and observe them in order to know God's blessing once again. The harsh theocracy of Geneva, Switzerland under the leadership of John Calvin is the model for Reconstructionists.

ECT (Evangelicals & Catholics Together) Accord – The designation of a document, spearheaded by Evangelical Charles Colson and Roman Catholic Richard John Neuhaus to find common ground. The implicit assumption in the document is that the Evangelical and Roman Catholic churches teach and proclaim the same Gospel. They assumed that the differences that separate them, while not unimportant, are of secondary importance in view of the fundamentals of the Gospel that they both supposedly affirm and embrace.

Ecumenism – A movement which seeks the organizational unity of all Christianity and ultimately of all religions. Its principal advocates are the World Council of Churches and the National Council of the Churches of Christ in the United States.

Evangelical – Historically this refers to the movement in modern Christianity that maintains a commitment to the fundamentals of the faith, the importance of evangelistic outreach and missionary zeal, without regard for denominational labels. Later, the term became much diluted through the movement historically known as Neo-Evangelicalism and its other aberrations.

EFMA (Evangelical Fellowship of Mission Agencies) – Identifies an organization founded in 1947 as a voluntary association of mission agencies committed to discipling the nations. It is composed of approximately 100 member agencies, representing more than 20,000 North American cross-cultural workers worldwide and is associated with the National Association of Evangelicals (NAE). The EFMA has historically differed from the IFMA (see separate entry) in that the EFMA included mission agencies from denominations and its doctrinal requirements were not as restrictive.

FOM (Fellowship of Missions) – An organization founded in 1969 as a voluntary association of 29 independent member agencies providing a biblical ministry outreach for Fundamental, Premillennial churches in North America. Membership is open to all fiscally responsible agencies who are committed to the biblical principles of personal and ecclesiastical separation (missions which do not engage in cooperative efforts with theological liberals, cults, Roman Catholics, or charismatics - nor with those who do).

Fundamentalism (Contemporary) – The designation of a movement within Fundamentalism, this is a relativistic term describing relationships. It demanded that all who would be called by the name Fundamentalist must not cooperate with any whose practices did not conform to their particular form of externalisms and must maintain a relationship with those who are separated from compromise in its many forms. It was characterized by its relationships.

Fundamentalism (Historic) – This term refers to the movement that began in the early Twentieth Century in the Presbyterian Church. It reaffirmed doctrinal orthodoxy and sought to defend it against the assailing fallacies of Modernism. Fundamentalism recognized five doctrines that had to be embraced in order for a person to be identified as a believer: inerrancy of the original manuscripts of Scripture, the Virgin Birth of Christ, the vicarious atonement of Christ, Christ's bodily resurrection, and the reality of miracles as recorded in Scripture. Fundamentalists practiced biblical separation for the purpose of maintaining the Fundamentals of the Faith. Its name derived from the twelve volume set of books entitled The Fundamentals published 1910-1915. It was characterized by its doctrine.

Fundamentalism (Popular) – This refers to a radical attitude among some Fundamentalists known for their intolerance and bigotry. It was characterized by its attitude.

GARBC (General Association of Regular Baptist Churches) - This term identifies an international network of independent Baptist churches of common Fundamentalist convictions that voluntarily partner for fellowship, witness, and ministry. It was founded in 1932 and is headquartered in Schaumburg, Illinois outside of Chicago.

Higher Criticism – The process of evaluating Scripture as literature, including the reliability of its sources. Because of the perspective of liberals, theological presuppositions caused the development of various hypotheses and theories which discounted the inspiration, inerrancy, and integrity of Scripture. An example is the "JEDP/Documentary Hypothesis."

JEDP/Documentary Hypothesis – An example of liberal Higher Criticism that approaches the first five books of the Bible as an evolutionary compilation by a late-date editor who synthesized four principle source documents called the Jehovistic, Elohistic, Deuteronomic, and Priestly documents. It denies Mosaic authorship and divine inspiration. This approach is often referred to as the Developmental Hypothesis.

ICCC (International Council of Christian Churches) – This is the militant Fundamentalist counterpart to the World Council of Churches. The ICCC organized in various regions of the world and set up Councils of Christian Churches (such as the American Council of Christian Churches). In all their meetings, the dominant issues were Modernism, unbelief, and ecumenism versus the inerrancy and full truthfulness of the Bible.

IFCA International – An international fellowship of Bible believing, independent, historically Fundamental churches, organizations and individuals. It serves as a source of interdependent, cooperative efforts in proclaiming the

Gospel of Christ and in the teaching of believers. It was founded in Cicero, Illinois in 1930 as the Independent Fundamental Churches of America and is now headquartered in Grandville, Michigan outside of Grand Rapids.

IFMA (Interdenominational Foreign Missions Association) – An organization founded in 1917 as a voluntary association of mission agencies designed to establish standards of accountability and integrity, to foster networking and strategic alliances for world missions, and to maintain a unified testimony and establish a united voice in mutual commitment to the Word of God and global evangelization. The IFMA has historically differed from the EFMA (see separate entry) in that the IFMA has not included mission agencies from denominations and its doctrinal requirements were more restrictive.

Modernism (Liberalism) – A movement of severe theological deviation from orthodox Christianity originating with German Rationalists who rejected the inerrancy of Scripture in favor of Developmental/Higher Critical Theories. This movement sought to synthesize major cultural epistemologies with Christian theology and denied all that was supernatural in Christianity.

NAE (National Association of Evangelicals) – An inclusive fellowship of member denominations, churches, organizations, and individuals, which attempts to demonstrate the unity of the body of Christ by standing for biblical truth, speaking with a representative voice, and serving the Evangelical community. It maintains as a core value, the idea of a growing biblical faith – that is, that prior to reaching heaven, because of our human frailty, we will not know for sure what is the unitary truth which is of God. Despite doctrinal differences, they include denominations that are Calvinist, Arminian, Wesleyan, Anabaptist and Charismatic.

NCC (National Council of Churches) – Identifies an organization founded in 1950, which replaced the Federal Council of Churches. It is the leading force for ecumenical cooperation among Christians in the United States. The NCC's 36 Protestant, Anglican, Orthodox, historic African American and Living Peace member faith groups include 45 million persons in more than 100,000 local congregations in communities across the nation.

Neo-Evangelical - This term refers to that movement within Evangelicalism characterized by a tolerance of and a dialogue with theological liberalism.

Its name was coined by Harold Ockenga in 1948. Its essence is seen in an emphasis upon the social application of the gospel and weak or unclear doctrines of: the inspiration of Scripture, biblical creationism, eschatology, dispensationalism, and separation. It is further characterized by an attempt to adapt biblical Christianity to make it acceptable to the modern mind.

New Perspective on Paul – This refers to a modern attempt first advocated by James D. G. Dunn (together with E. P. Sanders and N.T. Wright) to redefine the basic teachings of the Apostle Paul. This effort holds that traditional Christianity was overly influenced by the Sixteenth Century Reformation and has seriously distorted what the Apostle Paul taught about justification by faith. According to the New Perspective, when Paul wrote about justification, his concerns were corporate, national, racial, and social—not individual and soteriological. Thus, the issues of justification by faith and sole fide are seriously undermined by the minimizing individual sin.

Openness of God (Open Theism) – The theological position that redefines human free will, its relationship to God and the nature of the future. It asserts that God has granted free will to humanity and that in order for the free will to be truly free, the future choices of individuals cannot be known ahead of time by God. Thus, God's omniscience is limited to reality and He does not foreordain what is to be.

Scopes Trial – A trial in Dayton, Tennessee in the summer of 1925, at which a jury was asked to decide the fate of John Scopes, a high school biology teacher charged with illegally teaching the theory of evolution. The issue of John Scopes' guilt or innocence seemed to be diminished when the dominant issue became Secular Modernism versus Biblical Fundamentalism. Thus, the significance of the trial was that it became an interpretation of the national conflict between social, intellectual, and Biblical values.

Social Gospel – This refers to liberalism's attempt to deliver the underprivileged from their bondage to poverty through the application of biblical principles. It ignores the problem of the sinfulness of man and places the focus on economic and social need.

Syncretism – This term refers to the age-old attempt to combine or unite divergent religions so as to provide a basis for relationship. This was a persistent sin throughout the Old Testament as Israel was pressured to adopt the ways of the idolatrous nations around them. It was constantly denounced by the prophets of God throughout Old Testament history (Deuteronomy 12:30-31).

WCC (World Council of Churches) – This identifies the broadest and most inclusive among the many organized expressions of the modern ecumenical movement. It is a movement whose goal is Christian unity. The WCC brings together more than 340 churches, denominations and church fellowships in over 100 countries and territories throughout the world. They represent some 400 million Christians, including most of the world's Orthodox churches, scores of denominations from such historic traditions of the Protestant Reformation (such as Anglican, Baptist, Lutheran, Methodist and Reformed) as well as many independent churches. While the bulk of the WCC's founding churches were European and North American, today most are in Africa, Asia, the Caribbean, Latin America, the Middle East and the Pacific.

Young Evangelical – This term refers to the second generation of Neo-Evangelicals who joined the movement without a firm commitment to doctrinal orthodoxy and have subjected truth to contemporary cultural trends.

END NOTES

INTRODUCTION

1. Ernest Pickering, *Biblical Separation: The Struggle for a Pure Church* (Schaumburg, IL: Regular Baptist Press, 1979), 173.

2. Harold Lindsell, *The Battle for the Bible* (Grand Rapids, MI: Zondervan Corporation, 1976), 11.

3. John R. Edwards, "Unity Not of Our Making," *Christianity Today* (6 August 2001): 50.

4. R. C. Sproul, *Getting the Gospel Right* (Grand Rapids, MI: Baker Book, 1999), 24-25.

5. Philip Schaff, *History of the Christian Church*, 2nd ed. (Grand Rapids: Wm. B. Eerdman's, 1980), 7: 656.

6.Ibid. p. 650

CHAPTER ONE

7. See similar discussion in *Beware of the Pretenders* by MacArthur, pp. 40ff.

8. John MacArthur, *The MacArthur Study Bible* (Nashville, TN: Word Publications, 1997), 1418. Matthew 13:25

9. Fr. Francis Ripley, *Saint Peter's Catechism of Catholic Doctrine* (Bootle, Lancashire: Orell, 1972), paragraph 362, p. 33.

10. D. Martyn Lloyd-Jones, *The Puritans: Their Origins and Successors* (Edinburgh: Banner of Truth, 1987), 69.

11. Gervace Duffield, "Involvement," in *Evangelicals Today: Thirteen Stock-Taking Essays*, ed. John C. King (Guildford: Lutterworth Press, 1973), 163.

12. Kenneth Wuest, "Agapao Love," *Golden Nuggets, Wuest Word Studies* (Grand Rapids, MI: Wm. B. Eerdman's, 1980), 3:61.

13. J.P.Louw, *Greek-English Lexicon of the New Testament: Based on Semantic Domains*. (New York: United Bible Societies, 1996), 34.1.

14. Joe Maxwell, "Evangelicals Clarify Accord With Catholics," *Christianity Today* (6 March 1995): 53.

CHAPTER TWO

15. Ibid.

16. *Calvary Contender*, http://home.hiwaay.net/~contendr/5- 1-95.html\ Accessed on 24 January 2005.

17. *Encyclopedia Britannica*, 1985 ed.,19:288.

18. Ibid., 340.

19. See Appendix Two, "Facing Homosexuality in Your Community," *VOICE*, May/June 1996.

20. W.F. Arndt and F.W. Gingrich, *A Greek-English Lexicon of the New Testament and Other Early Christian Literature* (Chicago: University of Chicago Press, 1979), 62.

21. *Pantagraphy*, (September 20, 1970).

22. On May 21, 2003 Rep. Marilyn Musgrave, R-Colorado and five co-sponsors introduced H.J. Resolution 56 (Federal Marriage Amendment). A companion bill, S.J. Resolution 26 was introduced by Sen. Wayne Allard, R-Colorado on November 25, 2003.

CHAPTER THREE

23. C.F Hogg and W.E. Vine, *The Epistle to the Thessalonians*, (Fincastle, VA: Scripture Truth Book Company, 1959), 54.

24. Loraine Boettner, "Arianism," *Baker's Dictionary of Theology* (Grand Rapids, MI: Baker Book House, 1960), 63-64.

25. David Brought Knox, "Pelagianism," *Baker's Dictionary of Theology* (Grand Rapids, MI: Baker Book House, 1960), 399-400.

26. Ian H. Murray, *Evangelicalism Divided* (Carlisle, PA: Banner of Truth Trust, 2000), 35.

27. Ibid., 73-74. Murray's citation is from a television interview with Billy Graham by Robert Schuller on May 31, 1997

28. James D. Hunter, *Evangelicalism: The Coming Generation* (Chicago: The University of Chicago Press, 1987), 178.

29. Interdenominational Foreign Missions Association, *Historical Background*, http://wheaton.edu/bgc/archives/Guides/352.htm#3. Accessed 6 January 2006.

30. Ibid, paragraph 5.

31. Ibid.

32. Fellowship of Missions, http://www.fellowshipofmissions.org/history.html#1 Accessed on January 24, 2005.

33. Charles C. Ryrie, *What You Should Know About Social Responsibility* (Chicago: Moody Press, 1982), 14.

34. Ibid.

35. Kenneth Blanchard and Spencer Johnson, *The One Minute Manager*

(New York, William Marrow & Company, Inc., 1982), 40.

36. Warren Weirsbe, *The Integrity Crisis* (Nashville, TN: Oliver-Nelson Books, 1991), 117-118.

37. *Our Vision for the 21st Century* (Grandville MI: IFCA Press, 1996), 1.

CHAPTER FOUR

38. Robert Saucy, *The Church in God's Program* (Chicago: Moody Press, 1972), 11.

39. Charles Hodge, *1 & 2 Corinthians* (Carlisle, PA: Banner of Truth Trust, 1978), 652.

40. See Appendix Two, "Facing Homosexuality in Your Community," *VOICE*, May/June 1996.

41. *Constitution and By Laws of IFCA International* (Grandville, MI: IFCA Press, 2004), 3.

42. F.L Godet, *The Epistle to the Corinthians* (Grand Rapids, MI: Zondervan Publishing House, 1957), 64.

43. Snyder, James L., *A.W. Tozer On Worship and Entertainment* (Camp Hill, PA: Christian Publications, Inc., 1997), 14.

44. Ibid.,117.

45. Ron Owens, *Return to Worship*, (Nashville, Broadman and Holman, 1999), 198.

46. *Salvation by Grace Through Faith* (Grandville, MI, IFCA Study Committee on Saving Faith, IFCA Press, 1990).

47. Andy Crouch, "The Emerging Mystique," *Christianity Today* (November 2004): 38.

48. See Appendix Three, "Without Handles," *VOICE*, June 1999.

CHAPTER FIVE

49. "The Christian Divorce Culture," *Christianity Today* (4 September 2000): 47.

50. Ibid.

51. Shannon Derrick and Page Wise, *Divorce, How it Effects a Child*, [on line]; available from http://nh.essortment.com/divorcehoweffe_rhcq.htm; Internet; Accessed on 27 January 2005.

52. Barbara Dafoe Whitehead, "The Divorce Culture," *Christianity Today* (4 September 4 2000), 47.

53. Susan Orr, "Real Women Stay Married," *Washington Watch* (June, 2000).

54. Crown Ministries, "Single Parent Needs" [on line]; available from http://www.crown.org/singleparents/statistics.asp#Parent; internet; accessed 18 November 2004.

55. Keep Kids Healthy [on line]; available from http://www.keepkidshealthy.com/welcome/commonproblems/child_abuse.html; internet; accessed 18 November 2004.

56. David Semands, "CT Classic: A Marriage Counterculture," *Christianity Today* (28 August 2000).

CHAPTER SIX

57. Wiersbe, W. W., *Be What You Are: 12 Intriguing Pictures of the Christian from the New Testament* (Wheaton IL: Tyndale House, 1996), 67.

58. Ibid., 57.

59. Westminster Shorter Catechism [on line]; available from www.reformed.org/documents/index.html; internet; accessed 30 March 2005.

60. Wiersbe, op. cit., 71.

61. Medical Source [on line]; available from www.mymed.com/content/24/1836_50591.htm?lastselectedguid={5FE84E90-BC77-4056-A91C-9531713CA348}; internet; accessed 9 November 2004.

62. Ron Owens, *Return to Worship* (Nashville: Broadman and Holman, 1999), 39-40.

63. James L. Snyder, *A.W. Tozer onWorship and Entertainment* (Camp Hill, PA: Christian Publications, Inc., 1997) 14.

CHAPTER SEVEN

64. John H. Gerstner, "Good Works," in *Baker's Dictionary of Theology*, ed. Everett F. Harrison (Grand Rapids: Baker Book House, 1976), 253.

APPENDIX 1

65. Schaff, *History of the Christian Church*, 1:20.

66. Francis Schaeffer, *The Great Evangelical Disaster* (Westchester, IL: Crossway Books, 1984), 30.

67. Dennis McCallum, *The Death of Truth* (Minneapolis, MN: Bethany House Publishers, 1996), 12.

68. Schaeffer, *The Great Evangelical Disaster*, 35.

69. Ibid., 33.

70. David B. Calhoun, *Princeton Seminary, The Majestic Testimony* (Carlisle, PA: Banner of Truth Trust, 1999), 2:86.

71. Ibid., 244.

72. Dr. Allan MacRae, *Lectures on the Pentateuch* (Elkins Park, PA: Faith Seminary, 1960).

73. David O. Beale, *In Pursuit of Purity* (Greenville, SC: Unusual Publications, 1986), 41.

74. "The Practical Aims of a Liberal Evangelicalism," *The New York Times*, 19 May 1915, p. 8.

75. Auburn Affirmation of 1924 (Auburn, NY: The Jacobs Press, 1924), the full text available from www.covenantnetwork.org/aubaff.html. Accessed 30 March 2005.

76. J. Gresham Machen, *Christianity and Liberalism* (Grand Rapids, MI: Wm. B. Eerdmans, 1923), 2, 6-7.

77. Schaeffer, *The Great Evangelical Disaster*, 34.

78. Ibid., 37.

79. Arthur Steel, *Modern Religious Problems Lectures*, (Elkins Park, PA: Faith Seminary, 1961).

80. *A Brief History of The NAE*, available from http://www.nae.net. Accessed 20 September 2004.

81. Harold Lindsell, *The Battle for the Bible* (Grand Rapids, MI: Zondervan Corporation, 1976), Forward.

82. Iain H. Murray, *Evangelicalism Divided* (Carlisle, PA: Banner of Truth Trust, 2000), 73-74.

83. Ibid.

84. Christian Churches Together in the U.S.A., www.religioustolorance.org/chrcct.html. Accessed 24 January2005.

85. Ibid.

86. Ibid.

87. Ibid.

BIBLIOGRAPHY

Allen, Ronald and Gordon Borror. *Worship: Rediscovering the Missing Jewel.* Portland, OR: Multnomah Press, 1982.

Arndt, W.F. and F.W. Gingrich. *A Greek-English Lexicon of the New Testament and Other Early Christian Literature.* Chicago: University of Chicago Press, 1996.

Beale, David O. *In Pursuit of Purity.* Greenville, SC: Unusual Publications, 1986.

Blanchard, Kenneth and Spencer Johnson. *The One Minute Manager.* New York: William Marrow & Company, Inc., 1982.

Boettner, Loraine. "Arianism," *Baker's Dictionary of Theology.* Grand Rapids, MI: Baker Book House, 1960.

Calhoun, David B. *Princeton Seminary, The Majestic Testimony*, volume 2. Carlisle, PA: Banner of Truth Trust, 1999.

Carpenter, Joel A. *Revive Us Again. The Reawakening of American Fundamentalism.* New York: Oxford University Press, 1997.

Christian Churches Together in the U.S.A. Available from http://www.religioustolorance.org/chrcct.html. Accessed 30 March 2005.

Crouch, Andy. "The Emerging Mystique." *Christianity Today* 48, no. 11 (November, 2004): 36-41.

Derrick, Shannon and Page Wise. *Divorce, How it Effects a Child.* Available from http://nh.essortment.com/divorcehoweffe_rhcq.htm. Accessed 27 January 2005.

Duffield, Gervase. "Involvement." In *Evangelicals Today: Thirteen Stock-Taking Essays*, ed. John C. King. Guildford: Lutterworth Press, 1973.

Edwards, John R. "Unity Not of Our Making," *Christianity Today* (6 August 2001): 50.

Elwell, Walter A., ed. *Evangelical Dictionary of Theology*. Grand Rapids, MI: Baker Book House, 1984.

Ezell, Rick. *Strengthening the Pastor's Soul*. Grand Rapids, MI: Kregel Publications, 1995.

Gerstner, John H. "Good Works." In *Baker's Dictionary of Theology*, edited by Everett F. Harrison. Grand Rapids: Baker Book House, 1970.

Getz, Gene. *Elders and Leaders: God's Plan for Leading the Church*. Chicago, IL: Moody Publishers, 2003.

Godet, F.L. *The Epistle to the Corinthians*. Grand Rapids, MI: Zondervan Publishing House, 1957.

Godet, F. L. *Commentary on John's Gospel*. Grand Rapids, MI: Kregel Publications, 1978.

Gregory, Richard W. "One Church's Statement on Educational Choices", *VOICE* 82, no. 3 (May/June 2003): 28-30.

Gregory, Richard W. "Facing Homosexuality in Your Community." *VOICE* 75, no.3 (May/June 1996): 16-18.

Gregory, Richard W. "Without Handles." *VOICE* 78, no. 3 (May/June 1999): 14-15.

Hendriksen, William. *Exposition of the Gospel According to John*. Grand Rapids, MI: Baker Book House, 1953.

Hodge, Charles. *1 & 2 Corinthians*. Carlisle, PA: Banner of Truth Trust, 1978.
Hogg, C.F and W.E. Vine. *The Epistle to the Thessalonians*. Fincastle, Virginia: Scripture Truth Book Company, 1959.

Hunter, James D. *Evangelicalism*: The Coming Generation. Chicago, IL:

The University of Chicago Press, 1987.
Knox, David Brought. "Pelagianism." In *Baker's Dictionary of Theology*, edited by Everett F. Harrison. Grand Rapids, MI: Baker Book House, 1960.

Liddell, H. *A Lexicon: Abridged from Liddell and Scott's Greek-English Lexicon*. Oak Harbor, WA: Logos Research Systems, Inc., 1996.

Lindsell, Harold. *The Battle for the Bible*. Grand Rapids, MI: Zondervan Corporation, 1976.

Lloyd-Jones, D. Martin. *The Puritans: Their Origins and Successors*. Edinburgh: Banner of Truth, 1987.

Louw, J. P. *Greek-English Lexicon of the New Testament : Based on Semantic Domains* (LN 34.1). New York: United Bible Societies, 1996.

MacArthur, John, Jr. *Beware the Pretenders: Study Notes, Jude*. Panorama City, CA: Word of Grace Communications, 1984.

MacArthur, John, Jr. *The MacArthur Study Bible*. Nashville, TN: Word Publications, 1997.

MacArthur, John, Jr. *True Worship: Study Notes*. Panorama City, CA: Word of Grace Communications, 1982.

MacArthur, John, Jr. *The Ultimate Priority*. Chicago, IL: Moody Press, 1983.

Machen, J. Gresham. *Christianity and Liberalism*. Grand Rapids, MI: Wm. B. Eerdman's, 1923.

MacRae, Allan. *Lectures on the Pentateuch*. Elkins Park, PA: Faith Seminary, 1960.

Marsden, George M. *Reforming Fundamentalism*. Grand Rapids, MI: Wm. B. Eerdman's, 1987.

Marsden, George M. *Understanding Fundamentalism and Evangelicalism*. Grand Rapids, MI: Wm. B. Eerdman's, 1991.

Maxwell, Joe. *News: Evangelicals Clarify Accord With Catholics*. Available from http://www.leaderu.com/ect/ect3.html. Accessed 4 February 2005.

McCallum, Dennis. *The Death of Truth*. Minneapolis, MN: Bethany House Publishers, 1996.

Moritz, Fred. *Be Ye Holy: the Call to Christian Separation*. Greenville, SC: Bob Jones University Press, 2000.

Murphy, Lyle. *Grace Evangelistic Ministries Newsletter*. Lee's Summit: MO, May, 1994.

Murray, Iain H. *Evangelicalism Divided*. Carlisle, PA: Banner of Truth Trust, 2000.

Orr, Susan. "Real Women Stay Married," *Washington Watch*. Washington D.C.: Family Research Council, June, 2000.

Owens, Ron. *Return to Worship*. Nashville, TN: Broadman and Holman, 1999.

Pickering, Ernest. *Biblical Separation: The Struggle for a Pure Church*. Schaumburg, IL: Regular Baptist Press, 1979.

Pink, Arthur. *Exposition of the Gospel of John*. Grand Rapids, MI: Zondervan Publishing House, 1975.

Piper, John. *God's Passion for His Glory*. Wheaton, IL: Crossway Books, 1998.

Roberts, Richard Owen. *Repentance: The First Word of the Gospel*. Wheaton, IL: Crossway Books, 2002.

Ryrie, Charles C. *What You Should Know About Social Responsibility*. Chicago, IL: Moody Press, 1982.

Saucy, Robert. *The Church in God's Program*. Chicago: Moody Press, 1972.

Schaeffer, Francis. *The Great Evangelical Disaster*. Westchester, IL: Crossway Books, 1984.

Schaff, Philip. *History of the Christian Church*, 8 vols. 1910. Reprint. Grand

Rapids: Wm. B. Eerdman's, Volume 7, 1980.
Semands, David. "CT Classic: A Marriage Counterculture," *Christianity Today* (28 August 2000).

Snyder, James. *A. W. Tozer on Worship and Entertainment*. Camp Hill, PA: Christian Publications, Inc., 1997.

Sproul R. C. *Getting the Gospel Right*. Grand Rapids, MI: Baker Book House, 1999.

Tripp, Tedd. *Shepherding a Child's Heart*. Wapwallopen, PA: Shepherd Press, 1995.

Webber, Robert E. *The Younger Evangelicals*. Grand Rapids, MI: Baker Book House, 2002.

Webber, Robert E. *Worship Is a Verb*. Nashville, TN: Star Song Publishing Group, 1992.

Westminister Shorter Catechism. Available from www.reformed.org/documents/index.html.
Accessed 30 March 2005.

Wiersbe, W. W. *Be What You Are: 12 Intriguing Pictures of the Christian from the New Testament*. Wheaton IL: Tyndale House, 1996.

Weirsbe, Warren. *The Integrity Crisis*. Nashville, TN: Oliver-Nelson Books, 1991.

Wuest, Kenneth. "Agapao Love." *Golden Nuggets, Wuest Word Studies*. Grand Rapids, MI: Wm. B. Eerdman's, Volume 3, 1980.
Whitehead, Barbara Dafoe. "The Christian Divorce Culture." *Christianity Today* 44, no. 10 (4 September 2000): 47.

Auburn Confession of 1924 (Auburn, NY: The Jacobs Press, 1924). The full text is available at http://www.pcanet.org/history/documents/auburntext.html. Accessed 30 March 2005.

Constitution and By Laws of IFCA International. Grandville, MI: IFCA Press, 2004.

Our Vision for the 21st Century. Grandville, MI: IFCA Press, 1996.
Salvation by Grace Through Faith. Grandville, MI: IFCA Press, 1990.

"The Practical Aims of a Liberal Evangelicalism." *New York Times*, 19 May 1915, p. 8.